Peter Abelard

Ethical Writings

Peter Abelard

Ethical Writings:

His *Ethics* or *"Know Yourself"* and

His *Dialogue between a Philosopher, a Jew and a Christian*

Translated by
Paul Vincent Spade
With an Introduction by
Marilyn McCord Adams

Hackett Publishing Company, Inc.
Indianapolis/Cambridge

Peter Abelard: 1079–1142? (or 1144)

Copyright © 1995 by Hackett Publishing Company, Inc.
Printed in the United States of America

00 99   2   3   4   5   6

For further information, please address

Hackett Publishing Company, Inc.
P.O. Box 44937
Indianapolis, Indiana 46244-0937

Cover design by Listenberger & Associates
Text design by Dan Kirklin

Library of Congress Cataloging-in-Publication Data

Abelard, Peter, 1079–1142.
    [Ethica, English]
    Ethical writings: the complete texts of Ethics and Dialogue between a
philosopher, a Jew and a Christian/Peter Abelard; translated by Paul Vincent
Spade; introduction by Marilyn McCord Adams.
        p.   cm.
    Includes bibliographical references and index.
    ISBN 0-87220-323-9.   ISBN 0-87220-322-0 (pbk.)
    1. Ethics—Early works to 1800.   2. Judaism and
philosophy.   3. Christianity—Philosophy.   4. Natural law.   I. Spade, Paul
Vincent.   II Abelard, Peter, 1079–1142.   Dialogus inter philosophum,
judaeum et christianum. English.   III. Title.
BJ1240.A2313   1995
241—dc20   95-24270
                                                                CIP

Contents

Introduction by Marilyn McCord Adams   vii
Translator's Introduction   xxvii

Translation

Ethics
  Book I   1
  Book II   57

Dialogue between a Philosopher, a Jew and a Christian
  Preface   59
  Dialogue 1: Between the Philosopher and the Jew   63
  Dialogue 2: Between the Philosopher and the Christian   91

References   149
Bibliography   155
Index   163

Introduction

Abelard's Life and Works:

Among medieval thinkers, Abelard's is not only one of the most colorful and tragic of lives, but also one of the best attested because he left us his own partial autobiography, *The Story of My Troubles* (*Historia Calamitatum*).[1] Born in 1079 at Le Pallet, Brittany, Abelard thrived on book-learning and chose the pursuit of logic and philosophy over the promised glories of a military career. At Paris, his brilliance combined with personal arrogance to win him both throngs of students and life-long enemies. Twice a student of William of Champeaux, he humiliated his master by besting him in disputations, three times (between 1104 and 1108 or 1109) by setting up his own schools and attracting students away from William and his pupils by sheer force of dialectical skill. These conflicts were interrupted by Abelard's return home to arrange for his mother's (following his father's) entry into religious life. When he reappeared in Paris in 1113 to study theology, he began attending lectures on Ezekiel by the aging and much revered Anselm of Laon. True to previous form, Abelard found Anselm dull, opened his own counter-series on Ezekiel, and gained a large following. Anselm's loyal students Alberic of Rheims and Lotulf the Lombard persuaded their master to forbid Abelard from continuing, on the ground that he lacked previous theological training. Abelard went back to Paris to enjoy a lucrative teaching career, which was brought to a halt by his affair with Héloïse (ca 1117–1118). She was the niece of one canon Fulbert, and her intellectual gifts and literary preparation were notable in an age when neither was taken for granted in women. Abelard conspired to become her tutor, mutual passion took its course, and Héloïse became pregnant and gave birth to their son Astralabe. Their secret but career-threatening marriage to appease Héloïse's uncle failed in its purpose when the latter had Abelard castrated. Abelard considered this humiliation God's just judgment on his lust, and both partners entered religious orders. Shortly after taking up residence at St. Denis, Abelard was back to teaching both theology and secular subjects. Between 1118 and 1120 he wrote his *Theologia 'Summi Boni'* to satisfy

---

1. Translated by J.T. Muckle under the title *The Story of Abelard's Adversities* (Toronto: Pontifical Institute of Mediaeval Studies, 1964). I rely for this sketch of his life and works on Abelard's own autobiography, and on Eligius Buytaert's general introduction to the critical edition of Abelard's *Romans*-commentary, *Corpus Christianorum, Continuatio Mediaevalis*, vol. XI (Turnholti: Typographi Brepols Editores Pontificii, 1969).

student demand for rational explanations of how God can be three-in-one. In 1121, his old rivals Alberic and Lotulf arranged for the Synod of Soissons to be convened against him, and his book was condemned and burned without any serious examination of its actual doctrines. Released after a brief imprisonment at St. Medard, Abelard was welcomed at St. Denis into the arms of yet another controversy, this time occasioned by his observation that Bede contradicted their tradition that Dionysius the Areopagite had been bishop of Athens. After some negotiations, Abelard won his freedom, and in late 1122 built an oratory of reeds dedicated first to the Holy Trinity and then to the Paraclete. Once again students flocked to hear him, and enlarged the "campus" with more huts and buildings; once again, his enemies stirred trouble. In 1125, he escaped "out of the frying pan into the fire" when he accepted his surprise election as abbot of St. Gildas de Ruys, only to find the monks utterly undisciplined and to face multiple plots against his life. In 1129, he offered Héloïse and her nuns the Paraclete, and became their advisor and protector. Fleeing St. Gildas in 1132, Abelard became a peripatetic monk until 1135 or 1136, when he decided to return to Paris to teach and write theology. He had scarcely arrived when another old enemy, William of St. Thierry, informed Bernard of Clairvaux, the Cistercian reformer. After examining several of Abelard's works (including the *Ethics*), Bernard scheduled two meetings, and after the second extracted Abelard's promise to mend his ways. Abelard, however, was convinced that he had been misunderstood and retracted nothing substantive in his teachings or writings. Between 1139 and 1140, Bernard retaliated by persuading the archbishop of Sens to convene a synod in the season of Pentecost 1140 to hear Abelard's case. Abelard prepared several documents defending his orthodoxy, and rallied his many supporters to attend the scheduled disputation on June 2–3, 1140. On the actual occasion, however, when Bernard began to read the condemned theses and to dispute some of them, Abelard appealed to the pope. The synod granted the motion, but while Abelard was en route to Rome, Bernard persuaded Innocent II to condemn both Abelard and his writings without a further hearing. Defeated, Abelard turned to Peter of Cluny, who made peace among the conflicting parties. Once more, Abelard settled down to teaching and writing theology at Cluny, but his health soon failed. He died at St. Marcel on April 21, in either 1142 or 1144.

Despite such major disruptions in his career, Abelard has left an impressive corpus of philosophical and theological writings, as well as hymns, sermons, and letters of advice. The precise chronology of his works remains a vexed question for several reasons: their author repeatedly revised them; not many manuscripts remain; and Abelard's own cross-referencing is ambiguous.

Probably, his *Logica 'Ingredientibus,'* which contains his distinctive treatment of the problem of universals, along with the first version of *Dialectica*, were penned by 1118. Two versions of the *Theologia 'Summi Boni'* condemned at the Synod of Soissons were produced between 1118 and 1120, while the *Theologia Christiana* received attention during three interrupted periods (1122–1127, 1132–1135, and 1139–1140), and *Theologia 'Scholarium'* went through four versions between 1135 and 1140. The year 1137 marks the latest possible date for Abelard's *Romans*-commentary, and both the *Dialogue* and the *Ethics* stem from an extraordinarily productive period between 1136 and 1139. Certainly the *Ethics* postdates the *Romans*-commentary, while the *Dialogue* comes before the *Ethics*.

Contrasting Schemes of Human Evaluation:
Both of the present works reflect Abelard's concern to locate "true ethics" or "the discipline of morals" in relation to a variety of alternative schemes of human evaluation, including those imposed by civil government and religious institutions. In the *Dialogue*, the Philosopher and the Christian agree that the domain of ethics is defined by two principal questions:

(Q1) Where and what is the ultimate good? the ultimate evil?
(Q2) What is the route by means of which humans may arrive at the ultimate good [*DPJC* Pref. (4); *DPC* (148)–(150)]?[2]

Given the premiss that true happiness consists in the enjoyment of the ultimate good [*DPC* (150)], they infer that Q2 is equivalent to

(Q2') What is the route to human happiness [*DPJC* Pref. (4); *DPC* (150)]?

The Philosopher, Christian, and Jew all agree that "moral philosophy" is "the goal of all the disciplines" [*DPJC* Pref. (4); *DPC* (148)], the queen of the arts and the highest philosophy, served by all the others [*DPC* (148)–(152)]. By contrast with their late-twentieth-century counterparts, all three interlocutors are theists [*DPJC* Pref. (2)] and so readily redescribe interest in ethics as the desire to answer

(Q2″) What is the route to the salvation of my soul [*DPJ* (22)]?

2. *DPJC* abbreviates *Dialogue between a Philosopher, a Jew and a Christian; DPJ, Dialogue 1: between a Philosopher and a Jew; DPC, Dialogue 2: between a Philosopher and a Christian.* The boldface parenthetical arabic numeral indicates the number of the paragraph in the translation.

x   *Introduction*

Likewise, the Christian wins the Philosopher's agreement that the study of
ethics is the study of Divinity, because God is identical with the Ultimate
Good *simpliciter.*

As for the relation of ethics to civil and religious law or mores, the
Philosopher furnishes the helpful distinction between "natural justice" or
"natural right"—what human reason common to all races and nations dictates
ought to be done—and positive justice, which

> is what is instituted by human beings to protect either usefulness or honor more
> surely, or to increase them. It depends either on custom alone or on a written
> authority.

E.g., civil laws identifying crimes, regulating trials, and specifying punishments [*DPC* (283)–(285)]. The Philosopher's view is that both Jewish and
Christian religions represent Divine law as a mixture of moral precepts (as in
the Ten Commandments) and positive law (as in sacramental regulations,
specifying rites of initiation—e.g., circumcision for Jews and baptism for
Christians—and other precepts of the Hebrew Bible or canon law) [*DPC*
(285)]. This "philosophical" account seems to reflect Abelard's own view in
most passages: in general and for the most part, he seems at ease in distinguishing the purposes and precepts of ethics from positive civil and religious
law while conceding to each its own sphere of legitimacy.

Cross-Cultural Dilemmas:

Abelard's interlocutors share significant common ground: all agree that
human obligation to worship God is central to ethics. Nevertheless, their
"ancient and honorable" traditions—Judaism, Christianity, Hellenistic philosophy—generate partially incompatible answers to Q2/Q2'/Q2'': "we serve
[God] by different faiths and different kinds of life" [*DPJC* Pref. (2)]. The
Philosopher [later identified as a son of Ishmael and hence probably as a non-
Moslem Arab; *DPJ* (90)] exhibits the ambivalence many bring to such cross-
cultural exchange. On the one hand, he professes commitment to the rational
pursuit of the truth; he has initiated the discussion and has chosen the Jew and
Christian as partners, out of interest in the salvation of his soul [*DPJC* Pref.
(4)–(6)]. On the other, his express initial bias is that Jews are "fools" and
Christians "crazy" [*DPJC* Pref. (6)]. Both the Philosopher and the Christian
are capable of condescension (the Philosopher especially in his reply to the
Jew; the Christian in his lecturing of the Philosopher), scolding (the Philosopher scolds the Jew for misinterpreting Hebrew Scripture, and the Christian
for appealing to authority instead of reason), and name-calling (the Philoso-

pher of both the Christian and the Jew [*DPJ* Pref. (6)]; the Christian of the
Philosopher regarding the unity of the virtues [*DPC* (230)] and of the Jew
regarding literal readings for Scripture [*DPC* (358)].

The *Dialogue* presents the Jew as somewhat self-effacing, as disadvantaged
twice-over—in relation to the Christian who has two testaments in place of
one, and to the Philosopher who has greater experience in dialectic [*DPJ*
(19)–(22)]—and thus disinclined to *ad hominem* arguments. Nevertheless, the
Jew receives better treatment from Abelard than in other twelfth-century
Christian parallels. The Christian and the Jew never face off; each is matched
with the Philosopher. Moreover, Abelard is notorious for his contention that
the Jews who killed Christ did not sin, because they did not consent to *what
they believed unfitting*, but rather to what they (mistakenly) thought would
please God [cf. *Ethics* (110)–(112), (131)]. Still, in his discussion with the
Christian, the Philosopher is allowed to insult Jews twice more as "sensual"
"animals" who believe on the basis of "external" miracles and signs rather
than "reasons" [*DPC* (154), (157)]. And the Christian compares the Jew to
"an illiterate person" who attends to the literal rather than the mystical or
allegorical sense of Scripture [*DPC* (358)].

The interlocutors thus display semi-enlightened tolerance. By contrast,
Abelard the referee assumes his task expecting to "learn something from this,"
citing proverbs that no teaching is so false as to contain no truth, no disputation so frivolous that it cannot teach [*DPJC* Pref. (9)].

Initially the Philosopher seizes the agenda, challenging the Jew and the
Christian to "show" reasonable "cause why" he should move from an ethics
that restricts itself to natural law to adopt their religions. Natural law can boast
that it investigates "the truth by means of reasons, and in all things" follows
"not people's opinion but reason's lead" [*DPJC* Pref. (4)]. It is a common core
accessible to every human being and is prior in the order of time and
explanation to other laws and precepts [*DPJ* (11); *DPC* (159)]. He strongly
suspects religious adherence is fundamentally irrational ("fools" or "crazy")
for three reasons: (i) First, its socio-psychological roots are not reasons but
natural love for one's own people that first leads one to adopt and then
engenders bias toward and a sense of the superiority of their religion aptly
sloganized by "God loves only our group" [*DPJ* (16)–(17)]. (ii) Second, the
plurality and inconsistency of religious traditions forces a choice among or
rejection of them all. Selection should be driven by reasons that are naturally
prior to them all [*DPC* (164)]. (iii) Finally, many religious beliefs rest on
appeals to authority, traditionally the weakest sort of argument [*DPC* (165)].

In fact, the *Dialogue* follows (Pseudo-)Augustine's advice to "seek by disputation" and anticipates the later *quaestio* style of setting out a series of

positions, each with arguments pro and contra, and ending with a magisterial determination of the issue.[3] First, the Jew presents his position, with the Philosopher raising counterarguments which the Jew tries to answer. Contrary to the original proposal, the Christian manuveurs the Philosopher into going next, setting out the answers to Q1 and Q2/Q2'/Q2" offered by Hellenistic philosophy, to which the Christian objects. The Christian's corrections and the Philosopher's attempted reformulations gradually give way to the Christian's explanation of his position. The work ends with the Philosopher raising and the Christian answering a series of clarificatory questions.

Does Abelard mean thereby to put the Christian in the Master's role? Maybe. After all, the Philosopher seems to win his disputation with the Jew, while the Christian is allowed to revise and recontextualize the Philosopher's claims. Moreover, in *Theologia Christiana*, Abelard appeals to patristic sources to argue extensively that philosophers before Christ such as Socrates and Plato will receive eternal life. Abelard reasons that it is impossible to have good morals without faith. Yet many philosophers led holy lives out of love for Wisdom.[4] Therefore, God must have granted them faith in Christ and the Trinity.[5] And even though such doctrines are not *explicit* in their writings,[6] they can be detected via allegorical interpretation.[7] Perhaps Abelard intends the *Dialogue*'s Philosopher to be recapitulating the putative progress of ancient philosophers from natural law to Christian faith![8]

But maybe not. The answer ultimately turns on how we take the *Dialogue*'s apparently unfinished state. For the original agreement left the determination of the question up to Abelard himself. As it stands, the work ends with the Christian's invitation to the Philosopher to raise further questions or "hurry on to the remaining points" [*DPC* (425)] and so stops before Abelard's own piece gets said. Perhaps Abelard intended to close with his own *ex professo* response and simply didn't get around to it. Perhaps he considered it politically unwise to render his undoubtedly open-minded verdict. Alternatively, his

3. As Pierre Payer suggests in the introduction to his own translation of this work: *Abelard: Dialogue of a Philosopher with a Jew and a Christian*, "Introduction" (Toronto: Pontifical Institute of Mediaeval Studies, 1979), p.12.

4. *Theologia Christiana* I.54–55 (XII.94); II.67–68 (XII.159–161). References to Abelard's *Theologia Christiana* and to his *Romans*-commentary are to *Corpus Christianorum: Continuatio Mediaevalis*, volumes XI–XII, edited by Eligius Buytaert.

5. *Theologia Christiana* I.68 (XII.100ff); I.36 (XII.130–131).

6. *Theologia Christiana* II.15 (XII.139–140).

7. *Theologia Christiana* II.16 (XII.140); cf. II.26–36 (XII.143–147).

8. Cf. *Theologia Christiana* II.19–25 (XII.141–143)

omission may be pedagogical. In its present form, the *Dialogue* thrusts the reader into the magisterial role: the three interlocutors have presented their cases; those open to learn from cross-cultural discussions must decide the question for themselves.

The Jew's Defense, The Philosopher's Riposte:

Jew and Philosopher share a sense of obligation to obey the natural law. At issue is whether there is *reason* to regard other precepts and provisions of Jewish law as binding. These include the requirement of circumcision [*DPJ* (72)–(91)] and Sabbath rest, as well as the prohibition of exogamy and table-fellowship with non-Jews [*DPJ* (76)]. Most distinctive is the Holiness Code of Leviticus, which evaluates not only persons, but even places, things, and states of affairs as pure/clean vs. defiled on the basis of whether they fit or straddle clear-cut social or natural categories, of whether they preserve, blur or violate clear boundaries. Uncleanness is communicable by contact and is removable (if at all) by rituals. For example, certain animals are unclean and unfit for eating because they fail to conform to pre-established zoological kinds; dishes and utensils, if touched by certain insects; persons who have bodily emissions (through menstruation, ejaculation, or running sores) as well as beds and clothing touched by them; women after childbirth [*DPJ* (128)–(129)]. Important for present purposes is that the criteria for purity and defilement are utterly insensitive to the beliefs and/or intentions of persons. The man who accidentally and unwittingly bumps into a menstrous woman in a crowd is unclean nonetheless [*DPJ* (130)].[9]

The Jew concedes to the Philosopher that religious tradition is acquired under the influence of those one knows and loves, but offers [i] the following *pragmatic* argument that—once acquired—it can be reasonably retained. All agree that it would be fitting for God to give humans a law by which to make His will known. But it is at worst intellectually undecidable whether Jewish law is from God. Whether or not it actually is, observing it for God's sake would be pious and hence pleasing to God [*DPJ* (34)–(36)]—especially since it is burdensome [*DPJ* (42)–(43)] and pogroms even make observance a threat to life and limb [*DPJ* (38)–(41)]. Moreover, the Jew remarks, [ii] once Israel settled down in Canaan, these "extra" precepts had great social utility, serving to define the community by erecting a wall against cultural assimilation [*DPJ* (72)–(76)].

---

9. For a contemporary analysis from the point of view of social anthropology, see Mary Douglas, *Purity and Danger: An Analysis of Concepts of Pollution and Taboo* (London: Routledge & Kegan Paul, 1966).

Neither consideration is reason for a non-Jew to take up observance of Jewish law, however. For the pragmatic argument works as well or as badly for many inconsistent schools of thought, each of which thinks its practices makes them special friends of God, and so offers as much or as little reason to assent to each and all. Likewise, such positive laws [*DPC* **(284)–(285)**] can function to define community only if foreigners do not observe them. The Philosopher's principal objection is that circumcision, dietary laws, and the Holiness Code are irrelevant to "true ethics" because the former focus on "externals" rewarding (sanctioning) material conditions with earthly and temporal benefits (punishments), while God and morals look to the heart [*DPJ* **(126)–(135)**]. Hebrew Scriptures themselves give examples of Jews and Gentiles, before and after Sinai and settlement in the land, who are saved by observing the natural law to love God and neighbor, without adherence to the "extra" precepts [*DPJ* **(48)–(50), (63), (126)**]. External works or conditions aren't sufficient either, whether for Divine favor or moral uprightness, because without love they don't count [*DPJ* **(126)–(127)**].

Perspectives from Hellenistic Philosophy:
Having located the domain of ethics "within" the soul, the Philosopher turns to Hellenistic sources to identify the ultimate good and the human route thereto. (**Reply to Q1**) So far as the goal is concerned, he sees a mostly verbal dispute between Epicurus who identifies the ultimate good with the specific pleasure of

> a kind of inner tranquility of the soul whereby it remains calm and content with its own goods in disasters and good fortune alike, while no sense of sin consumes it [*DPC* **(180)**]

and Stoics who contend that it is virtue and that virtue is its own reward [*DPC* **(188)**]. For "the 'blessed' " is

> one who is "well-suited," so to speak—that is, deals well and easily in all things. Thus, being blessed is the same as being strong in good morals, that is, in the virtues [*DPC* **(188)**].

Both put the individual's good "inside" in such a way as to be within his/her power. Their moral-psychological assumption was that each individual had the capacity to learn so to choose and to build up habits that the person would have inner peace and the dignity of self-control and self-mastery no matter what happened on the outside. Expanding on the Stoic formulation, the Philosopher explains that a virtue (vice) is an excellent (worse) habit of mind, that is to say an entrenched non-natural disposition acquired by striving and deliberation [*DPC* (254)]. Moreover, he claims, virtues (vices) are good (evil) substantially and of their own nature in such a way that they cannot become evil (good) [*DPC* (257)]. The Philosopher also rehearses the Ciceronian theses of the unity and equality of the virtues—the person who has one virtue has them all; all sins are equal and therefore all evil persons are equally evil; all good persons are equally good—and sketches a mostly Ciceronian analysis of prudence, justice, fortitude, and temperance [*DPC* (256)–(298)]. (**Reply to Q2/Q2′/Q2″**) Unsurprisingly, the route to virtue is moral education that strengthens a good will [*DPC* (186)].

The Semantics of 'Good':
   Both Philosopher [*DPC* (297)–(308)] and Christian [*DPC* (395)–(424)] conclude that order cannot be brought out of the confusion of this topic without clearly distinguishing different ways in which the term 'good' is used. 'Good' (*bonum*) can occur as a neuter adjective, in which case it can signify a *good thing;* or as an adjective modifying a noun (a good *F*), in which case the criteria for goodness vary with the noun in question; or as modifying the occurrences of things or states of affairs (it is good that *p*). The Christian offers [D1] and [D3] explicitly, [D2] by implication:

(D1.1)   a good thing = that which, while it's fit for some use, mustn't impede the advantage or worthiness of anything [*DPC* (397)];

(D1.2)   an evil thing = that which either is unfit for some use or impedes the advantage or worthiness of something or both [*DPC* (397)];

(D1.3)   an indifferent thing = a thing that's neither good nor evil = a thing such that no good is necessarily delayed or impeded by its existence [*DPC* (397)].

(D2)   a good *F* = an exemplary member or version of *F*-kind [*DPC* (396)].

(D3)   it is good that *p* = it is necessary for filling out some optimal arrangement of God's even if that arrangement is completely hidden from us [*DPC* (421)].

Apparently endorsing the controversial thesis of the harmony of all positive goods, the Christian counts all substances as paradigm-case *good things* "because, while they're able to impart some usefulness, no worthiness or advantage is necessarily hampered through them" [*DPC* (420); cf. *Ethics* (101)]. (One wonders, for example, whether naturally carnivorous lions do not interfere with the advantage of their prey, insect-eating swallows with that of swarming bugs!) Turning to [D1.2], he notes, even some Hellenistic philosophers

> ... count poverty, illness, death and other troubles of adversities or sufferings as evils. And because of things contrary to the virtues, there are many vices both of the soul and of the body. They're to be no less regarded as evils. For instance, the body's lameness or blindness, the mind's dullness or forgetfulness ... [*DPC* (200)]

That [D1.1] 'good thing' is distinct from [D2] 'good *F*' is clear, because when God creates a three-legged horse He creates a good thing, but not a good horse. Likewise, a wrongdoer is a good thing qua created by God but a bad human being because not equipped with good morals [*DPC*, (304)]. Looking to other dimensions of human being, the Philosopher wonders whether naturally irascible or lustful, stupid or feeble humans would not be bad humans although good things [*DPC* (305)–(306)]. In the neighborhood of [D2] is another notion of **[D4]** what is *good for* a thing, which could mean **[D4.1]** what makes it a better thing, but probably (e.g., in discussions of the human good) is understood as **[D4.2]** what makes it [D2] a better thing *of its kind*.

That [D1] diverges from [D3] is shown from universal Divine providence: because "God's ultimate goodness" "permits nothing to happen without a cause" and "preordains even evils well, and even uses them for the best, to such an extent that [D3] it's even good for evils to exist, although nevertheless [D1.2] evil isn't [D1.1] good at all" [*DPC* (402)]. Likewise, [D3] it is just and hence good that wrongdoers be punished, although punishment is not [D1.1] a good thing [*DPC* (307)–(308)].

Most important for ethics, however, are the evaluations of agents and their actions. Here Christian and Philosopher concur in a thesis Abelard will defend in his *Ethics:* that all actions are of themselves [D1.3] indifferent things. Nor can **[D5]** the evaluation of an act be "read off" its consequences: to do well it is not enough to produce [D1.1] a good thing, but it must be done with a good intention [*DPC* (404)]. For

> it often happens that the same thing is done by different people in such a way that the one does it well and the other evilly, according to their intention ... [*DPC* (404)]

Thus, two men hang a criminal, but one does it out of hatred and the other from zeal for justice; Scripture says that both God and Satan take away Job's positions; that the Father, Jesus, the devil, and Judas all hand Jesus over to be crucified [cf. *Ethics* (57)–(59); *DPC* (404)–(406)]. For the same reason, it can be [D3] good that Judas betrayed Christ and/or [D3] good that Satan destroyed Job's goods, children, and health, although Judas and Satan [D5] act wickedly because from bad intentions. Ironically, then, willing what God wills to occur is not sufficient for [D5] acting well if "they don't do or want to do it because they believe God wants it to be done . . ." [*DPC* **(406)**]. Conversely, "sometimes there's even a good will when someone wants evil to be done by someone else, because he wants it with a good intention"—as when for good and sufficient reason God wills the devil or a tyrant to afflict the innocent or sends a lying spirit into the false prophets who deceive Ahab [*DPC* **(407)**–**(409)**]. If bad intention is sufficient for bad action and good intention necessary for good, is good intention also sufficient? The Christian muddies these waters, leaving us unclear whether well-intended actions are therefore well done and/or whether the agent must also accurately assess and so conform to actual Divine intentions and ordinances in the matter in order to have a good intention [*DPC* **(421)**–**(423)**]. Abelard will revisit this issue briefly in Book II of the *Ethics*.

Christian Revisions:
  On balance, the Christian finds the Philosopher "not far from the Kingdom of Heaven," and undertakes by a series of arguments and objections, modifications and refinements to bring him much closer to Christian truth. **(i)** So far as [D1.1] good things are concerned, it will not do to identify the ultimate good with human perfection (virtue, Epicurean pleasure, or happiness), because God or Divine happiness is unsurpassably greater [*DPC* **(217)**–**(224)**, **(297)**]. Indeed, Abelard claims elsewhere that the aggregate of God with no matter what collection of creatures cannot be better than God all by Himself [*Ethics* **(101)**–**(104)**]! **(ii)** Nor is *ante mortem* virtue apt to be sufficient for human happiness because there are many *ante mortem* [D1.2] evils of body and soul which diminish *ante mortem* peace of mind and happiness. If the Philosopher holds that freedom from bodily afflictions is not sufficient for happiness because virtues are necessary [*DPC* **(192)**–**(193)**], the Christian maintains that an affliction-free environment is conducive to growth in virtues and necessary to maximizing them [*DPC* **(194)**–**(206)**]:

> . . . the better life is the one that surely is both altogether devoid of these evils and so absolutely removed from sin that not only *does* one not sin but one *cannot* sin either . . . [*DPC* **(206)**]

The Christian then offers his own *pragmatic* argument, that Christianity is preferable to Hellenistic philosophy. For both agree that humans ought to live a moral life. All recognize that hope is psychologically necessary for perseverance.

Hellenistic philosophy exhorts us to virtue for its own sake in an *ante mortem* environment which allows us neither perfect virtue nor freedom from affliction, while Christianity calls us "to the virtues with a better reason or hope"— freedom from affliction, impeccability, and beatific vision of God in a future life [*DPC* (210)–(212)]!

(iii) The Christian agrees with the Philosopher that moral education in virtue is the route to happiness, and seems willing to go along with the notion that prudence and its daughter virtues justice, fortitude, and temperance play a formative role. He even concedes that "virtue" "understood properly" as "what obtains merit with God" is one and identical with charity or love of God above all [*DPC* (234)]. But he rejects as ridiculous the twin Ciceronian theses of the unity and equality of the virtues. On the contrary, prudence, temperance, and courage are habits distinct from one another and from charity [*DPC* (234), (240)]. Likewise, reason, experience, and authority all declare that virtues come in degrees and different humans exemplify them in different patterns [*DPC* (235)–(236)].

(iv) Just as the Philosopher slid from defining "the ultimate good" as "that which when attained makes one blessed" [*DPC* (178)] to equating it with human happiness, so he moved from a definition of "the ultimate evil" as "that the attaining of which makes one wretched" [*DPC* (178)] into its identification with "the ultimate misery or penalty of any creature whatever . . . undergone in proportion to its merits," indeed "all the tortures people undergo there in proportion to their merits" [*DPC* (298)]. The Christian first persuades him that punishment cannot be the *ultimate* evil because it cannot be worse than the fault that merits it [*DPC* (299)–(311)]. Returning to the spirit of the original definitions, the Christian first defines "ultimate human good" as "that by which the person is made better" and identifies it with ultimate love of God; "ultimate human evil" with "that by which the person is made worse," viz., "ultimate hatred of God" [*DPC* (313)–(315)]. The Christian explains that these are reached via *post mortem* developmental processes: love of God combines with *post mortem* beatific enjoyment of God to generate a gracious spiral of ever-increasing love and bliss, while hatred of God joins with punishment and despair of any relief to produce a vicious spiral of hatred and torment. Thus, there is a natural integration between what pleases God more (less) and what benefits (harms) us [*DPC* (315)–(317)]. Indeed, we come closer to the truth if we say that

. . . God himself, who alone is properly and absolutely called the ultimate good, is also the ultimate human good. That is, we're made truly blessed by the participation we enjoy in the vision of it that we've spoken of . . . [*DPC* (335)]

The Locus of Imputability:

Abelard's slightly later work *Ethics*, alternatively entitled *Know Yourself!*, continues the task of differentiating "true" "ethics" or "morals" from other frameworks of human evaluation. Where the *Dialogue* concentrates on identifying the ultimate good and the human route thereto, *Ethics* concerns itself with the locus of moral imputability: for what, properly speaking, can we be held morally accountable, appropriate subjects of moral praise or blame [*Ethics* (3)]? Here as before Abelard counts the latter equivalent to the theological queries, what is sin? by reason of what do we merit "a crown of glory that never fades away" [1 Peter 5:4; cf. *Ethics* (6), (10), (22)]?

Abelard's own intuitions resonate with the Philosopher's Hellenistic (Stoic and Epicurean) sources: i.e., he agrees that moral/ethical/religious imputability is directed at what is inside and within the individual's power! In Book I, Abelard begins with the negative, with sin properly speaking. Formally, it is a negative symbolic value—viz., that of scorning or showing contempt for God [*Ethics* (7)–(8)]. Materially, after several false starts [*Ethics* (7)–(8)], he settles on the following definition:

(D6) Sin is [i] consent to [ii] what we believe [iii] is unfitting (i.e., consent to not doing what we believe ought to be done by us for God's sake, or consent to doing what we believe ought not to be done by us for God's sake.

[i] That Abelard wants to locate sin in *consent* rather than in the deed itself is explicit in many places [*Ethics* (29), (47)–(48)]. [ii] Ignorance excuses, because it devalues the act as currency for showing contempt [*Ethics* (49)]. Most notorious is Abelard's claim that the Jews who believed that persecuting Christ would please God would have sinned if they had refrained from consenting to that act [*Ethics* (110)–(112), (131)]. Perhaps equally remarkable (if for different reasons) is the example of a man's sleeping with another's wife believing her to be his own [*Ethics* (49)]. Abelard also infers from [ii] that infants and children below the age of reason, as well as the mentally incompetent, are not capable of sin properly speaking [*Ethics* (44)]. [iii] Abelard clarifies that the ultimate standard of what is unfitting is not God's explicit commands but His intentions, since the Bible records how God sometimes issues commands that He does not intend for us to obey [*Ethics* (60)–(66)].

Abelard assigns consent a *dispositional* element, when he stipulates that we consent to an act when we are fully prepared to perform it if given the chance [*Ethics* (29)]. Later on, he speaks indifferently of intention or consent [*Ethics*

(106)–(109)]; and if 'intention' implies disposition, 'consent' suggests an occurrent element as well. It is not clear whether Abelard thinks consent must be fully conscious (e.g., when voluntary actions aren't preceded by conscious deliberation), but certainly it is important to him that consent is within our power. Indeed, Abelard sees consent as voluntary in the double sense that it is not necessary or inevitable, and that it proceeds from the will [*Ethics* (34)] within whose power it lies [*Ethics* (51)]. Even where circumstances make withholding consent extremely difficult by attaching consequences that run contrary to our strong desires, consent is never necessary or coerced properly speaking [*Ethics* (33)–(34)].

In defending [D6], Abelard distinguishes sin from [a] vices of the soul, [b] an evil will, and [c] evil deeds. [a] Vices of the soul that pertain to morals— e.g., irascibility or lust [*Ethics* (4)]—are those that make us *disposed* to do [*Ethics* (1)] or to consent to doing what is unfitting [*Ethics* (3)]. [b] For Abelard, 'evil will' does not mean 'evil choice or decision' but rather 'evil desire or want' [*Ethics* (29)]—e.g., the desire to lie with another man's wife [*Ethics* (21)–(27)] or to eat delicious fruit that belongs to someone else [*Ethics* (28)]. Abelard contends that sin can be identified with none of these.

Symptomatic is the fact that [a] vice of the soul or [b] an evil will may offer some positive advantage to the agent. For it is always within a person's power not to follow such vices and evil desires by consenting to what is unfitting [*Ethics* (72)–(73)]. One who has such vices and evil desires is thereby in a position to earn more merit than one who lacks them, because it will represent victory in a more challenging struggle to consent only to what God is believed to intend [*Ethics* (5)–(6), (22)–(23)]. Likewise, neither [a] vices, nor [b] evil will/desires, nor [c] external omissions and commissions suffice as sin, because all are common to the good and the bad alike [*Ethics* (3)]. As in the *Dialogue*, "deeds . . . are equally common to reprobates and to the elect" and are "in themselves all indifferent" [*Ethics* (90)].

Abelard's principal reason for refusing to identify any of [a]–[c] with sin, however, is that very often these are not within one's voluntary control, while sin properly speaking is so much within our power that we could (albeit with difficulty) entirely avoid it during our *ante mortem* lives [*Ethics* (133)]. He observes that humans may be initially no more responsible for [a] irascibility or lust than for lameness [*Ethics* (2)–(4), (6)]; that our *ante mortem* weakness renders most of us unable entirely to eliminate [b] evil desires in this life [*Ethics* (27)]; and that circumstances or ignorance may prevent us from [c] doing or refraining from doing what is fitting that we should do or refrain from doing [*Ethics* (52)–(53)]. But "things less in our power are less worth commanding" [*Ethics* (51)]!

In fact, all that follows from the fact that they are common to good and bad people alike is that none of these is sufficient for sin. Without the further premiss

> **(P1)** What isn't sufficient by itself to count as morally good (evil) cannot qualify as morally good (evil) *properly* speaking, through relation to something else, nor can it contribute to anything else's qualifying as morally good (evil) properly speaking.

it doesn't follow that these are not necessary *partial* constituents of sin or that they cannot make something else more sinful than it would otherwise be.

Abelard does not so much argue that [a] vices, [b] evil desires, and [c] outward acts/omissions are not necessary, as that consent is *sufficient*. Provided that someone consents to what the person believes unfitting, it makes no difference whether or not the consent was preceded by [a] vice or [b] an evil desire [*Ethics* (10)]; the person sins. Since consent involves a state of readiness to act if given the opportunity, [c] the action is not required for sin either. By definition, once one has consented, one acts if given the chance; and if not, it remains that one has done everything in one's power toward the action and is prepared to do more—which is quite enough to show contempt for God.

Abelard also insists that actual performance of the action cannot *increase* sin or reward [*Ethics* (92)–(99)], apparently assuming the principle that

> **(P2)** What is not substantially/essentially morally good (evil) cannot increase the goodness (evil) of a whole of which it becomes a part.

Probably this principle also underlies **(P1)** above. An outward action cannot qualify as substantially or essentially sinful because it can be performed in ignorance or under coercion [*Ethics* (49)–(50)]. Therefore it cannot add to the sinfulness of any whole of which it is a part. At most it can be accidentally sinful by relation to something else—viz., the consent which causes it. Similarly, he insists that since carnal pleasure does not suffice for sin (as is proved by a separation argument from cases where it accompanies thoroughly innocent acts), it cannot increase sin either [*Ethics* (47)–(48)].

Just as only consent or intention is sin properly speaking, so only consent or intention is good in itself [*Ethics* (91), (106)]. Abelard seems to advance the following criterion for an intention's counting as a good intention:

> **(D7)** An intention to do A (refrain from doing A) is a good intention if and only if [i] doing A (refraining from doing A) is pleasing to God; [ii] one

believes doing A (refraining from doing A) is pleasing to God; and [iii] one intends to do A (refrain from doing A) for the love of God.

The persecutors of Christ and the tormenters of Christian martyrs cannot be said to have had *good* intentions simply by virtue of [ii] believing their actions would be pleasing to God, because not-[i] their actions were not *in fact* pleasing to God [*Ethics* (109)]. Nevertheless, the persecutors of Christ *did not sin*, because they were consenting only to [ii] what they believed would please God [*Ethics* (110)]. Presumably, [i] and [ii] will not suffice, because conformity to apparent Divine intentions out of fear of punishment or in hope of reward but not out of love for God would not render the intention fully good (cf. Abelard's discussion of penitence [*Ethics* (151)–(152), (167)–(168)]). By contrast, later Aristotelians recognize degrees of virtue according to which satisfying [i] and [ii] would be enough to count as good; but a higher degree is reached when [iii] is satisfied as well. As for actions that proceed from good intentions, Abelard's main concern is to emphasize that good intentions and good actions are not two good things; rather the actions are morally indifferent in themselves and as such add no goodness over and above that of the intentions [*Ethics* (105)–(106)]. Once again, he fails to clarify whether even the goodness of the intention is sufficient or only necessary for the goodness of the action in a derivative and extended sense of 'good.'

Morality versus Civil Law:

In the *Dialogue between the Philosopher and the Jew*, the Philosopher rejects the Jewish Holiness Code as morally irrelevant, primarily on the ground that its evaluations were based on externals which are often beyond the scope of the individual's intention and knowledge and hence control. On the other hand, the Jew's analysis of the function of such legislation in maintaining social cohesion proved quite astute. Likewise, in the *Ethics*, Abelard has located the morally imputable inside at the point of consent/intention, which is allegedly within an agent's control. In the rest of the work, he confronts the issue of how ethical evaluation is related to that of civil and ecclesiastical law.

An objector challenges (D6) Abelard's definition of 'sin' on the ground that it doesn't square with civil law, whose penal code assigns heavier punishment to *deeds* than to intentions. Abelard's reply is that state and morals have different functions. Human penal institutions are in the service of organizing and maintaining a stable society. Accordingly, they are designed to prevent public injury and promote the common utility [*Ethics* (85), (88)]. While consent not carried into action corrupts the soul, it does not usually result in public injury or detract from public utility [*Ethics* (86)]. Often humans are not in a position to know the intentions of others; only God knows the heart [*Ethics* (85)–(86)]. On the other hand, whether or not accompanied by consent, deeds may have harmful consequences [*Ethics* (79)–(80)] and can set a bad example for others [*Ethics* (86)]. Likewise, since humans can—in principle—know the outward acts of others, laws prohibiting or requiring them can be enforced. Thus, human legal institutions reward and punish deeds according to their harmful or good consequences (potential or actual) in order to deter people from producing the former and encouraging them to produce the latter [*Ethics* (100)]. Not only do human institutions punish lesser sins with greater punishments and vice versa [*Ethics* (88)], but also by following them a judge may be forced to punish someone who is entirely innocent from a moral point of view (e.g., the accused whom the judge knows but cannot by the rules of law prove to be innocent [*Ethics* (81)]). Abelard acknowledges that these penal customs are unjust from a moral point of view, but he does not say that the institutions themselves are unfitting (contrary to God's intentions) in their focus on social organization and public utility. His overall tone is that these institutions have a legitimate place, but—once again—they are distinct from morals.

Morality and the Church:
Abelard's contrast between morality and civil law combines with his identification of morality with divinity to make relations between morality and ecclesiastical norms problematic. For in the *Ethics*, Abelard stresses how "God looks on the heart." One might therefore expect that Divine law, which directs humans to the salvation of their souls, would be sensitive to moral evaluation and not to "external" considerations. Yet, at the institutional level, the Church bears many analogies to civil government: first, canon law specifies what counts as sin and classifies sins as to seriousness; second, it attaches penalties ("penances") proportioned to the crime; third, it defines the powers of various officials, in particular clergy who could serve as judges rendering the verdict and assigning the penance. Abelard recognizes that bishops sometimes mete out punishments with an eye to communal utility rather than guilt (e.g., the poor woman who smothers her baby in trying to keep it warm [*Ethics* (79)–(80)]). And, like Jewish law, canon law imposes "external" requirements on citizens in good standing, including rites of initiation and other sacramental practices.

Pulled in two directions, Abelard mixes "internalist" and "externalist" considerations in his sketch of the degrees of sin, its punishment and remedies. [i] If—pace Cicero—sins come in degrees [*Ethics* (145)–(146)], then Abelard's formal definition of sin as contempt for God would lead us to expect the seriousness of sin to vary both [a] with the intensity of the normative Divine intentions, and [b] with how much of ourselves we put into it. Abelard identifies two criteria for [a] the former: what goes more against the Second Great Commandment of neighbor-love; and how much punishment God assigns to the corresponding deed [*Ethics* (146)]. Focusing on [b], Abelard counts as "venial" or "light" consent to what we *dispositionally* know or believe but don't remember to be unfitting, but classifies as "damnable" or "serious" sins done deliberately [*Ethics* (134)–(136)]. Murder, adultery, and perjury get listed as paradigm "heavy" sins, because (he claims) unlike overeating they cannot be done otherwise than *deliberately*. Again, Abelard classifies as "criminal" sins done deliberately that detract from one's reputation and/or scandalize the Church. But inward intentions by themselves aren't public enough to cause scandal. A few lines down, he corrects himself, indicating that it is *consent* to such deeds that constitutes "heavy" or "criminal" sin [*Ethics* (137); cf. *Ethics* (51)–(52), where he emphasizes that Decalogue prohibitions really forbid *consent* rather than the deeds themselves].

[ii] Abelard gives a thoroughly internalist account of penitence as "the mind's sorrow over what it has failed in" when "it troubles someone that he's gone out of bounds in some way" [*Ethics* (151)]. The wicked and the damned can repent out of fear of punishment. But fruitful penitence proceeds out of love for God, and is incompatible with lingering consent to anything unfitting: e.g., I cannot repent of overeating out of love for God while still spreading rumors about my archenemy, because my love for God will spill over into sorrow about any and every way that I show contempt for Him [*Ethics* (165), (167)]. Moreover, Abelard declares, penitence out of love for God is sufficient for a baptized person to escape the punishment of hell [*Ethics* (166)]! Taking an anti-institutionalist turn, Abelard insists that true penitence will show itself more in restoring what was defrauded and alms-giving than in keeping money for heirs to buy masses for the dead [*Ethics* (158)–(160)].

[iii] Abelard's discussion of confession weaves internalist and institutional threads together. On the one hand, he commends the institution of confession before a priest as useful for individual salvation. For Abelard endorses the Church's view that God requires us to make satisfaction (e.g., by fasting, vigil-keeping, and mortification of the flesh) for our sins; and that *ante mortem* penalties will be lighter than those in *post mortem* purgatory [*Ethics* (200)]. We go to confession in order that the priest may assign such penances to us. Again, confessing before others facilitates the internal transformation of the sinner: the humility involved in confessing is a greater part of the satisfaction we perform, in that it reverses our posture of contempt for God. Finally, by confessing our sins to other Christians, we put ourselves in a position to be helped by their prayers.

Nevertheless, Abelard does not treat this institutional process as absolutely necessary for salvation. For example, Abelard speculates that Peter delayed confession of his sin in denying Christ for a long time—presumably in the interests of institutional stability—but his very tears constituted satisfaction for the sin [*Ethics* (186)–(189)]. Further, he insists, corrupt or ignorant priests can neither open the door to eternal life for the unrepentant nor bar it for those sincerely sorry. Not everyone institutionally authorized but only those who imitate Peter's merits inherit his power of "binding and loosing" [*Ethics* (208)–(222)]. Faced with deficient clerics, Abelard advises penitents to turn to others [*Ethics* (192)] and/or to listen to the sermons without imitating the examples of clerics who preach but do not practice [*Ethics* (196)]. In any event, those who obey wicked priests will not be condemned because God looks to the heart, and their true penitence will reconcile them to God.

Overall, then, Abelard's treatment of penitence, satisfaction, and confession seems to commend the Church's institutional penitential structures to the extent that they are at all useful, but to maintain the distinction between institutional and Divine empowerment, between the decrees of prelates and the judgment of God Who looks on the heart.

Morality and Divine Government:

All the same, there are other passages which jeopardize the consistency of Abelard's identification of morality with divinity.

[i] For God is the provident governor of the universe. Abelard is convinced that justice obliges God everywhere and always to optimize, to do what is maximally reasonable and best [*Ethics* (62)].[10] Moreover, he reckons, Divine as much as human punishment policies in this world may be dictated by considerations of utility more than by the agent's actual fault. Severe afflictions may be visited upon the relatively innocent [a] as a trial test, or [b] as an occasion of glorifying God when they are lifted (e.g., the blind man in John 9), or [c] as a warning to others. Likewise, collective punishment (e.g., of Israel by foreign conquest) makes children suffer great harms along with their sinful adult parents [*Ethics* (119)]. Yet, Abelard reassures, such "condemnations" to bodily death irrespective of guilt are distinct from a sentence of eternal damnation [*Ethics* (122)].

[ii] Cause for confidence seems to evaporate entirely when he admits that although

---

10. Cf. *DPC* (410)–(412); *Romans*-commentary II (v,19) (XI.169, lin. 526–534).

what they did out of ignorance, or even the ignorance itself, isn't properly called sin, that is, scorn for God, so neither is disbelief, although this necessarily closes off access to eternal life for adults who are already using reason. Indeed for damnation it is enough not to believe the Gospel, to be ignorant of Christ, or not to receive the Church's sacraments, even though this happens not through malice so much as through ignorance . . . [*Ethics* (124), (125), (129)]

Appealing to Scripture and experience, and noting that God sometimes rejects those who are more disposed to believe and draws the reluctant instead, Abelard quips that "God's judgments are a great abyss!" [*Ethics* (127)] Likewise, infants cannot sin properly speaking by showing contempt for God [*Ethics* (44), (113), (122)], and yet they contract the punishment from their parents [*Ethics* (45)]. It seems, therefore, that God does not look to the heart in awarding eternal life or damnation after all!

[iii] Abelard also wrestles with the damnation of unbaptized infants in his *Romans*-commentary. By contrast with philosopher-saints before Christ, infants are incapable of intention or consent; when God looks on their hearts, He finds neither guilt nor merit. After Christ such children can be saved only by sacramental participation. Here Abelard tries to soften this conclusion with the bold contention that the damnation of unbaptized infants is accompanied by many Divine graces. First, their punishment is the mildest: they are merely deprived of a vision of Divine Majesty without hope of recovering it![11] At the same time, the severity of their punishment serves as a warning and a prod to others—sometimes, for example, moving the parents to conversion.[12] Yet, if Abelard's God allows general or specific utility to override moral desert where not merely bodily death but eternal damnation is at stake, then surely Divine and moral evaluations break apart! Abelard's final but undeveloped suggestion for reuniting them appeals to God's counterfactual knowledge that the unbaptized infants would have compiled even worse moral records and thereby incurred even more severe punishments had they lived.[13]

Marilyn McCord Adams
Yale University

11. *Romans*-commentary II (v,19) (XI.169–170).
12. *Romans*-commentary II (v,19) (XI.170–172).
13. *Romans*-commentary II (v,19) (XI.170, lin. 549–554).

Translator's Introduction

For Abelard's *Ethics*, I have used the critical Latin edition by D. E. Luscombe.[1] Of course I consulted his excellent translation in preparing my own; it would have been hard not to, since his edition and translation are on facing pages. Nevertheless I found that I disagreed with Luscombe's sense of the text in a few instances. All departures from his Latin edition are marked with an asterisk as described below.

For the *Dialogue*, I have used the critical Latin text by Rudolf Thomas. While this edition is reliable on the whole, it does contain a significant number of typographical errors and several dubious readings. For help with these, I have occasionally consulted the earlier edition in Migne's *Patrologia latina*, always keeping in mind that it is by and large an inferior text. I compared my own translation with Pierre Payer's at each step of the way, although in the end my translation differs markedly from his, both in style and sometimes in sense. It goes without saying that I am enormously indebted to both Payer and Luscombe, without whose earlier translations I would have had far more difficulty coming up with my own.

Both these texts are studded with references to Scripture and to patristic and classical authors. A full translation must identify these references so that readers can pursue matters further if they wish. Nevertheless, in order to keep such references from intruding on the text itself, and in order to keep the number of footnotes to a manageable minimum, I have gathered all external references into a separate section following the translations, where they are keyed to paragraph numbers in the text.

Readers should realize that Abelard's quotations from Scripture are often patchworks of discontinuous verses. I have tried to list all relevant verses in the table of references, but I have done nothing to indicate visually within a given quotation, for example by ellipsis marks, where the "seams" of Abelard's patchwork lie; the list of references provides enough information for readers to work that out for themselves if they are so inclined.

Abelard sometimes employs a method of glossing Scriptural passages in a way modern readers may find confusing at first: he will break up a text into short phrases of only a few words each, following each phrase with his own explanation or comment. A good example of this technique may be found in

---

1. For full bibliographical references here and in the translation, see the Bibliography at the end of this volume.

the *Ethics,* paragraph (16). Such passages should pose no further difficulty once the reader realizes what Abelard is doing.

Internal cross-references *within* each of the texts translated here are incorporated into the translation itself, and are given by paragraph number within square brackets. There are no explicit cross-references *between* the two texts, but there are nevertheless occasional parallel passages that need to be pointed out; these have been indicated in the footnotes.

In several instances, I could not plausibly construe the Latin editions as they stood, and have accordingly had to depart from their readings. In some cases, this involved simply adopting a reading recorded as a variant in the apparatus to the edition. In other cases, it involved correcting a typographical error, conjecturing a palaeographically plausible variant (for example, *'nunc quam'* for *'nunquam'* in one instance), or (in the *Dialogue*) preferring a reading in Migne for a dubious reading in the Thomas edition. All such departures are marked with an asterisk (*) in the translation. Readers with access to the Latin should be able to tell at once from my translation what I have done, so that I have not bothered to explain each such case individually. On the other hand, where it is *not* obvious how I have departed from the editions, I have added a brief explanation in a footnote.

The division and numbering of the paragraphs are my own. Material in square brackets is my own addition; it has no manuscript authority. Section titles not in square brackets are as found in the critical editions. Although they are useful for marking changes of topics, such titles occur too sporadically (especially in the *Dialogue*) to serve as the basis for an analytical table of contents.

I have tried to adopt a fairly literal but flexible approach to these translations. On the one hand, mere paraphrase, no matter how accurate, is not the same thing as translating. I have therefore resolutely avoided the temptation to "improve" Abelard's sometimes obscure text by simply retelling it "in my own words," thereby shielding readers from very real difficulties that ought to be faced; intelligent readers have a right to demand more than that from a translation. On the other hand, I have recognized that it is not always possible, or even desirable, to map the important Latin terms onto English equivalents one to one, as though the goal were to produce a translation from which, by a kind of algorithm, it would be possible to *reconstruct* the original Latin. I have tried to strike a happy medium between these two extremes, sinning if necessary on the side of literalness.

Latin contains a number of conjunctions and adverbs (*'nam,' 'autem,' 'quidem,'* etc.) that by Abelard's day sometimes served as little more than punctuation. Where they seem to convey some genuine nuance (and they usually do), I have tried to capture the sense in my translation, but otherwise I have felt free just to ignore them. Again, Abelard's sentences are sometimes long and ornate in a way modern readers (including me) often find tedious and pompous. Where it was possible to break up a long sentence without losing sight of the connections among the parts, I have done so. But in other cases I have not hesitated to translate a long, complicated sentence literally where I thought this was the only or the best way to capture what Abelard was saying.

Abelard's Latin in these two works contains a number of other difficulties too. Thus subjects and their verbs don't always agree in number, and the tenses of Abelard's verbs often shift suddenly and unpredictably (perhaps most noticeably at the very beginning of the *Dialogue,* paragraph [1]). Where such infelicities are not too obtrusive, I have preserved them in my translation for the sake of accuracy. But where I thought they were confusing or made the text needlessly difficult, I have tacitly "fixed" them without comment.

In an effort to minimize some of the formalities of Abelard's Latin for the modern reader, I have adopted what I hope is a "conversational" tone in the translations, particularly in the *Dialogue,* including the regular use of contractions as observed in colloquial speech. On the other hand, in quotations from Scripture or other authoritative sources, I have studiously avoided such informality.

Abelard sometimes uses the word 'law' to refer to *revealed* law in particular, and other times to refer generally to any law. In the former cases, I have capitalized the word, whereas in the latter I have left it in lower case. Sometimes it is unclear which Abelard intends, and there I have had to use my best judgment. I intend this typographical convention as an aid to reading, but readers should not make too much of it and should feel free to reverse the sense if they think I have it backwards in any given passage.

I have used the capitalized form 'Apostle' where the word is being used as an honorary title for St. Paul. Elsewhere I have used the lowercase form 'apostle.'

Whereas English uses the word 'man' to mean both human being in general and the male of the species in particular, Latin has two quite different words, *'homo'* and *'vir'* respectively, and never confuses them. In an effort to maintain some such distinction in my translations, I have resorted to expressions like 'human being' or 'person' as translations for *'homo.'* On the whole this works without sounding too artificial, but there is a danger the reader should be alerted to. In mediaeval theological vocabulary, 'person' has a technical sense one must be aware of in contexts involving the Trinity or the Incarnation. These doctrines hold that there are three "persons" in the Trinity, and one "person" but two natures in Jesus; obviously the word 'person' cannot be read as a substitute for 'man' in these cases. Again, angels count as "persons,"

Translator's Introduction

although obviously not as human beings. Fortunately, in the texts translated below, there are few opportunities for such confusion, so that the word 'person' is available to be used as a translation for '*homo.*' There is one exception, however: In paragraph **(101)** of the *Ethics*, 'person' is used in the theological sense employed in discussing the Incarnation.

I am indebted to Professor Peter King, Mr. Charles Bolyard, and an anonymous reader for their considerable help and advice in making these translations much more readable and accurate than they would have been otherwise.

Paul Vincent Spade
Indiana University

Ethics

The Beginning of Master Peter Abelard's Book Called "Know Yourself"

[Book I]

(1) We call "morals" the mind's vices or virtues that make us disposed to bad or good deeds.

(2) Not only are there the mind's vices or goods, but also the body's. For example, weakness of the body or the strength we call vigor, sluggardness or nimbleness, lameness or walking erect, blindness or sight. That is why when we said "vices" we prefixed the words "the mind's," in order to exclude such bodily vices. Now these vices (that is, the mind's) are contrary to virtues. For example, injustice to justice, laziness to perseverance, immoderateness to moderation.

On mental vice relevant to morals

(3) But there are also some vices or goods of the mind that are unconnected to morals and don't make a human life deserving of censure or praise. For example, mental obtuseness or a quick wit, being forgetful or having a good memory, ignorance or knowledge. Since all these things turn up among reprobates and good people alike, they are irrelevant to the make-up of morals and don't make a life shameful or respectable. Thus when we said "the mind's vices" above [(1)], we were right to add, in order to exclude such morally irrelevant vices, the words "that make us disposed to bad deeds"—that is, they incline the will to something that isn't properly to be done or renounced at all.[1]

What difference is there between a sin and a vice inclining one to evil?

(4) This kind of mental vice isn't the same as a sin. And a sin isn't the same as a bad action. For instance, being hot-tempered—that is, disposed or easily

---

1. The sentence is elliptical. The sense is that they incline the will either to *do* something that should *not* be done, or else to *forgo* something that *should* be done.

given to the turmoil that is anger—is a vice. It inclines the mind to doing something impulsively and irrationally that isn't fit to be done at all. Now this vice is in the soul in such a way that the soul is easily given to getting angry even when it isn't being moved to anger, just as the lameness whereby a person is called "lame" is in him even when he isn't limping around. For the vice is present even when the action is absent.

(5) So also the body's very nature or structure makes many people prone to wantonness, just as it does to anger. But they don't sin by the fact that they are like this. Rather they get from it material for a fight, so that victorious over themselves through the virtue of moderation they might obtain a crown.[2] Thus Solomon says, "The long-suffering man is better than the mighty man, and the one who rules his mind than the capturer of cities." For religion doesn't think it shameful to be defeated by a human being, but by a vice. The former surely happens to good people too, but in the latter we depart from goods.

(6) In recommending this victory to us, the Apostle says, "No one will be crowned unless he struggles according to the Law." Struggles, I say, in resisting not people so much as vices, lest they drag us away to improper* consent. They don't stop assaulting us, even if people do stop, so that the vices' attack against us is more dangerous the more it is repeated, and victory is more glorious the more difficult it is. But no matter how much people influence us, they force nothing shameful on our life unless, having so to speak been *turned** into vices for us, they subject us to shameful consent the way vices do. There is no risk to true liberty while others rule the body; we don't run into any abominable slavery as long as the mind is free. For it isn't shameful to serve a human being but to serve a vice, and it isn't bodily slavery that disfigures the soul but submission to vices. For whatever is common to good and bad people equally is irrelevant to virtue or vice.

What is mental vice, and what is properly called "sin"?

(7) So it is vice that makes us disposed to sin—that is, we are inclined to consent to what is inappropriate, so that we do it or renounce it.[3] This consent is what we properly call "sin," the fault of the soul whereby it merits damnation or is held guilty before God. For what is this consent but scorn for God and an

2. That is, a reward or prize.
3. Again the sentence is elliptical. The idea is that we either do what should *not* be done, or go without doing what *should* be done.

affront against him? God cannot be offended by injury but he can by scorn. For he is the ultimate power, not diminished by any injury but wreaking vengeance on scorn for him.

(8) Thus our sin is scorn for the creator, and to sin is to scorn the creator— not to do for his sake what we believe we ought to do for his sake, or not to renounce for his sake what we believe ought to be renounced. And so when we define sin negatively, saying it is *not* doing or *not* renouncing what is appropriate, we show clearly that there is no substance to a sin; it consists of non-being rather than of being. It is as if we define shadows by saying they are the absence of light where light did have being.

(9) But perhaps you will say that *willing* a bad deed is also a sin; it renders us guilty before God, just as willing a good deed makes us just. As a result, in the same way as there is virtue in a good will so there is sin in a bad will, and there is sin not only in non-being but also in being, just as with virtue.[4] For just as by willing to do what we believe pleases God we do please him, so by willing to do what we believe displeases God we do displease him, and appear to affront or scorn him.

(10) But I say that if we look more closely, we have to view this matter quite otherwise than it appears. For sometimes we sin *without* any bad will. And when a bad will is curbed without being extinguished, it wins the palm-branch of victory for those resisting it, and provides the material for a fight and a crown of glory. It shouldn't itself be called a "sin" but a kind of illness that is now[5] necessary.

(11) Look, here is some innocent person. His cruel master is so enraged with fury at him that with bared blade he hunts him down to kill him. The innocent man flees him for a long time, and avoids his own murder as long as he can. Finally, under duress and against his will, he kills his master in order not to be killed by him.

(12) Whoever you are, tell me what bad will he had in doing this deed! If he wanted to flee death, he also wanted to save his own life. But was this willing a bad one?

(13) You will say: It isn't *this* will, I think, that is bad, but the will he had for killing the master who was hunting him down.

(14) I reply: You speak well and astutely, if you can point to a will in what you are saying. But, as was already said [(11)], it was against his will and under duress that he did what kept his life intact as long as possible. Also, he knew

---

4. The point is that while some sins (*e.g.*, sins of omission) are non-beings, others (*e.g.*, certain acts of will) are beings.

5. That is, in this life.

danger would threaten his own life as a result of this slaying. How then did he *willingly* do what he did with this danger even to his own life?

(15) If you reply that this too was done because of a willing, since obviously he was brought to this point by willing to escape death, not by willing to kill his master, we aren't contesting that. But as was already said,[6] this willing isn't to be condemned as bad. As you say, through it he wanted to escape death, not to kill his master. Yet he did wrong in consenting (even though he was under duress from the fear of death) to an unjust slaying he should have borne rather than inflicted. He certainly took up the sword on his own; he didn't have it entrusted to him by some power.

(16) Hence Truth says, "Everyone who takes up the sword will perish by the sword." "Who," he says, "takes up the sword" out of presumptuousness, not someone to whom it was entrusted for the sake of administering punishment. "Will perish by the sword"—that is, brings upon himself damnation and the slaying of his own soul by this foolhardiness. And so, as was said, he wanted to escape death, not to kill his master. But because he consented to a killing he shouldn't have consented to, his unjust consent that preceded the killing was a sin.

(17) Now if perhaps someone says this person wanted to slay his master for the purpose of escaping death, he cannot without qualification infer from this that he wanted to kill him. It is as if I tell someone, "I want you to have my cap, for the purpose of your giving me fifty cents,"[7] or "I cheerfully want it to become yours for that price." I don't therefore grant that I want it to be yours. And if someone confined in jail wants to put his son there instead of himself, so that he might look for his own ransom, do we therefore grant without qualification that he wants to send his son to jail—an event he is forced to accept, with great tears and many groans?

(18) Surely a so called "willing" like this, one that consists of great mental sorrow, isn't to be called a "willing" but instead a "suffering." To say he "wants" one thing because of another is like saying he tolerates what he doesn't want because of something else he does desire. So too a sick person is said to "want" to be cauterized or to be operated on in order to be cured. And the martyrs "wanted" to suffer in order to reach Christ, or Christ himself "wanted" to suffer that we might be saved by his suffering. But we aren't thereby forced to grant without qualification that they wanted this. For there

6. In fact Abelard has not quite said this. But see the rhetorical questions in (12) and (14).
7. Fifty cents = literally, five *solidi*—shillings or French sous. The exact value varied, but it was not very much. I have translated by an appropriate but approximate small sum.

cannot be a "suffering" at all except where something happens against one's will; no one "suffers" when he accomplishes his will and when what happens delights him. Surely the Apostle who says, "I long to be dissolved and to be with Christ"—that is, to die in order to reach him—elsewhere comments, "We do not want to be disrobed but to be clothed over, so that what is mortal be absorbed by life."[8]

(19) Blessed Augustine also mentions this view, stated by the Lord where he says to Peter, "You will hold out your hands, and someone else will gird you and lead you where you do not want to go." In accordance with human nature's assumed[9] infirmity, the Lord also says to the Father: "If it is possible, let this chalice pass from me. Yet not as I will, but as you do." Surely his soul was naturally terrified at the great suffering of his death, and what he knew would be a penalty couldn't be a matter of "willing" for him. Even though elsewhere it is written about him, "He was offered up because he himself willed it," either this has to be taken in accordance with the nature of divinity,[10] the will of which included the assumed man's suffering, or else "willed it" is here used in the sense of "arranged it," in accordance with the Psalmist's statement, "He has done whatever he willed."

(20) Hence it is plain that sin is sometimes committed without any bad will at all, so that it is clear from this that willing isn't said to be what sin is.

(21) Of course, you will say, this holds where we sin under duress, but it doesn't hold where we sin willingly. For example, if we want to commit some deed we know shouldn't be committed by us. In that case, surely, the bad willing and the sin appear to be the same. For example, someone sees a woman and falls into lust. His mind is stirred by the pleasure of the flesh, with the result that he is set on fire for the shamefulness of sex. So, you say, what else is this willing and shameful desire but sin?

(22) I reply: What if this willing is curbed by the virtue of moderation but not extinguished, stays for the fight, holds out for the struggle, and doesn't give up even when defeated? For where is the fight if the material for the fight is absent? Where does the great reward come from if there is nothing serious

---

8. That is, we do not want to die but, without dying, to receive a glorified, immortal body *over* our present body, if that were possible. In that case our mortal body would be so to speak "absorbed" by the immortal one (by "life").

9. "Assumed" here and later in the paragraph is a technical term from the theology of the Incarnation, in which the second person of the Trinity, in addition to the divine nature it already had, "assumed"—that is, took on—a human nature in becoming the man Jesus.

10. That is, the "willing" refers to the *divine* will in Jesus, not his human will.

we put up with? When the struggle has passed, there is no fighting left but only the receiving of the reward. We struggle by fighting here in order that, triumphant in the struggle, we might receive a crown elsewhere. But to have a fight it's proper to have an enemy who resists, not one who gives up altogether. Now this* enemy is our bad will, the one we triumph over when we subject it to the divine will. But we don't entirely extinguish it, so that we always have a will we might strive against.

(23) For what great deed do we do for God's sake if we don't put up with anything opposed to our willing but instead accomplish what we will? Indeed who thanks us if, in what we say we are doing for his sake, we are accomplishing our own will?

(24) Rather, you will say, what do we merit before God from what we do, either willingly or unwillingly?

(25) I reply: Nothing, of course, since in giving out rewards he takes account of the mind rather than the action. The action doesn't add anything to the merit, whether it springs from good or bad willing, as we shall show later on [(30), (35)–(48)].

(26) But when we prefer his will to ours, so that we follow his rather than ours, we do obtain great merit before him, according to the perfection of Truth, "I did not come to do my will but his who sent me." In encouraging us to do this, he says "If anyone comes to me and does not hate his father and mother, indeed even his own soul, he is not worthy of me." That is, unless he refuses their suggestions or his own will and submits himself entirely to my commands. Therefore, if we are ordered to hate our father but not kill him, so too for our will; the order is that we not follow it, not that we destroy it entirely.

(27) For he who says, "Do not pursue your lusts, and turn away from your will," commanded us not to *satisfy* our lusts, but not to do without them altogether. For satisfying them is wicked, but going without them is impossible in our feeble state. And so it isn't the lusting after a woman but the consenting to the lust that is the sin. It isn't the will to have sex with her that is damnable but the will's consent.

(28) Let's look at gluttony with respect to what we said about wantonness. Someone is going by another person's garden and on seeing the delicious fruits falls to craving them. But he doesn't consent to his craving so that he takes something away from there by theft or plunder, although his mind has been inflamed to a great desire by the deliciousness of the food. Now where there is desire, no doubt there is will. So he desires to eat the other person's fruit, and he doesn't doubt there is pleasure in eating it. Indeed he is driven by the very nature of his feeble state to desire what he may not take without its owner's

knowledge and permission. He curbs his desire; he doesn't destroy it. But because he isn't drawn into consent, he doesn't fall into sin.

(29) What is the point of this? In brief, to make it clear that in such cases too[11] the sin isn't said to be the willing itself or the desire to do what isn't allowed, but rather the consent, as we said [(7)]. Now we consent to what isn't allowed when we don't draw back from committing it and are wholly ready to carry it out should the opportunity arise.

(30) So whoever is found in this condition has incurred complete guilt. Adding on the performance of the deed doesn't add anything to increase the sin. Instead, for God, someone who tries as hard as he can to go through with it is just as guilty as one who does go through with it insofar as he is able. It is just as if he too had been apprehended in the very deed, as blessed Augustine remarks.

(31) But although the willing isn't the sin and sometimes we even commit sins *against* our will, as we said [(11), (14)], nevertheless some people say every sin is "voluntary." In so doing they find a kind of difference between the sin and the willing. For one thing is called the "will," and another thing is called "voluntary"; that is, the will is other than what is committed *by* the will. But if we call a sin what we have said above is properly called a sin [(7)–(8)]—namely scorn for God, consenting to what we believe should be renounced for his sake—then how do we say the sin is "voluntary"? That is, how do we say we *want* to scorn God (which is what sinning is), or to grow worse or to be made deserving of damnation? For although we might want to do what we know ought to be punished, or that whereby we might be deserving of punishment, nevertheless we don't want to be punished. In this respect we are plainly being unfair, because we want to do what is unfair but don't want to yield to the fairness[12] of a penalty that is just. The penalty, which is just, displeases; the action, which is unjust, pleases.

(32) Often too it comes about that although, attracted by her appearance, we want to have sex with someone we know is married, nevertheless we wouldn't want to commit adultery with her; we would want her *not* to be married. Conversely, there are many who for the sake of their own fame yearn more for the wives of powerful men, *because* they are the wives of such men, than they would if the same women were unmarried. They are more eager to commit adultery than fornication, to deviate more rather than less.

11. That is, in matters of gluttony, as well as matters of wantonness as discussed in (21)–(27).

12. There is a wordplay here that is hard to translate satisfactorily. *Iniquum* = wicked, but etymologically = unequal, hence unjust, *unfair*. It is therefore opposed to *aequitas* = equality, hence equity, justice, *fairness*.

(33) There are also people who entirely regret being drawn into consenting to lust or into an evil will, and are compelled by the flesh's weakness to want what they don't *want* to want at all.

(34) Therefore, I really don't see how this consent that we don't want is going to be called "voluntary" so that, following some people as was said [(31)], we call *every* sin "voluntary"—unless we understand the "voluntary" as merely excluding the necessary (since no sin is inevitable), or call the "voluntary" whatever arises from some will (for although he who killed his master under duress didn't have a will for killing, nevertheless he committed it from *some* will, since he wanted to escape or put off death).

(35) Some people may be more than a little upset because they hear us say [(30)] that doing the sin doesn't add anything to the guilt or to the damnation before God. For they object that in acting out a sin there follows a kind of pleasure that increases the sin, as in sex or in the eating we talked about [(28)].

(36) It wouldn't be absurd of them to say this, if they proved that this kind of bodily pleasure is a sin and that no one can commit anything like that without sinning. If they actually accept that, then surely it is illicit for *anyone* to have this bodily pleasure. Hence not even married couples are exempt from sin when they are brought together by this bodily pleasure that is permitted to them, and neither is one who enjoys a delicious meal of his own fruit. All sick people too would be at fault who favor sweeter foods for refreshment, in order to recuperate from their illness. They surely don't take these foods *without* pleasure; otherwise if they took them they wouldn't help.

(37) Finally, even the Lord, the creator of foods as well as of our bodies, wouldn't be without fault if he inserted into those foods flavors such as would necessarily force those who eat them into sin by their pleasure in them. For why would he make such foods for our eating, or permit us to eat them, if it were impossible for us to eat them without sin? And how can sin be said to be committed in doing what is permitted?

(38) For if what were at one time illegal and prohibited deeds are later permitted and so legalized, they are committed now without any sin at all. For example, eating the flesh of pigs and many other actions once prohibited to the Jews but now permitted to us. So when we see even Jews who have been converted to Christ freely eating the kinds of foods the Law had prohibited, how do we defend them as without fault except by maintaining that this is now permitted to them by God?

(39) Hence if in such eating, formerly prohibited to them but now permitted, the permission itself excuses the sin and takes away scorn for God, who can say anyone sins in doing what divine permission has made legal for him? Therefore, if having sex with one's wife or eating delicious food has been

permitted to us from the first day of our creation, which was lived without sin in paradise, who will argue that we have sinned if we don't go beyond the bounds of permission?

(40) But again, they say sex in marriage and the eating of delicious food are only permitted in such a way that the pleasure itself is *not* permitted. Rather, they should be done entirely *without* pleasure. But surely if this is so, then they were permitted to be done in a way such that they cannot be done at all. An authorization that permitted their being done in a way that they certainly *cannot* be done is unreasonable.

(41) Furthermore, why did the Law at one time urge marriage so that each one would leave behind his seed in Israel, or why did the Apostle require married couples to fulfill their duty to one another, if these things cannot be done without sin? Why does he talk about "duty" here, where already there is necessarily sin? How is anyone supposed to be *required* to do what will offend God by sinning?

(42) In my judgment, it is plain from these considerations that no natural bodily pleasure is to be counted as a sin. It isn't to be regarded as a fault that we take pleasure in what is such that, when it has occurred, pleasure is necessarily felt. For example, if someone forces someone in religious orders, bound by chains, to lie among women, and he is led into pleasure—but *not* into consent—by the bed's softness and the touch of the women around him, who can venture to call this pleasure nature has made necessary a "sin"?

(43) Now suppose you object that, as it appears to some people, even bodily pleasure in lawful sex is regarded as a sin. For David says, "For behold, I was conceived in iniquities." And when the Apostle said, "Come back together again, that Satan not tempt you because of your lack of self-restraint," he adds, "Now I say this as an indulgence, not as a commandment." These texts seem to bind us, more by authority than by reason, to grant that bodily pleasure is itself a sin. For it is well known that David wasn't conceived in fornication but in marriage. And indulgence—that is, forgiving, as they say—doesn't occur where fault is completely missing.

(44) But as far as appears to me, the fact that David says he had been conceived in iniquities, or "sins," and didn't specify whose, refers to the general curse of original sin, the sin whereby everyone is made subject to damnation by the fault of his own parents. This accords with what is written elsewhere, "No one is clean of stain if his life is on earth, not even the day-old infant." For as blessed Jerome has remarked, and as plain reason has it, the soul lacks sin as long as it is in infancy. Therefore, if it is clean of sin, how is it unclean with the stain of sin, unless it's because the former is to be understood with respect to fault, the latter with respect to punishment?

(45) Surely one who doesn't yet perceive by reason what he ought to do doesn't have any fault because of scorn for God. Yet he isn't immune to the stain of his earlier parents' sin, from which he already incurs punishment even if not fault; he preserves in his punishment what they committed in their fault. Thus when David says he was conceived in iniquities or sins, he perceived that he was subject to the general pronouncement of damnation from the fault of his parents. And he referred these offenses not so much to his immediate parents as to earlier ones.

(46) Now what the Apostle called "indulging" isn't to be taken, as they wish it to be, in the sense that he called forgiving a sin "indulging" in the sense of "allowing." Surely his expression, "as an authorization, not as compulsory," is as if he had said "by way of allowing, not by coercing." For if a married couple wishes, and they have decided by mutual consent, they can completely abstain from carnal practice; they are not to be forced into it by a commandment. But if they haven't decided this, they have the "indulgence"—that is, they are allowed—to turn away from the more perfect life to the practice of a more lenient life. Therefore, the Apostle in this passage didn't understand "indulging" as forgiving a sin, but as the authorization of a more lenient life in order to avoid fornication, with the result that the inferior life would prevent a great amount of sin, and is less in merits so that it not become greater in sins.

(47) We have brought up these matters so that no one, perhaps wanting every pleasure of the flesh to be a sin, would say that sin itself is increased by the action when one extends the mind's consent to the point of performing the deed, so that one is defiled not only by consent to shamefulness but also by the stains of the act. As if what occurred outside in the body could defile the soul!

(48) Therefore, any kind of carrying out of deeds is irrelevant to increasing a sin. Nothing taints the soul but what belongs to it, namely the consent that we've said is alone the sin, not the will preceding it or the subsequent doing of the deed. For even if we want or do what is improper, we don't *thereby* sin, since these things frequently occur without sin, just as, conversely, consent occurs without these things. We have already shown this in part: the point about the will without consent, in the example of the man who fell into lust for a woman he saw, or for someone else's fruit, yet wasn't enticed to consent [(21)–(28)]; the point about bad consent without a bad will, in the example of the person who killed his master unwillingly [(11)–(17)].

(49) Now as for things that ought not to be done, I don't think it escapes anyone how often they *are* done without sin, for example when they are committed through force or ignorance. For instance, if a woman subjected to force has sex with someone else's husband, or if a man somehow deceived sleeps with a woman he thought was his wife, or if by mistake he kills someone

he believed *should* be killed by him in his role as a judge. So it isn't a sin to lust after someone else's wife, or to have sex with her; the sin is rather to *consent* to this lust or to this action.

(50) Indeed the Law calls this *consent* to lust "lust" when it says, "Thou shalt not lust."[13] For it isn't the *lusting* that had to be prohibited (which we cannot avoid and wherein we do not sin, as was said [(27)]), but rather the *assent* to it. The Lord's words too, "He who shall look at a woman in order to lust after her," have to be understood in this way: he who shall look at her in order to fall into *consent* to lust "has already committed adultery in his heart," even if he hasn't committed adultery in deed. That is, he already has the guilt for the sin, even if he is still lacking the performance of it.

(51) If we look carefully, wherever deeds appear to be included under a command or prohibition, they are to be referred more to the will[14] or the consent to the deeds than to the deeds themselves. Otherwise, nothing relevant to merit would come under the scope of a command. For things less in our power are less worth commanding. There are surely many things we are prevented from doing, but we always have will and consent within our power of choosing.

(52) Look, the Lord says "Thou shalt not kill," "Thou shalt not bear false witness." If we take these at face value, as being only about the deed, guilt isn't proscribed at all. Neither is fault prohibited, but only the action associated with the fault. For it isn't a sin to kill a human being or to have sex with someone else's wife. These acts can be committed sometimes without sin. If this kind of prohibition is taken at face value, as being about the deed, then he who *wants* to bear false witness, or even he who *consents* to saying it, as long as he *doesn't* say it and keeps quiet for whatever reason, doesn't become guilty before the Law. For it wasn't stated that we should not *want* to bear false witness, or not *agree* to bearing it, but only that we should not bear it.

(53) Or again, when the Law forbids us from taking our sisters in marriage, or from joining together with them, there is no one who can keep this commandment, since often someone cannot recognize his sisters—no one, I say, if the prohibition is made with respect to the act rather than to the consent. So when someone out of ignorance accidentally takes his sister in marriage, does he break the commandment because he does what the Law forbade him to do?

13. Lust = *concupisces*. The usual translation here is "covet," which is broader than sexual lust. But Abelard has hitherto been using the word in primarily sexual contexts.

14. The occurrence of this word here is surprising. Abelard has been at pains to *distinguish* the will from the consent to it.

(54) You will say he doesn't break it, because* he didn't *consent* to breaking it insofar as he acted unknowingly. Therefore, just as he who does what is forbidden isn't to be called a lawbreaker, but rather he who consents to what is agreed to be forbidden, so neither is the prohibition to be taken with respect to the deed, but with respect to the consent. Thus, when it says "Do not do this or that," it's like saying "Do not *consent* to doing this or that"—as if it said "Do not knowingly venture to do this."

(55) Blessed Augustine too thought about this closely and reduced every command or prohibition to charity or greed rather than to deeds. He says, "The Law commands nothing but charity, and forbids nothing but greed." Hence too the Apostle says, "All the law is fulfilled in one statement: You shall love your neighbor as yourself." And again, "The fulfillment of the Law is love."

(56) Surely it has no bearing on merit whether you give alms to one in need. Charity may make you prepared to give alms and your will may be ready, although the means are absent and the power to do so doesn't remain in you, no matter what chance event it is that impedes you. Surely it is plain that deeds appropriately done or not are equally carried out by good people as by bad. The intention alone separates the two cases.

(57) Indeed, as the aforesaid Doctor[15] remarks, in the same deed in which we see God the Father and the Lord Jesus Christ, we also see Judas the traitor.[16] When the Father handed over the Son and the Son handed himself over, as the Apostle mentions, and Judas handed over his master, certainly the handing over of the Son was done by God the Father; it was also done by the Son, and it was done by the traitor. Therefore, the traitor did what God did too. But did he do *well* to do it? For even if it was good, it was not at any rate done well, or something that ought to have been beneficial to him. For God doesn't think about the things that are done but rather in what mind they are done. The merit or praiseworthiness of the doer doesn't consist in the deed but in the intention.

(58) Often in fact the same thing is done by different people, through the justice of one and the viciousness of the other. For example, if two people hang a criminal, one out of a zeal for justice and the other out of hatred springing from an old feud,[17] then although the hanging is the same action, and although

15. "Doctor" literally means "teacher." Here Abelard is referring to Augustine (see [(55)]), who was often referred to as one of the "Doctors of the Church."

16. The reference is to Judas' betrayal ("handing over") of Jesus. With this paragraph, compare Abelard's *Dialogue* (406).

17. Compare Abelard's *Dialogue* (404).

they certainly do what is good to be done[18] and what justice demands, nevertheless through the difference in their intention the same thing is done by different people, one badly and the other well.

(59) Finally, who doesn't know that the Devil himself does nothing but what he is permitted to do by God, when he either punishes an unjust person deservedly or else is allowed to afflict a just person, either to purify him or else to offer an example of patience? But because it is at the instigation of his own viciousness that he does what God permits him to do, his power is said to be good or even just, while his will is always unjust. The former he gets from God; the latter he has from himself.

(60) Also, who among the elect can be the equal of the hypocrites in matters pertaining to deeds? Who puts up with or does so many things from the love of God as they do from greed for human praise?[19] Finally, who doesn't know that sometimes things God forbids to be done are rightly performed anyway, or *should* be done, just as sometimes, contrariwise, he commands some things that nevertheless aren't fit to be done? For look, we know that when he was curing illnesses, some of his miracles he forbade to be revealed, as an example of humility, so that no one would crave fame from perhaps having a similar grace bestowed on himself. Yet nonetheless, those who received the benefits didn't stop publicizing them for the honor of him who both did them and forbade their being revealed. It is written of those people, "As much as he commanded them not to tell, so much more did they proclaim it," etc.

(61) Will you judge such people guilty of breaking the law? They acted contrary to the command they received, and even did so knowingly. What will excuse them from lawbreaking except the fact that nothing they decided to do to honor the one who gave the command did they do out of scorn for him? Tell me, please, did Christ command what should not have been commanded? Or did they reject a command that should have been kept? What wasn't good to be done was nevertheless good to be commanded.

(62) No doubt you'll find fault with the Lord even in the case of Abraham. He first commanded Abraham to sacrifice his son, but afterwards prevented it himself. Did God not do *well* to command to be done what wasn't good to be done? For if it *was* good, why was it forbidden later on? But if the same thing was both good to be commanded and good to be forbidden (for God neither

---

18. The construction is awkward in English, but Abelard is carefully avoiding the active voice here; he conspicuously does *not* say it is "good *to do* it." So too in (61)–(62), (65)–(66) below.

19. The idea is that if deeds were what mattered, the "hypocrites" would end up being the most meritorious of all.

permits anything to happen nor consents to do it without reasonable cause), you see that only the intention of the commandment excuses God, not the doing of the deed. He did well to command what wasn't good to be done. For God didn't intend this or command it to be done in order that Abraham would *really* sacrifice his son, but in order that his obedience and the steadfastness of his faith or of his love for him might be sorely tried and left as an example to us.

(63) Surely the Lord himself plainly acknowledged this later on, when he said, "I have recognized now that you fear the Lord"—as if he had said openly, "What you have shown yourself prepared to do, this I commanded of you, so that I might make others know what I myself had known about you before the ages."

(64) Thus, this intention of God's was right, in the case of a deed that was *not* right. So too his prohibition was right in the matters we mentioned [(60)]. He forbade them not in order that the prohibition be observed but in order that examples of shunning empty glory might be given to us invalids.

(65) So God commanded what wasn't good to be done, just as conversely he forbade what *was* good to be done. And as in the former case [(62)] the intention excuses him, so too in the latter [(60)] it excuses those who didn't fulfill the commandment in deed. They surely knew he hadn't commanded it for the sake of the commandment's being kept, but in order that the abovementioned example be set out. Keeping the will of the order-giver, they didn't scorn him whose will they understood they weren't going against.

(66) Therefore, if we think of deeds rather than of the intention, we will see not only that sometimes one *wills* something to be done contrary to God's command, but even that it *is* done, and done knowingly, without any of the guilt belonging to sin. When the intention of the one to whom the command is given doesn't depart from the will of the command-giver, the will or the action isn't to be called "bad" just because it doesn't keep God's command in deed. For just as the intention of the order-giver excuses him who commands to be done what nevertheless isn't fit to be done, so too the intention of charity excuses him to whom the command is given.

(67) To gather all that has been said into one short conclusion, there are four things we have set out above in order that we might carefully distinguish them from one another: (a) the mental vice that makes us disposed to sin [(2)–(7)]; after that (b) the sin itself, which we have located in consent to evil or in scorn for God [(8)]; then (c) the will for evil [(9)–(34)]; and (d) the doing of the evil [(35)–(66)]. Now just as willing isn't the same as accomplishing the will, so sinning isn't the same as carrying out the sin. The former is to be taken as the mind's consent by which we sin, the latter as the result of the doing, when we accomplish in deed what we have consented to earlier.

(68) Thus, when we say sin or temptation comes about in three ways—by suggestion, pleasure and consent—it is to be understood that we are often seduced into doing sin by these three things, as happened with our first parents. For the devil's persuading came first, when he promised immortality would come from tasting of the forbidden tree. Pleasure followed when the woman, seeing the fine wood and understanding it was sweet to eat,[20] was set on fire with a craving for it by the pleasure she believed she would take from the food. Although to keep the commandment she should have curbed her craving, she was drawn into sin by her consenting to it. And while she should have corrected the sin by repenting, to merit forgiveness, in the end she brought it to completion in her deed. And so she progressed in three phases to performing the sin.

(69) So too we often reach the point, not of sinning but of *performing* the sin, by these same steps: (a) by suggestion, at the instigation of someone who urges us from outside to do something improper. But if we know it is pleasurable to do it, then (b) even before it is done our mind is carried away by the pleasure of the deed, and in the thought itself we are tempted by pleasure. When (c) we approve of this pleasure by consent, we sin. By these three steps, we finally reach the point of performing the sin.

(70) There are some people who want the suggestion of the flesh, even if a suggesting *person* is absent, to be included under the name "suggestion." For example when a woman is seen, if someone falls into lust for her. But actually, it seems that this "suggestion" ought to be called nothing but pleasure. In fact this pleasure, which comes about necessarily so to speak, and others like it that we remarked above [(42)] are *not* a sin, the Apostle calls "human temptation" when he says: "Let temptation not grab hold of you, unless it is human temptation. Now God is faithful. He will not allow you to be tempted more than you are able to bear. Rather along with the temptation he will also make a way out for you, so that you can withstand it."

(71) Now temptation in general is said to be any inclination of the mind to doing something improper, whether that inclination is a will or a consent. But a temptation without which human frailty is now[21] hardly or never able to go on is called "human." For example, carnal lust or desiring delicious food. The one who said, "Release me from my needs, Lord" asked to be freed from them— that is, from these temptations of lusts that now come about so to speak naturally and necessarily, so that they not draw me into consent, or so that I will lack them entirely when this life full of temptations is over.

---

20. Presumably Eve thought it would be sweet to eat the *fruit*, not the *wood*.
21. That is, now after the Fall of Adam.

(72) Therefore, the Apostle's statement, "Let temptation not grab hold of you, unless it is a human temptation," is much like saying, "If the mind is inclined by a pleasure that is a 'human' temptation, as we have called it, let it not lead the mind as far as the consent sin consists of." He says, as if someone had asked what power of ours enables us to resist these lusts: "God is faithful. He will not allow you to be tempted." It is as if he had said, "Rather than trusting in ourselves, we should place our confidence in him who promises us aid and is truthful in all his promises." This is what it is for him to be faithful, so that faith in him is to be extended in all matters. If we do this, he doesn't allow us to be tempted more than we are able to bear, since he so tempers this human temptation with his mercy that it doesn't pressure us into sin more than we can endure by resisting it.

(73) But more than that, he then turns this temptation itself into an opportunity for us, when he exercises us by it so that thereafter it can be less hard on us when it occurs, and so that even now we may fear less the assault of an enemy we have already conquered and know how to endure. Surely, every fight we haven't yet been through is harder to withstand and is feared more. But when it comes to be routine for the victors, its strength and terror alike disappear.

On suggestions by demons

(74) Now suggestions come not only from people but also from demons. For they too sometimes urge us to sin, not so much by their words as by their deeds. They are skilled in the nature of things, both by the subtlety of their abilities and by long experience. For this reason they are called "demons"—that is, knowers.[22] They know the natural forces of things whereby human frailty can be easily aroused to lewdness or to other impulses.

(75) Thus sometimes, with God's permission, they put people into a state of lethargy, and afterwards bring cures to those who beg them to. Often when they stop injuring them, they are believed to cure them. In the end, they were permitted to work many amazing tricks against Moses in Egypt by means of magicians, by the natural force of the things they knew. They aren't to be called "creators" of what they made so much as "arrangers." For example if

22. In his *Etymologies*, Isidore of Seville had offered the following derivation (*Etymologiae*, VIII. 11. 15–16): "They are called 'demons' by the Greeks, *'daimonas'* as it were—that is, skilled and knowledgeable of things. For they foreknow many future things, and so are accustomed to give replies to questions. For the knowledge of things inheres in them more than in human weakness, in part because of the acuity of their superior sense, in part because of the experience of their extremely long life, and in part by an angelic revelation through an order by God."

someone, following the lesson in Vergil and pounding bull-meat, brought it about thereby that bees were produced by his labor, he shouldn't be called the "creator" of the bees so much as a "preparer" of nature.

(76) So by this skill they have with the natures of things, demons arouse us to lust or other mental passions and bring them to us, by whatever art, while we don't realize it, putting them either in our sense of taste or in our bed, or stationing them somehow or other inside us or outside. For in herbs or seeds, or in the natures of both trees and stones, there are many forces apt to arouse or pacify our minds. Those who would come to know them closely could do this with ease.

Why the doing of sin is punished more than the sin itself

(77) There are people too who get more than a little upset when they hear us say [(30), (35)–(48)] the *doing* of a sin isn't properly said to be the sin, or doesn't add anything to enlarge the sin. Why, they ask, is a harder atonement exacted of penitents for performing the deed than for being guilty of the fault?

(78) I give them this reply first: Why aren't you especially surprised at the fact that sometimes a great penalty is imposed as atonement where *no* fault occurred, and that sometimes we ought to punish those we know are innocent?

(79) For look, some poverty-stricken woman has a little baby at the breast and doesn't have enough clothes to be able to meet the needs both of the little one in the crib and of herself. So, moved by pity for the little baby, she puts him by her side to warm him with her own rags. In the end, overwhelmed in her own feebleness by the force of nature, she is driven to smother the one she embraces with the greatest love.

(80) Augustine says, "Have charity and do whatever you want." Yet when she comes to the bishop for atonement, a heavy penalty is exacted from her, not for a fault she committed but to make her or other women more careful about anticipating such dangers.

(81) Sometimes too it happens that someone is accused by his enemies before a judge. They attribute to him something such that the judge thereby knows he is innocent. Yet because they pursue the matter and demand a hearing in court, they begin the proceedings on the assigned day. They bring forward witnesses, although false ones, to convict the one they are accusing. Yet since the judge cannot in any way refute the witnesses by clear reasons, he is forced by the law to accept them. Admitting their proof, he punishes the innocent. Therefore, he should punish one who shouldn't be punished. He should do it anyway, because it is in accordance with the law that the judge does justly here what the person didn't deserve.

(82) So it is clear from these cases that sometimes a penalty is reasonably exacted from one in whom no fault has occurred. What then is there to wonder at, if where a fault *has* occurred, the ensuing deed increases the penalty before human beings in *this* life, but not before God in the future one? For human beings don't judge about what is hidden but about what is plain. They don't think so much of the guilt belonging to the fault as of the performance of the deed. Rather God alone, who pays attention not so much to the deeds that are done as to the mind with which they are done, is truly thinking about the guilt in our intention and tries the fault in a true court.

(83) Thus he is called the tester of the heart and reins, and is said to see in darkness. For where no one sees, there he sees most of all, because in punishing sin he doesn't pay attention to the deed but to the mind, just as conversely we don't pay attention to the mind that we don't see but to the deed we know. Thus often we punish the innocent or free culprits, either by mistake or through being forced by the law, as we said. God is called the tester and knower of the heart and reins—that is, of any intentions coming from an emotion of the soul or from bodily weakness or pleasure.

On spiritual or carnal sins

(84) Now since all sins belong to the soul alone, not to the flesh, surely sin and scorn for God can exist where knowledge of him and reason can reside. Nevertheless some sins are called spiritual, others carnal. That is, some come from the soul's vices, others from the flesh's weakness. And although lust belongs only to the soul, as will does too (for we cannot lust after or desire something except by willing it), nevertheless there is said to be a lust of the flesh as well as a lust of the spirit. "For the flesh," the Apostle says, "lusts against the spirit and the spirit against the flesh." That is, the soul, from the pleasure it has in the flesh, is eager for certain things it nevertheless shrinks from in reason's judgment, or rates as things one should not be eager for.

Why God is called the examiner of the heart and reins

(85) Therefore, God has been called the "tester of the heart and reins"— that is, the examiner of the intentions or consents stemming from there— with respect to the two things we've just mentioned: lust of the flesh and lust of the soul. But we, who aren't in a position to discriminate or decide this, turn our judgment mostly to the deeds. We don't punish the faults so much as the deeds, and are eager to punish not so much what it is in someone that injures his soul as what can injure others, so that we prevent public

damages more than correcting individual ones, according to what the Lord said to Peter, "If your brother shall sin against you, reproach him between you and him only."

(86) What is "shall sin against you"? Is it, so to speak, "*not* against someone else," so that we ought to correct or punish harms inflicted on us more than on others? Far from it. "If he shall sin against you," the Lord says, as when your brother openly does something whereby he can corrupt you by example. For he sins in himself alone, so to speak, when his hidden fault makes him alone guilty and does not in itself draw others into guilt by example. In fact even if there are no people who imitate his action or even know about it, nevertheless the action itself more than the mind's fault should be rebuked before people, because it was able to make the greater and more ruinous offense come about by example than could a fault lying hidden in the mind. For everything that can contribute to common ruin or to public disadvantage is to be punished with the greater rebuke. What causes greater offense deserves a heavier penalty among us, and the greater scandal for people incurs the greater punishment among people—even if a slighter fault preceded it.

(87) Indeed, let us assume someone has corrupted a woman by having sex with her in a church. When it has been brought to the ears of the people, they are upset not so much by the violation of the woman, a true temple of God, as by the breach of the corporeal temple, even though it is more serious to exploit a woman than mere walls and to bring harm to a human being than to a place. Yet we punish house-burnings with a greater penalty than we do for carrying out fornication, when before God the latter is regarded as much more serious than the former.

(88) These things are done not so much out of duty to justice as out of the proper balance needed for its administration, so that, as we said, in preventing public injuries we have regard for general expediency. Hence we often punish the least sins with greater penalties, not paying so much attention with the fairness of justice to what fault preceded as thinking with the discretion of foresight how great a disadvantage can come from them if they are punished mildly. So, saving the mind's faults for divine judgment, with our own judgment we pursue their results, which are ours to judge. In such cases we pay more attention to administering—that is, to the standpoint of foresight we mentioned—than to pure fairness.

(89) But God arranges everyone's penalty according to the extent of the fault. Those who scorn him equally are punished afterwards with an equal penalty, no matter what their circumstances or profession. For if a monk and a layman come to consent equally to fornication, and in addition the mind of the layman is so on fire that if he were a monk, he wouldn't out of reverence for

God refrain from this shamefulness either, then he deserves the same penalty as the monk does.

(90) This is what should be maintained too in the case of two persons, one of whom, sinning openly, scandalizes many people and corrupts them by his example, while the other, since he sins secretly, harms himself alone. For if he who sins secretly has the same purpose as the other, and the same scorn for God, so that the fact that he doesn't corrupt others comes about more by chance than by his giving up something for God's sake (he doesn't restrain himself for God's sake),[23] then he is surely bound by an equal guilt before God. Indeed God pays attention only to the mind in rewarding good or evil, not to the results of the deeds. He doesn't* think about what *arises* from our fault or from our good will, but judges the mind itself in its intention's purpose, not in the result of the outward deed. In fact deeds, which we said above [(6)] are equally common to reprobates and to the elect, are in themselves all indifferent. They are not to be called good or bad, except according to the intention of the doer—that is to say, not because it is good or bad for them to be done, but because they are well or badly done, that is, done with the intention whereby they are done properly, or not. For, as blessed Augustine remarks, it is good for evil to exist, since God uses even it well, and doesn't permit it to exist otherwise, although nevertheless it itself isn't good at all.

(91) So when we call a person's intention good and his deed good, we are distinguishing two things, the intention and the deed, but we are talking about *one* goodness—that of the intention. For example, if we say "good person" and "good person's son," we represent two people, certainly, but not two goodnesses. Therefore, just as (a) a person is called good from his own goodness, but when "good person's son" is said, the son isn't thereby shown to have anything good in him, so too (b) one's intention is called good in itself, but his deed isn't called good *from itself,* but rather because it proceeds from a good intention. So the goodness whereby both the intention and the doing are called good is one, just as there is one goodness by which a good person and a good person's son are so called, or one goodness by which a good person and a person's good will are so called.

(92) So let those accustomed to object that acting on an intention is worth rewarding too, or brings about some increase in the reward, realize that their objection is futile. Two things are good, they say, the good intention and the result arising from the good intention. And good conjoined to good ought to be worth something more than each of them alone.

23. The passage from "so that" to the end of the parentheses is very obscure and syntactically awkward in the Latin. My translation is conjectural.

(93) I reply to them that if we assume the whole to be worth more than each of its parts, are we for that reason forced to grant that it is worth a greater reward? Certainly not. For there are many things, both animate and inanimate, such that a group of them is useful for more things than is each one of the things included in that group. For look, an ox joined with another ox or with a horse, or a piece of wood joined with a piece of wood or with iron, is surely a good thing. And the grouping of them is worth more than each of the parts, although the combination doesn't have any more reward.

(94) That's so in fact, you will say, because they aren't such that they can *deserve* merit, since they are lacking in reason.

(95) But does our deed have reason so that *it* can deserve merit?

(96) Not at all, you will say. But yet the deed is said to deserve merit because it makes *us* deserve merit—that is, be worthy of reward, or at least of a greater one.

(97) But surely we've denied that above [(56)]. And in addition to what we've said, understand *why* it is to be denied: There are two people with the same plan of building homes for the poor. One of them accomplishes the performance of his devotion. But the other has the money he's prepared stolen from him violently and isn't allowed to finish what he proposed, being prevented by no fault of his own but hindered only by that violence. Could what is enacted externally lessen his merit before God? Or could another person's malice make him who did as much as he could for God's sake less acceptable to God?

(98) If these things could be so, a large amount of money could make anyone better and more worthy—that is, if it itself could bring about merit or an increase of merit. People could become better the richer they were, since out of the bountifulness of their riches they could add more in deeds to their devotion.

(99) But to think this, that wealth is able to contribute something to true happiness or to the soul's worthiness, or to remove something from the merits of the poor, is sheer craziness. If however the possession of things cannot bring about a better soul, surely it cannot make it dearer to God or earn anything of merit in happiness.

On the reward for external deeds

(100) Nevertheless, we aren't denying that in this life something is awarded for these good or bad deeds, in order that we may be further encouraged to good deeds or kept from bad ones by present repayment as profit or penalty, and in order that some people should take their examples from others in doing things that are proper or shunning those that are improper.

That the combination of God and man, united in Christ, is not anything better than God alone

(101) To return finally to the above claims, where it was said that good added to good brings about something better than each one of them is by itself [(92)], watch out that you aren't led to the point of saying that Christ—that is, God and man united to one another in the person—is something better than Christ's divinity or humanity is, that is, than God himself is, united to man, or man himself is, assumed[24] by God. Surely it is undisputed that in Christ both the assumed man and the assuming God are good, and that both substances can only be understood as good, just as in individual humans both the corporeal and the incorporeal substance is good, even though the body's goodness is irrelevant to the soul's worthiness or merit.

(102) But now who will dare to put the whole that is called "Christ"—that is, God and man together—or for that matter any group of things at all, ahead of God, as though there can be something better than one who is both the supreme good and such that all things get whatever good they have from him? For even though there seem to be some things so necessary, in order to do something, that God cannot do it without them as aids or primordial causes, nevertheless nothing can be called better than God, no matter how big a group of things it is. For although a number of good things plainly exists, so that there is goodness in several things, it does not come about for that reason that the goodness is *greater.*

(103) For instance, if there is abundant knowledge in several people, or the number of sciences grows, it is not for that reason necessary that *every* person's knowledge grows, so that his knowledge becomes greater than before. So too, since God is good in himself and creates innumerable things that have being and being-good only through him, therefore goodness is in several things through him, so that the number of good things is greater. Yet no goodness can be put ahead of his goodness or made equal to it.

(104) Indeed, there is goodness in man and goodness in God, and although the substances or natures in which goodness inheres are diverse, nevertheless no thing's goodness can be put ahead of or equal to the divine goodness. And therefore nothing is to be called better (that is, more good) than God, or equally good.

That a group of goods is not better than one of the goods

(105) On the other hand, in a combination of a deed and an intention there doesn't appear to be a plurality of either goodnesses or good things. For when

24. See n. 9 above.

one talks about a good intention and a good action (that is, one proceeding from a good intention), only the intention's goodness is referred to. The name "good" is not held to the same signification in the two occurrences, in such a way that we could speak of several goods. For when we say a human being is simple[25] and a word is simple,[26] we are not for that reason granting that they are a plurality of simple things, since the name "simple" is taken in one sense in the latter case and in another sense in the former case. So no one should force on us the claim that when a good action is added to a good intention, good is added onto good, as though there were *several* goods, for which the reward should grow accordingly. For, as was just said, we cannot correctly call things "several goods" where the word "good" doesn't fit them in a single sense.

That a deed is good by means of a good intention

(106) Indeed we call an intention good (that is, right) in itself. We don't however say that a "doing" takes on any good *in itself,* but that it proceeds from a good intention. Hence even if the same thing is done by the same person at different times, nevertheless because of the diversity of the intention, his doing it is called now good, now bad. So it appears to shift between good and bad, just as the proposition "Socrates is sitting" (or the understanding of it) shifts between true and false according as Socrates is now sitting, now standing. Aristotle says this alteration, the shift between true and false, occurs in these cases not in such a way that the things that shift between true and* false take on anything in their changing, but rather that the subject thing, namely Socrates, is in himself moved from sitting to standing or conversely.

On what basis should an intention be called good?

(107) Now there are people who suppose an intention is good or right whenever someone believes that he is acting well and that what he is doing pleases God. For instance, even those who persecuted the martyrs, about whom Truth says in the Gospel, "The hour is coming when everyone who slays you will suppose he is offering obedience to God." In fact, the Apostle pities such people's ignorance when he says, "I testify for them that they have an ardor for God, but not one in accordance with knowledge." That is, they have a great fervor and desire to do what they believe pleases God. But because they

25. That is, sincere or without guile.
26. That is, not a complex or compound expression.

are deceived in this zeal or eagerness of the mind, their intention is mistaken and their heart's eye is not simple in such a way that it could see clearly—that is, keep itself from error.

(108) So when the Lord distinguished deeds according to whether their intention is right or not right, he was careful to call the mind's eye (that is, its intention) "simple" and so to speak pure of dirt so it can see clearly, or conversely "cloudy." He said, "If your eye is simple, your whole body will be shining." That is, if the intention is right, the whole mass of deeds arising from it—which, like corporeal things, can be seen—will be worthy of light, that is, will be good. So too the other way around.

(109) Thus an intention isn't to be called good because it *appears* good, but more than that, because it *is* such as it is considered to be—that is, when if one believes that what he is aiming at is pleasing to God, he is in addition not deceived in his evaluation. Otherwise the infidels themselves would also have good deeds, just as we do, since they too believe no less than we do that through their deeds they are saved or are pleasing to God.

That there is no sin except against conscience

(110) Nevertheless, if someone should ask whether the martyrs' persecutors, or Christ's, sinned in doing what they believed was pleasing to God, or whether without sin they could have given up what they thought shouldn't be given up, then insofar as we earlier [(7)–(8)] described sin to be scorn for God or consenting to what one believes shouldn't be consented to, we certainly can't say they were sinning. No one's ignorance is a sin, and neither is the disbelief with which no one can be saved.

(111) Consider people who are ignorant of Christ, and for that reason spurn the Christian faith because they believe it is contrary to God. What scorn for God do they have in what they do *because* of God, and for that reason suppose they are doing well, especially since the apostle says, "If our heart does not reprove us, we have trust in God"? It is as if he had said, "Where we do not go against our conscience, there is no point to our fear of being set before God, guilty of a fault."

(112) On the other hand if such people's ignorance is hardly to be counted as a sin at all, then why does the Lord himself pray for those crucifying him, saying "Father, forgive them, for they do not know what they are doing"? Or why does Stephen, instructed by this example and praying for the people stoning him, say "Lord, do not set this sin against them"? For where no fault preceded, there doesn't appear to be anything to be excused. And being "excused" is usually said to be nothing but being let off from the penalty that a

fault deserved. Furthermore, Stephen plainly calls what happened from igno-rance a "sin."

How many ways is something called a "sin"?

(113) But to reply more fully to objections, one needs to know that the name "sin" is taken in different ways. (a) Properly, sin is said to be scorn for God or consent to evil, as we remarked above [(7)–(8)]. Children and those who are naturally fools are exempt from this. Since they lack reason so to speak, they don't have any merits, nothing is charged against them as a sin, and they are saved only through the sacraments.

(114) (b) The *sacrifice* for sin is also called "sin," insofar as the Apostle says that the Lord Jesus Christ was made "sin."

(115) (c) The *penalty* for sin is also called "sin" or a "curse," insofar as we say a sin is forgiven (that is, the penalty is excused), and insofar as we say the Lord Jesus Christ endured our sins (that is, he took on the penalties for, or arising from, our sins). Now when we say, following the Apostle, that children have original sin or that we all have sinned in Adam, it is as if to say we have acquired from his sin the source of our penalty, or the judgment of damnation.

(116) (d) Sometimes the *deeds* of sin themselves, or whatever we don't do or will correctly, we also call "sins." For what is it for someone to have committed a sin except to have carried out the performance of the sin? No wonder we speak this way, since conversely we also call the sins themselves "actions," in accordance with Athanasius' statement: "And they will give an account of their own actions. And those who have done good things will go into eternal life, while those who have done evil things will go into eternal fire." Now what is the meaning of "of their own actions"? Is it as if judgment will be made only about what they have carried out in deed, so that he who will do more in deed will receive more in reward, or he who was lacking in the performance of what he intended is exempt from damnation—for example, the Devil himself, who didn't achieve in practice what he anticipated in desire?

(117) Hardly! And so Athanasius says "of their own actions" with reference to the *consent* to what they decided to accomplish, that is, the sins that are counted for the Lord as the doing of an action, since he punishes them as we punish the deeds.

(118) Now when Stephen [(112)] calls "sin" what the Jews perpetrated against him out of ignorance, he was either calling sin the penalty they bore* from the sin of our first parents, as well as other penalties stemming from that, or else the unjust action they undertook in stoning him. He begged that this not "be set against them," that is, that they not be physically punished for it.

For God often physically punishes people here when no fault of theirs requires it. Yet he doesn't do this without cause. For instance, when he casts afflictions even on the just as a kind of purification or test of them, or when he permits some people to be afflicted so that afterwards they may be freed from it and he may be glorified for the favor he has bestowed—as he did with the blind man of whom he said, "Neither he nor his parents sinned so that he was born blind; rather he was born blind so that God's deeds might be made plain in him."

(119) Also, who denies that innocent offspring are sometimes endangered or afflicted together with their evil parents because of the latter's fault, as happened in Sodom or as occurs among many peoples, so that the more the penalty is broadened the more the evil people are frightened? Blessed Stephen, who noted this carefully, prayed that the sin—that is, the penalty he endured from the Jews, or what they wrongly did to him—not be "set against them," that is, that they not be physically punished because of this.

(120) The Lord as well was of this view when he said, "Father, forgive them"—that is, don't take vengeance on what they're doing to me, with even a physical penalty. Certainly that could reasonably have been done, even if no fault of theirs had preceded, so that others who saw this, or even they themselves, would recognize from the penalty that they hadn't behaved rightly in this. But it suited the Lord by the example of his prayer to exhort us most of all to the virtue of patience, and to showing ultimate love, so that by his own example he displayed to us in deed what he taught in words, namely for us to pray for our enemies too.

(121) Thus when he said "forgive," it referred not to any preceding fault or scorn for God they had in this case, but to the reason for bringing a penalty on them, which as we said [(118)] could have followed not without cause, even though there hadn't been any preceding fault. This is just what happened with the prophet who, by eating when he was sent against Samaria, did what the Lord had prohibited. Yet in doing so, since he didn't undertake to do anything out of scorn for God, but was instead deceived by another prophet, his innocence brought on death not from any fault's guilt so much as from committing the deed.

(122) "Surely God," as blessed Gregory remarks, "sometimes changes his ruling, but never his resolve." That is, he often arranges not to carry out what for some reason he decided to command or threaten. But his resolve remains fixed—that is, what he arranges to do in his foreknowledge is never lacking in effectiveness. Therefore, just as he didn't hold to the command for Abraham to sacrifice his son, or to the threat made against the Ninevites, and thus as we said changed his ruling, so too the prophet just mentioned, when God had forbidden him to eat while on the road, believed God's ruling to be changed

and that he would be delinquent in the extreme if he didn't listen to the other prophet, who claimed he was sent by the Lord to refresh his fatigue with food. Therefore, he did this without fault insofar as he resolved to *avoid* fault. Unexpected death didn't harm him; it released him from the present life's distresses. It also benefited many people as a warning, since in this way they saw a just man punished without any fault, and thereby saw the realization of what is said to the Lord elsewhere, "Since you, Lord, are just, you arrange all things justly, even though you condemn him who does not deserve to be punished."[27] "Condemn," he says, not to eternal but to physical death. For just as some people, children for example, are saved without any merits and gain eternal life by grace alone, so it isn't absurd for some people to bear physical penalties they haven't merited, as is plain again with children who die without the grace of baptism and who are damned with both a physical and an eternal death, many of whom are afflicted even though they are innocent.

(123) So what wonder is there if the Lord's crucifiers could have incurred a temporal penalty from that unjust action (not unreasonably, as we said [(118)]), even though their ignorance excuses them from guilt? And for this reason he said "Forgive them," that is, don't impose the penalty that (not unreasonably as we said) they could have incurred in this case.

(124) Just as what they did out of ignorance, or even the ignorance itself, isn't properly called sin, that is, scorn for God, so neither is disbelief, although this necessarily closes off access to eternal life for adults who are already using reason. Indeed for damnation it is enough not to believe the Gospel, to be ignorant of Christ, or not to receive the Church's sacraments, even though this happens not through malice so much as through ignorance. Truth says of such people, "He who does not believe is already judged." And the Apostle says, "And he who does not know will not be known."

(125) Now when we say we "sin" unknowingly, that is, do something improper, we are taking "sin" not for any scorn but for the action. For philosophers too say that doing or saying something inappropriately is sinning, even though that seems irrelevant to offending God. Thus Aristotle in the chapter on relation, when he was talking about the wrong assignment of relatives, said, "But now sometimes it will not seem to be converted unless what it is said of is assigned appropriately. For if the one who makes the assignment sins, so that for example 'wing' is assigned to 'bird,' it will not be

---

27. The Vulgate Bible has (Wisd. of Sol. 12: 15), "and you regard it as outside your virtue to condemn him who does not deserve to be punished." The text as Abelard cites it has completely reversed the sense. Yet the lines that follow indicate that this reversed sense is indeed what Abelard intends.

converted so that the bird is 'of a wing.' "[28] If therefore in this way we call "sin" everything we do wrongly or everything we have that is contrary to our salvation, then by all means we will call both disbelief and ignorance of the things that have to be believed for salvation "sins," although there appears to be no scorn for God there. Nevertheless I think what is properly called "sin" can nowhere occur without fault.

(126) But being ignorant of God, or not believing him, or doing things that aren't rightly done, can happen without fault to many people. For if someone doesn't believe the Gospel or Christ because their preaching didn't reach him, then in accordance with the Apostle's statement: "How will they believe him whom they have not heard? But how will they hear without someone who preaches?" What fault can be attributed to him because he doesn't believe? Cornelius didn't believe in Christ until Peter was sent to him and informed him about him. Even though he had earlier recognized and loved God by the natural law, thereby earning a hearing for his prayer and an acceptance of his alms by God, nevertheless if he had happened to pass on from this light before having faith in Christ, we wouldn't dare promise him life, no matter how good his deeds seemed. We wouldn't count him among the faithful but rather among the faithless, no matter how busy he had been with his eagerness for salvation.

(127) "God's judgments are a great abyss." Sometimes he drags along those who are reluctant or less concerned for their salvation, and in the deepest plan of his administration of the world spurns those who offer themselves or are more prepared to believe. For thus he reproached the man who offered himself saying, "Master, I will follow you wherever you will go," and didn't tolerate for even an hour the other man, with his dutiful excuse, who excused himself because of the concern he had for his father. And finally, in upbraiding certain cities' obstinacy, he said: "Woe unto you, Chorazin! Woe unto you, Bethsaida! For if the powers that were worked in you had been worked in Tyre and Sidon, they would already have done penance in sackcloth and ashes long ago."

(128) Look, he offered them not only his preaching but also a display of miracles. Yet he knew beforehand that neither one was going to be believed. On the other hand, he didn't count other Gentile cities, which he knew would be quick to accept the faith, as then worth his visiting. Surely when some people in these cities died with the word of preaching withdrawn from them, yet were prepared to accept it, who will charge this to a fault of theirs? We see that it happened through no negligence. Nevertheless, we say this disbelief of

28. That is, when correlatives are properly identified, they are "convertible." For example, "the parent of the child" and "the child of the parent." But where they are not properly identified, this may fail. For example, "winged bird," but *not* "birded wing."

theirs in which they died is enough for damnation, even though the cause of the blindness in which the Lord left them is less visible to us. Indeed, if someone attributes this to a faultless sin on the part of the disbelievers, that will perhaps be all right, since it seems absurd to him that such people are damned without sin.

(129) Yet as we have already mentioned many times [(7)–(8), (29), (48), (67), (113)], we judge that only what consists in the *fault* of negligence is properly called "sin." This fault cannot be in any people, no matter of what age, without their meriting damnation thereby. But I don't see how not believing in Christ (which is what disbelief is) should be attributed to a fault in children or those it wasn't announced to, or how anything done out of invincible ignorance or that we were unable to foresee should be attributed to a fault in us. For instance, if someone perhaps slays with an arrow a person he doesn't see in the forest, while meaning to shoot wild beasts or birds. While we nevertheless say he "sins" out of ignorance just as sometimes we confess to "sinning" not only in consent but also in thought, speech and action, in this context we aren't using the word properly for a fault, but are taking it broadly for what is not fit for us to do—whether it is done out of error, out of negligence or in any other inappropriate way.

(130) Therefore this is what sinning out of ignorance is: not to have any fault in it, but *doing* what isn't appropriate for us. Sinning in thought (that is, in will) is willing what isn't appropriate for us. Sinning in speech or in action is speaking or doing what we ought not, even if this happens out of ignorance, against our will.

(131) Thus those who persecuted Christ or his followers, and believed they *should* be persecuted, we say sinned through action. Nevertheless, they would have sinned more seriously through fault if they had spared them contrary to conscience.

Is every sin forbidden?

(132) Now it is asked whether God forbids us every sin. If we accept this, it seems he does so unreasonably, since this life cannot be led at all without at least venial sins. For if he commands us to avoid all sins, but we can't avoid them all, then surely he doesn't, as he himself promised, impose "a sweet yoke" on us or "a light burden," but one that goes far beyond our powers and that we cannot carry at all, as Peter the apostle declared about the yoke of the Law.

(133) For who can always take measures to guard himself from even a superfluous word so that, in never going too far in this respect, he achieves the perfection of which James says, "If someone does not offend in word, he is a

perfect man"? Since he had also already said, "We all offend in many things," and since another apostle, one of great perfection, said, "If we say we do not have sin, we mislead ourselves and the truth is not in us," I think it doesn't escape anyone how hard, indeed impossible, it seems in our feeble state for us to stay completely devoid of sin—I mean if we are taking the word "sin" broadly, as we said [(116)], and are also calling sins *whatever* we do inappropriately. But if we are understanding "sin" properly and say that only scorn for God is a sin, then this life can indeed be led without it, although only with the greatest difficulty. Surely nothing else* is forbidden us by God, as we remarked above [(51)], except consent to the evil whereby we scorn God, even when it seems the command is made with respect to a deed, as we explained above [(51)–(54)], where we also showed that otherwise his commands cannot be observed by us at all.

(134) Now some sins are called venial, the light ones, so to speak; others are called damnable or serious. Again, among damnable sins some are called crimes, namely* those that can make a person notorious or criminal if people come to hear of them. But others are not like that.

(135) Sins are venial or light when we consent to what we know isn't to be consented to, but yet what we know doesn't come up in memory at the time. Surely we know many things even while we are sleeping or when we aren't recalling them. For in sleeping we don't lose our knowledge and aren't made into fools, and we aren't made wise when we wake up. So sometimes we consent to bragging or to needless eating or drinking, which we know shouldn't be done. But we don't at that time recall that it shouldn't be done. And so consents like this, which we rush into on account of forgetfulness, are called "venial" or "light" sins. That is, they shouldn't be corrected by a penalty involving great atonement, like our being punished for them by being put out of the Church or weighed down by a heavy abstinence.

(136) In fact to get penitents forgiven for these negligences, we repeat the words of daily confession, in which no mention should be made of more serious faults, but only of the lighter ones. For we shouldn't say there, "I have sinned by perjury, homicide, adultery," and things like that, which are called "damnable" and "more serious" sins. We certainly don't rush into *these* on account of forgetfulness, as we do the former; instead, we commit them so to speak by design and out of deliberation, and are even made abominable to God, according to the Psalmist, "They have been made abominable in their designs"—made, so to speak, loathsome and quite odious from what they have knowingly undertaken.

(137) Now among these damnable sins, some are called "criminal." They are known through their result, they stain a man with the blemish of a great

fault, and they very much damage his reputation. For example, consents to perjury, homicide and adultery that scandalize the Church very much.

(138) But when we give ourselves up to food more than is needed, or decorate ourselves out of vainglory with immoderate elegance, even if we dare to do it knowingly, these things don't count as a crime. With many people they earn more praise than criticism.

Is it better to refrain from lighter faults than from more serious ones?

(139) There are people who say it is more perfect, and so better, to look out for venial sins than for criminal ones, insofar as it seems harder and requires the care of a greater effort. I answer them first according to Cicero, "If it is hard work, it is not for that reason glorious." Otherwise, those who bore the Law's heavy yoke would have more merit before the Lord than do the people who serve in evangelical freedom. For fear, which perfect charity banishes, involves pain, and those under the Law work harder at whatever is done out of fear than those people do whom charity makes spontaneous in doing it.

(140) Thus the Lord encourages those who are laboring and burdened to take on a sweet yoke and a light burden, so that they may pass over from serving the Law whereby they were oppressed to the freedom of the Gospel, and so that they who began from fear may be brought to completion by the charity that without difficulty suffers all things and withstands all things.

(141) Surely nothing is hard for one who loves, especially since the non-carnal, spiritual love of God is stronger the truer it is. Who also doesn't know it's harder for us to be prepared against a flea than against an enemy host, or against the hindrance offered by a little stone than by a big one? But do we judge for this reason that it is better or more beneficial to avoid what is harder? Of course not. Why not? Because what is harder to avoid is less able to cause harm.

(142) So therefore, although we maintain it is harder to look out for venial sins than for criminal ones, it is more proper to shun the latter, which are more dangerous and earn the greater penalty, and which we believe God is more offended by and are more displeasing to him. For the more we cling to him through love, the more anxiously we ought to avoid what he is more offended by and more disfavors. For anyone who truly loves someone has his hands full avoiding not so much hurting himself as offending or scorning his beloved, in accordance with the Apostle, "Charity does not seek things that are its own." And again, "Let no one seek what is for himself, but what is for someone else."

(143) Therefore, if we ought to avoid sins not so much on account of the harm to ourselves as on account of the offenses to God, then surely the ones he

is more offended by ought to be more avoided. And if we turn to the poetic judgment about the worthiness of morals—"Good people hate to sin, from the love of virtue"—then all things are to be taken with greater hatred the more they are regarded as shameful in themselves, the more they depart from the character of virtue, and the more they are naturally offensive to all.

(144) Finally, in order for us to discriminate sins more carefully by comparing individual sins with one another, let us put venial sins together with criminal ones, for example unnecessary eating together with perjury and adultery, and ask in which infraction there is the greater sin or the worse scorn and offense for God.

(145) I don't know, perhaps you will respond, since some philosophers regard all sins as on a par. But if you want to follow this philosophy—rather, this plain foolishness—then it is equally good to refrain from criminal and from venial sins, because it is equally bad to commit the latter as the former. Why then does anyone dare to give precedence to refraining from venial sins over refraining from criminal ones?

(146) If someone perhaps demands to know on what basis we are able to guess that the infraction of adultery is more displeasing to God than excessive eating is, I think the divine law can teach us. It hasn't established any atonement as a penalty to punish the one,* but has decreed that the other be condemned not by just any penalty but by the extreme distress of death. For where love of neighbor (which the Apostle calls "fulfillment of the Law") is more seriously injured, there is more done contrary to it and the sin is greater.

(147) If individual venial and criminal sins alike are compared with one another like this, then we want to compare also *all* the one kind with *all* the other kind together, so we can be completely thorough.[29] I'm not running away from that fact at all. Therefore, let's assume that someone avoids all venial sins with great care, and doesn't worry about shunning criminal ones, and while he avoids all the former, undertakes to do the latter. Who will judge that in doing this he is sinning more lightly, or that it is better if in taking precautions against the former he rushes into the latter? So once the comparison of individual sins is made, as we have said, as well as the comparison of all sins with one another together, I think it's obvious that avoiding venial sins is not better or of any greater perfection than avoiding criminal ones.

(148) Yet if when someone has avoided criminal sins first, he is afterwards able to avoid venial ones, I confess that his virtue has indeed reached perfec-

---

29. That is, we need to consider not just the case where someone avoids one particular venial sin but commits another, criminal one; we need also to consider the case where someone avoids *all* venial sins but nevertheless commits criminal ones.

tion in so doing. Nevertheless the latter, which the fulfillment of virtue is based on,[30] are not for that reason to be given precedence to the former. They don't deserve as much reprisal either. For in constructing a building, often those who finish it do less than those who worked on it beforehand do. By putting the last beam in place and completing the task, they finish the building, so that in this way the house that wasn't a house* while it was unfinished might come to be finished.

(149) For now I think we have worked hard enough to get a knowledge of sin as far as comes to memory, so it can be better avoided the more accurately it is known. Familiarity with evil surely can't be lacking in a just person. One can't avoid vice unless he knows it.

On reconciling sins

(150) Since we've presented the soul's injury, let's apply ourselves to showing the remedy to cure it. Thus Jerome says, "Physician, if you are an expert, then just as you have given the cause of disease, so point out the cause of health." Thus when we have offended God by sinning, there are still ways we can be reconciled to him. So there are three steps in reconciling sinners to God: penitence, confession and atonement.

What is properly called penitence?

(151) The mind's sorrow over what it has failed in is properly called penitence, namely when it troubles someone that he's gone out of bounds in some way. This penitence sometimes arises from the love of God and is fruitful, but sometimes it arises from some injury we don't want to be burdened with. The penitence of the damned is like this. It is written of them: "Seeing this,[31] they will be upset with a horrible terror, and will marvel at the suddenness of a salvation they had not expected. Doing penance and sighing from the anguish of their spirit, they will say to themselves, 'These are the ones we at one time held in derision.' " We read also of Judas' penitence over the fact that he betrayed the Lord. We believe his penitence occurred not so much because of the fault of the sin as because of his own cheapness; he realized he was damned in the judgment of all. For when one person has dragged into ruin someone else who has been corrupted by money or some other way, no one regards the tempter as a cheaper traitor, no one trusts

---

30. That is, the fulfillment of virtue is based on *avoiding* the latter.

31. That is, seeing the just person vindicated at the final judgment (Wisd. of Sol. 5: 1).

himself to him less, than does the person who is more fully experienced in the traitor's unfaithfulness.

(152) Indeed, every day we see many people who are about to leave this life, repenting over the disgraceful deeds they have committed and wailing with grave remorse, not so much from the love of God whom they have offended, or from hatred of the sin they have committed, as from fear of the punishment they are afraid of being thrown into headfirst. In this respect they also *continue* to be immoral, since the immorality of their fault doesn't bother them as much as the penalty's just severity does. They don't regard with hatred what they have committed, because it is evil, so much as they do God's just judgment, which they fear as penalty. They hate fairness more than unfairness. For a long time they have been blinded and called to be converted from their maliciousness, until finally divine justice so turns them over to a "reprobate mind" and casts them, struck blind, away from his face, that they do not have any notion of salutary penitence and are unable to perceive how atonement is to be made.

(153) How many people we observe every day, dying and wailing momentously, blaming themselves much for loan-sharking, pillaging, acts of oppressing the poor, or* whatever wrongs they have committed, and consulting a priest to fix these things. If, as ought to happen, the advice they are given first is that they sell all they have and give back to others what they have taken away from them—in accordance with Augustine's advice: "If a thing belonging to someone else is not returned to him when it *can* be returned, then penitence is not done but faked"—they immediately reveal by their reply how empty their penitence is. They say: "Then what would my household live on? What would I leave to my children, what to my wife? How would they be able to manage?"

(154) The Lord's reproach applies in the first instance to them: "Fool, tonight they demand your soul of you. But whom will the things you have made ready belong to?" You miserable person, whoever you are like this—in fact, most miserable of all the miserable, most foolish of all fools—are you looking after not what you will keep for yourself but what you will stockpile for others? By what presumptuousness do you offend God, whose horrifying judgment you will be dragged off to, in order to appease your own people, whom you are making rich by ravaging the poor? Who won't laugh at you if he hears that you hope others will be better disposed toward you than you yourself are? You put trust in the alms of your family, whom you set up as equal heirs in your immorality because you believe you have successors. You leave them what belongs to others, to be possessed as booty. You tear the life away from poor people by taking from them the means of sustaining themselves, and you maneuver to kill Christ again in them, according to what he said himself, "What you did to one of the least of mine, you did to me."

(155) You who are wrongly dutiful to your family, and cruel to yourself and to God alike, what do you expect from a just judge to whom you are rushing off to be judged, like it or not, and who demands an account not only for ravaging but even for an idle word? By the punishment imposed on earlier men, he has regularly demonstrated how strict his vengeance is.

(156) Adam sinned once, and by comparison with our sins, as blessed Jerome remarks, his sin was a very light one. He didn't oppress anyone through violence and didn't rob anyone of anything. He tasted the fruit once, and it was replaceable. Yet even in the case of so light an infraction, which through its penalty redounded to all posterity, the Lord decided to show in advance what he would do with greater faults. The rich man descended into hell, the Lord says, not because he seized what belonged to other people but because he didn't share his own meals with the poor man Lazarus, and ate them like lawful meals. He plainly teaches us what penalty people will be struck with who do seize what belongs to others, if he who didn't give away his own goods was so damned and buried in hell.

(157) When your memory is buried with you and the tears of the people you had at your funeral have quickly dried (in accordance with Apollonius the rhetorician's remark, "Nothing dries up faster than a tear"), your wife will soon get herself ready* for a new wedding and* will serve* the pleasures of a new husband with the spoils you left her. She will warm the bed your body's been in up to now for someone else, while in misery you are punished in the flames of Gehenna[32] for these pleasures.

(158) The same thing is to be expected from your children. If someone asks them perhaps why they don't atone for you by their alms in your memory, they seem able to excuse themselves for many reasons. They would answer like this: "Since he didn't want to be well disposed toward himself, what foolishness it was to hope others would be well disposed toward him, and to entrust the salvation of his soul to others. He most of all should have been looking after it himself. Who did he believe was going to be better disposed toward him than he was himself? He who was cruel to himself, whose mercy was he relying on?" In the end they can hold out his greed as an excuse and say, "Besides, we know the things he left us are not the kind we ought to use as alms." All who hear of these things will laugh, and laugh they should! But the miserable man, who compelled the despoiled poor to weep hourly, will weep there[33] in perpetuity.

(159) There are those who want to conceal their negligence from human beings but not from God, and who "in order to make themselves excuses for

32. That is, hell. The term entered late Latin from Hebrew via Greek.
33. *I.e.*, in Gehenna or hell.

sins" say they have despoiled so many people that they are completely unable to recognize or find them again. Since they aren't worried about this, they come under the judgment of the apostolic decree, "And he who ignores will be ignored." They don't find them because they aren't looking for them. The right hand of the God they scorned will find them! It is written of it, "Your right hand will find all who hate you." The same prophet who said this was intensely afraid of that hand, and considering that there was no place to escape it, elsewhere said: "Where will I go, away from your spirit? Where will I flee, away from your face? If I climb up to heaven, you are there. If I go down to hell, you are present."

(160) And because a priest's covetousness is very often no less than the people's (according to the prophet, "And the people will be as the priests"), priests' greed misleads many of the dying, promising them a vain security if they offer in sacrifice what they have and buy masses they would never have gotten for free. In this commerce, in fact, it is well known that there is a fixed price among them: a penny for a mass, fifty cents for masses and all the liturgical hours for a period of thirty days, or six dollars a year.[34] They don't counsel the dying to *give back* their spoils but to "offer" them as in sacrifice, even though on the contrary it is written, "He who offers a poor person's property as sacrifice is like someone who makes a sacrificial victim of a son before the father's eyes." For the killing of a son weighs more on the father if it is done in front of him than if he didn't see it. And, so to speak, a son is killed as an offering when a poor man's property, which his life consisted of, is put to sacrifice. Preferring mercy to sacrifice, Truth says: "Go, learn what it is. I want mercy and not sacrifice." Now as we remarked above in the case of the rich man's damnation [(156)], it is worse to keep the spoils than not to bestow mercy—that is, to take what belongs to the poor than not to bestow what is our own.

On fruitful penitence

(161) Since we have spoken about unfruitful penitence, let us consider the fruitful kind more closely insofar as it is more beneficial. In inviting to this fruitful penitence everyone who is obstinate and pays no attention to God's terrifying judgment, the Apostle says: "Do you scorn the riches of his goodness and patience and long-suffering? Do you not know that God's kindness leads you to penitence?" He shows plainly by these words what kind of penitence is beneficial and comes from the love of God rather than from fear, so that we may be sorry to have offended God or to have scorned him,

34. Penny = *denarius*, fifty cents = five *solidi*, six dollars = sixty *solidi*. See n. 7 above.

more because he is good than because he is just. For the longer we scorn him because we believe he doesn't immediately judge contempt for him—as on the contrary worldly princes do who don't know how to restrain themselves or to delay revenge for their injuries—the more justly our scorn for him brings about a heavier penalty. The more patient he was in waiting, the stricter he is in his revenge. The Apostle we just mentioned pointed this out later, saying "According to your hardness and your impenitent heart you are storing up wrath against yourself, for the day of wrath." Indeed, it will be the day of wrath then, but of gentleness now, because then it will be the day of vengeance, but now it is the day of patience. As justice demands, he will there take vengeance more severely on scorn for him the less he *ought* to have been scorned, and the longer he put up with it.

(162) We fear offending people, and out of shame we avoid the ones we don't run away from in fear of having offended them. We look for a hiding place when we fornicate, so that we aren't seen by people; we cannot stand the glance of even one human being then. We know God is there, from whom nothing can be hidden. We aren't embarrassed to be seen by him and the whole of heaven's court in this act of shamefulness—we who would get all bewildered at one little human being's glance. We are extremely afraid to venture anything before an earthly judge, by whom we know we are to be judged with only a temporal penalty, not an eternal one. Carnal desire compels us to do or bear many things, but spiritual desire only a few. If only we did or put up with as much for God's sake, to whom we owe all things, as we do for the sake of wife or children or any whore!

(163) With what penalty should this injury be judged, I ask you, that we put even a whore ahead of him! Through the prophet, he himself complains that love isn't shown to him as to a father, or fear as to a lord. "A son," he says, "honors the father, and a servant fears his lord. If I am a father, where is my honor? And if I am the Lord, where is the fear of me?" He complains that a father or a lord is given preference to him. So think how outraged he is that even a whore is put ahead of him, and that he is scorned all the more for the surpassing patience of his goodness, where he ought to have been more loved!

(164) According to the Apostle's urging quoted above [(161)], those who repent to their benefit, and who look to this goodness and long-suffering patience, are moved to remorse not so much by fear of the penalties as by love for him. He was carefully describing beneficial penitence when he said the opposite:[35] "The riches of his goodness," that is, the rich and plentiful

---

35. That is, he was implicitly describing it by describing its opposite in Rom. 2:4. In the following sentence, Abelard is in effect glossing the verse phrase by phrase by incorporat-

goodness, or the abundant "kindness" of "long-suffering patience," by which
he puts up with you for so long, "do you scorn" it, that is, because he doesn't
quickly punish, "not knowing," that is, not observing, that his "kindness" in
itself "leads you to penitence," that is, makes the very fact that you have
scorned someone who is so kind the reason why, by observing that kindness,
you should be converted to penitence? Now this is the really fruitful penitence
for sin, when this sorrow and mental contrition arises from the love of God
whom we observe to be so kind, rather than from fear of the penalties.

(165) Now sin—scorn for God or consent to evil—doesn't persist together
with this groaning and contrition of heart we call true penitence. For God's
charity, which inspires this groaning, is incompatible with any fault. In this
groaning we are at once reconciled with God and obtain forgiveness for the
preceding sin, in accordance with the prophet, "In whatever hour the sinner
groans, he will be saved"—that is, made worthy of his soul's salvation. He
doesn't say "in what year" or "what month" or "what week" or "what day," but
"what hour," to show that the sinner is worthy of forgiveness without delay and
doesn't deserve the eternal penalty the condemnation of sin consists of. For
even if he is prevented by some crisis of necessity and doesn't have any
opportunity to get to confession or finish atoning for the sin, nevertheless in no
way does he fall into Gehenna when he departs this life in this state of
groaning. This is what it is for a sin to be pardoned by God: for the sinner to
become such as he isn't yet worthy of being, just as earlier he was worthy of
being eternally punished by God on account of his preceding sin.

(166) Now when God pardons penitents' sin, he does not excuse them from
all penalty but only the eternal kind. For there are many penitents who,
prevented by death, haven't done the atonement of penitence in this life
and are held back for purgatorial penalties, not damning ones, in the future
life.[36] Thus it is uncertain how much time the supreme day of judgment will
take, when many of the faithful will be punished unexpectedly,[37] even though

---

ing bits of it into his own text. This form of "commentary" was quite common throughout
the Middle Ages. The Latin word order of the original passage does not lend itself to
translating Abelard's text very gracefully here. It may help if the reader compares the
words in quotation marks with the original quotation as given in (161) above.

36. That is, they are sent for a while to Purgatory, not permanently to hell.

37. Unexpectedly = *repente*. There are two ways to translate this—both problematic.
Luscombe (p. 89) has "suddenly." But the topic is how judgment day can take an
indefinitely long time. My "unexpectedly" suggests that the faithful didn't know it was
coming, that it surprised them, which seems wrong too. An anonymous reader has
plausibly suggested that the faithful's surprise will be over how they have failed.

the *resurrection* will take place "in a moment, in the blink of an eye." So they will make as much atonement there as God has determined, for faults they have either put off making atonement for or else haven't been permitted to make it.

Can someone repent of one sin but not another?

(167) There are people who ask whether someone can repent of one sin and not of another—for instance, of murder and not of the fornicating one has still not stopped doing. But if we understand the fruitful kind of penitence as the kind the love of God introduces in us and that Gregory describes when he says, "Penitence is bewailing deeds one has committed and not committing deeds that are to be bewailed," then whenever even one instance of scorn for God is retained, our state of mind can't be called the "penitence" that the love of God drives us to. For if, as it must, the love of God brings me to this penitence and draws my mind to sorrow for this sinful consent only because in it I have offended God, then I don't see how the same love doesn't for the same reason force me to repent of the other scorn for God—that is, set my mind on the resolution that, whatever deviation of mine occurs to memory, I am likewise sorry for it and am ready to make atonement.

(168) So wherever there is true penitence—that is, coming only from the love of God—there remains no scorn for God, especially since Truth says, "If someone loves me, he will keep my word, and my Father will love him and we will come to him and make our lodging with him." Therefore, all who persist in the love of God are necessarily saved. This salvation wouldn't have occurred if even one sin, one case of scorn for God, were retained. On the other hand, when God finds no sin in the penitent any longer, he finds there no cause for damnation. So it is necessary that once the sin has ceased, the damnation—that is, the torment of a perpetual penalty—doesn't remain.

(169) This is what it is for an earlier sin to be pardoned by God, namely that God takes care of the eternal penalty the sinner earned for the sin, as we said [(166)]. For although God doesn't find in the penitent what he ought to punish forever, nevertheless he is said to pardon the penalty for the earlier sin, since by the fact that he inspired the groan of penitence in him he made the penitent worth making an allowance for—that is, made him such that no eternal penalty is due him then, and such that he has to be saved if he departs this life in this state. But if perhaps he relapses into the same scorn, then just as he goes back to sinning, so too he will revert to the debt of the penalty so that he, who by repenting earlier earned his not being punished, ought to be punished once more.

(170) If someone perhaps should say that for a sin to be pardoned by God is like saying God will not damn the person for what has been committed, or that God has decided for himself that he would not damn him on account of this, then indeed it seems it must be granted that even before the penitent sinned God had pardoned the sin—that is, had decided for himself that he wouldn't damn him on account of it. Certainly God hasn't decided or determined for himself anything recently! Rather whatever things he is going to do, both matters concerning pardoning any sin and those concerning other things that happen, are settled from eternity in his predestination and are prearranged in his providence.

(171) So it seems to be better for us that God be understood as pardoning sin in the sense that, as we have said [(169)], he makes someone worth making an allowance for through a groan of penitence inspired in him—that is, makes him such that damnation isn't due him then or ever after, if he continues in such a resolution. Thus God pardons sin when, by inspiring penitence, the very one by whom the penalty should have been imposed produces the reason why it now doesn't *need* to be imposed.

It is not an injustice for a worthy person not to be given his reward

(172) But perhaps you demand to know if one who repents, who isn't worthy of damnation, is now worthy of eternal life. If we grant this, the objection is raised against us that one who dies in a state of relapsing after repenting[38] *was* worthy of eternal life while he was repenting, and so it seems that God is to be charged with wrongdoing. He didn't even grant him his reward then, when he was worthy of it, so as thereby to prevent his damnation. For just as the penitent would have been saved if he had died then, worthy of eternal life on account of the resolution he had, so too even if he relapsed later he nevertheless *was* worthy to be saved on account of the same state of mind he had before.

(173) But I say that often many people are worthy of damnation and yet don't die in their iniquity in such a way that the damnation they earned might be given to them by God. Nevertheless just as God isn't to be charged with injustice because he didn't give them the penalty they earned, so too he isn't to be charged with injustice in giving rewards that are promised only to those who persevere. Truth bears witness, "He who will persevere to the end, he will be saved."

(174) Therefore, we aren't forced to grant that because someone was at some time worthy of reward or penalty, therefore it is worthy or just for God to bestow

38. And so is condemned because he did not die in a state of penitence.

it on him. For he who uses even evil things well, and arranges all the worst things for the best, foresaw that he would use that person better some other way.

(175) If someone perhaps says that one who truly repented and loved God at the time, but who nevertheless didn't persevere in this penitence or love, wasn't therefore worthy of the reward of life, then certainly, since it is granted that he wasn't at that time worthy of damnation either, it will be seen that at that time he was neither just nor a sinner.

On inexcusable sin

(176) Now since every sin gets excused right away through penitence, as we said [(165)], it is asked why Truth called a certain sin "inexcusable," that is, one that will never get excused or receive a pardon. The sin of blasphemy against the Holy Spirit is like this. Matthew relates that he[39] said the following about this: "People will be excused every sin and blasphemy. But blasphemy against the Spirit will not be excused. And whoever says a word against the Son of Man will be excused for it. But he who says it against the Holy Spirit will *not* be excused for it, either in this age or in the future." Mark explained why he said this. He says, "Because they said, 'He has an impure spirit.' "

(177) This sin some people call "despairing of forgiveness," when someone because of the extent of his sins completely gives up hope in God's goodness, which is what is meant by the "Holy Spirit," with the result that he is unable to gain forgiveness either by repenting or by any atonement.

(178) But if this is what we call sinning or blaspheming against the Spirit, what will we call sinning against the Son of Man? As far as I can see, disparaging the excellence of Christ's humanity is what in this passage is called "sinning" or "blaspheming" against the Son of Man, as if, because of the flesh's visible feebleness, we were denying that Christ's humanity was conceived without sin or assumed by God. Surely *that* could not have been found out by any human reasoning, but believed only by God's revealing it. Therefore, his statement: "People will be excused every sin and blasphemy. But blasphemy against the Spirit will not be excused," is as if to say God has decided that only this blasphemy will not be disregarded for any people. "And whoever will say a word against the Son of Man, he will be excused for it"— that is, no one who disparages the assumed man's dignity,[40] as we said, will be damned on account of it if other causes of damnation do not enter in.

---

39. That is, Jesus (= "Truth").

40. That is, the dignity of the humanity taken on by God in the Incarnation. See n. 9 above.

(179) For no scorn for God can be observed here if such a person contradicts the truth by mistake and doesn't act against his conscience, especially since the matter is such that it can't be investigated by human reason, but appears rather to be contrary to reason. But blaspheming against the Spirit is defaming the deeds of the manifest grace of God in such a way that things they[41] *believe* to come about mercifully through the Holy Spirit (that is, by divine goodness) they *assert* are done through a devil, as though they said that he whom they believe is the Spirit of God is instead a vile spirit, and thus that God is a devil.

(180) So those who have sinned like this against Christ, by saying against their conscience that he casts out demons "in virtue of Beelzebub the Prince of Demons," are so utterly banished from the kingdom of God and entirely shut off from his grace that none of them deserves an allowance to be made through penitence. Of course we aren't denying they can be saved *if* they were to repent; we are only saying that they *will* not pursue acts of penitence.

Do those who repent carry the groan of sorrow away with them from here?

(181) Perhaps someone asks whether people who depart from this life while repenting, in this heart-groan and contriteness of sorrow where the true sacrifice to God is offered—in accordance with the psalm, "A troubled spirit is a sacrifice to God"—whether, I say, such people, passing over from this life, carry away with them this groan and sorrow, so that in that heavenly life too, where as is written, "Sorrow and groaning and sadness run away," they are sorry for having committed these sins. Certainly, just as our sins are displeasing to God or the angels without any of sorrow's pain,[42] insofar as they don't approve of what they regard as evils, so things we have done wrong will then be displeasing to us too. But whether we will *want* those things to have been done (we know they are well arranged by God and know also they worked together in us to good effect, in accordance with the Apostle, "We know that for lovers of God all things work together to good effect"), that is another question, which we answered in the third book of our *Theology* to the extent of our powers.

41. That is, the blasphemers, who believe one way but say the opposite, and so act "against their conscience."

42. That is, *they* are not the ones who feel the pain of sorrow, whether *we* do or not.

On confession

(182) It behooves us to deal with the confession of sins. Exhorting us to it, the apostle James says: "Confess your sins to one another, and pray for one another so that you may be saved. For a just person's constant praying is worth much."

(183) There are people who think only God should be confessed to. (Some ascribe this to the Greeks.) But I don't see what confession is worth before a God who knows all things, or what allowance the tongue gains for us, even granted that the prophet says, "I have made my misdeed known to you and have not hidden my injustice."

(184) The faithful confess their sins to each other for many reasons, according to the apostle's exhortation cited above [(182)], both (a) for the reason given above, that we might be helped more by the prayers of those we confess to, and also (b) because in the humility of confession a great part of the atonement is done, and in the release that goes with penitence we gain greater allowance. It is as is written about David. When he was accused by the prophet Nathan he responded, "I have sinned," and at once heard from the same prophet the reply, "And the Lord has taken your sin away." For the greater the king's exaltedness was, the more acceptable to God was his humility in confessing. Finally (c), the priests (to whom are entrusted the souls of those who confess) have to prescribe for them the atonements of penitence, so that those who used their free choice badly and pridefully in scorning God are corrected by another power's choice, and so that they do this more securely insofar as they follow not their own will so much as their superiors',[43] the more they obey them. If perhaps his superiors didn't direct the penitent correctly when he was ready to obey, this is to be blamed on them rather than on him.

(185) "We are not ignorant" of Satan's subtleties, the Apostle says. His viciousness here should not be overlooked, whereby he drives us to sin and holds us back from confession. Indeed, while urging us to sin he strips us of fear and shame alike, so that there is nothing left any more that keeps us from sin. For there are many things we don't dare commit out of fear of the penalty, and many we are embarrassed to try because of the loss to our reputation, even if we could do it with impunity. Therefore anyone wrongly released from these two shackles, so to speak, will be made reckless about perpetrating any sin at all. Indeed, in this way what Satan earlier took away from the sinner, so that he

43. *"Praelatus,"* from *"praefero,"* can mean anyone who is "set over" another—a "superior," someone "in charge"—or it can mean "prelate" in the ecclesiastical sense. I have generally translated it as "superior," except where the ecclesiastical sense is the only one that will work.

would carry out the sin, he afterwards returns to him in order to keep him away from confession. The sinner is afraid or embarrassed to confess then what he *wasn't* afraid or embarrassed to do at first, when he should have been. He is afraid that, found out through confession, he will perhaps be punished by human beings—he who wasn't afraid of being punished by God. He is embarrassed that the deed, which he wasn't embarrassed to commit before God, should be known by humans. But if someone wants medication for a wound, then no matter how disgusting the wound is, no matter how much it stinks, it has to be disclosed to the doctor so that the appropriate cure is used. Now the priest by whom the atonement is to be established, as we said [(184)], plays the role of the doctor.

That confession can sometimes be omitted

(186) Yet it should be known that confession can sometimes be avoided with a salutary dispensation, as we believe in the case of Peter. We know about the tears over his denial of Jesus, but we don't read about any other atonement or confession on his part. Thus in commenting on Luke, Ambrose too says about Peter's denial and about his weeping: "I do not find what he said; I do find that he wept. I read about his tears; I do not read about atonement. The tears wash away the misdeed that it is a disgrace to confess out loud, and the weeping takes care of the forgiveness and shame. The tears speak without terror about the fault. They confess without detriment to the feeling of shame. The tears do not beg forgiveness but earn it. I find why Peter kept silent: so that his begging forgiveness so soon not be all the more offensive."

(187) We need to see what this shame is, this apprehensiveness about confession such that Peter atoned more by weeping than by confessing. For if he was ashamed to confess for the single reason that once his sin was known he would be regarded as baser, then he was surely prideful and was looking after the glory of his reputation more than his soul's salvation. On the other hand, if not his own shame but the Church's was being shielded, that's not to be blamed. Perhaps he anticipated that he would be appointed by the Lord as prince[44] over the Lord's people and was afraid that if his threefold denial got to be publicized through his confession of it, the Church would be scandalized seriously and disconcerted by intense embarrassment at the Lord's putting at its head someone so quick to deny and so fainthearted.

---

44. Prince = *princeps*. In the twelfth century, the word can also mean simply "bishop," which is also appropriate here. Luscombe (p. 103) translates "leader," which is likewise good.

(188) Therefore, if he delayed confessing not so much for the sake of saving his own reputation as because of this general embarrassment of the Church, he did it with foresight, not with pride. And his fear, for the injury of the Church more than for the damage to his own repute, was for a reasonable cause. Certainly he knew the Church was especially entrusted by the Lord to him when the Lord said to him, "And once you are converted, strengthen your brothers." Thus condemned by his own confession, if so horrible a failure of his came to the ears of the Church, who wouldn't easily say, "We do not want him to rule over us"? Who wouldn't easily reject the Lord's decision that selected him who was first to fall short to strengthen the brothers?

(189) By this kind of foresight many other people could also delay confession or do completely without it without sin, if they believed it would be more harmful than beneficial. For where we don't scorn God, we commit no offense against him arising from a fault. Peter delayed confessing his sin, since until Peter's strength had been tested by his preaching or his miracles, the Church was still fragile in the faith and weak. But afterwards, once that had already been established, Peter himself was able to confess this to counter the despair of the fallen without any scandal to the Church, so that it was even left written down by the Evangelists.

(190) Perhaps there are people for whom it appears that Peter, who was in charge of all the others and didn't have a superior to whom his soul was entrusted, had no need to confess his sin to a human being at all, in the sense that atonement would be set for him by that other person, as though he obeyed the other person's command like a superior's. But if he didn't *have* to confess to someone for the sake of having atonement exacted, nevertheless it *could* have been done, not inappropriately, on account of the support of prayer that would result. On this point, in fact, when it was said [(182)], "Confess your sins to one another," there was added, "and pray for one another so that you may be saved." There is also nothing to prevent superiors from picking one of their subjects to make confession to or for assigning them atonement, so that the atonement done becomes more acceptable to God insofar as it is performed more humbly. Who in such cases will prohibit anyone from picking someone more religious or more discreet, to whose decision he might entrust his atonement and be much helped by his prayers? Thus even though it was said above, "And pray for one another so that you may be saved," it was at once added [(182)], "For the just person's constant praying is worth much."

(191) Just as many people become incompetent doctors whom it is dangerous or useless for the sick to be sent to, so too with the Church's prelates. There are many found who are neither religious nor discreet, and who are furthermore quick to divulge the sins of those who confess to them, with the

result that confessing to them appears not only useless but even destructive. Such people certainly have no intention of praying and don't merit being heard in their prayers. Since they are ignorant of the regulations in the canons[45] and don't know how to manage the assignment of atonements, they often promise an empty security in such cases and deceive those confessing with a futile hope, in accordance with Truth's remark, "They are blind leaders of the blind," and again, "If a blind person is set as leader over a blind person, both fall into the ditch." Since they also frivolously disclose the confessions they receive, as we said, they move penitents to outrage, and those who ought to have cured sins bring about new wounds of sins and scare the people who hear about it away from confession.

(192) Sometimes too, in revealing sins out of either rage or frivolousness, they seriously scandalize the Church and put those who have confessed into great perils. Hence people are in no way to be blamed who have decided to avoid their superiors because of these improprieties, and pick other people whom they believe are more appropriate in such cases. Instead they are more to be commended for going off to a more skillful doctor.

(193) Yet if they can get their superiors' agreement in doing this, so that they are directed by their superiors to other confessors, they behave more properly insofar as they do this more humbly through obedience. On the other hand, if prideful superiors forbid them this—as though holding themselves poorer doctors if better ones are needed—nevertheless let the sick person who is concerned about his health look with greater concern for what he believes is the better medicine and let him comply most with the better advice. For no one, if he finds out that the leader assigned to him by someone is blind, ought to follow him into a ditch. To get where he is going, it is better to pick a leader who sees than it is to follow someone over the cliff by mistake who has been assigned to him by mistake.

(194) For anyone who assigned him such a leader, as if he were going to show him the way, did it either knowingly out of spite or else innocently out of ignorance. If out of spite, then care should have been taken that his spite not be fulfilled. If out of ignorance, then it isn't going against his will if we don't follow the blind person into danger whom he gave us as a leader.

(195) Nevertheless, it is useful for us first to consult the people to whom we know our souls are entrusted, and once their advice has been heard it is more beneficial not to abandon it if it is the medicine we hoped for.[46] This is

---

45. That is, the canonical rules set down for the "care of souls."

46. The syntax of the Latin is very clumsy throughout this sentence. The idea is that we should look to the *content* of the confessor's advice rather than to his personal integrity. If it is good advice, do not dismiss it even if it comes from an incompetent.

especially so when we believe they do not know the Law,[47] so that* they are not only concerned about what to do but also ignorant of what to be sorry for. They are to be regarded as worse than those of whom Truth says: "The Scribes and Pharisees have sat in Moses' seat. Therefore, whatever things they have said, keep them and do them. But be unwilling to do according to their deeds." It is as though he had said: "Such people get a mastery of the Law, but their deeds are to be spurned since they are evil. Nevertheless God's words, which they pronounce from Moses' seat—that is, from their mastery of the Law—are to be accepted, so that we reject the deeds which are theirs, and keep the words which are God's."[48]

(196) Therefore, such people's teaching isn't to be scorned—that is, people who preach well but live badly, who educate by word but don't edify by their example. They show the way they are unwilling to follow. They are to be judged not so much for their ignorance's blindness as for their negligence's fault. But as for those *unable* to show their subjects the way, who should entrust themselves to *their* leadership and ask for instruction from people who don't know how to teach?

(197) Nevertheless their subjects are not to despair of God's mercy when they are fully prepared to make atonement, when they turn themselves over to their superiors' decision (even though the latter are blind), and when they carefully carry out through obedience what little their superiors assign. For the superiors' mistake doesn't damn their subjects, and the former's vice is no complaint against the latter. There is no longer any state of fault remaining in the subjects wherein they might die. Penitence, as we said [(165)], has already reconciled them with God in advance, before they came to confession or received their atonement.

47. That is, when we think they are acting out of ignorance, not out of spite or malice.
48. The last part of this difficult paragraph is clear enough. Again, the main idea is that we should look to the *content* of the teaching, not to the person of the teacher. But how does this fit with the earlier part of the paragraph? Here at the end, we are talking about people who have a "mastery" of the law. Earlier we were talking about people we believe are *ignorant* of the law, and it was said we should be *especially* careful in that case to separate their words from their example and to follow the former if they contain sound advice. But why should it be more important to follow good advice from people who don't know what they are talking about than from people who do? Again, if ignorant teachers are "worse" than the Scribes and Pharisees, then why should we be *especially* careful not to reject their advice if it is worthy? Perhaps the point is simply that since we are understandably inclined to be suspicious of incompetents, especially if they are evildoers in addition [(196)], we need to be particularly careful to recognize and follow good advice when it comes from such people.

(198) Yet if some penalty assigned in atonement is less than it should be, then God who lets no sin go unpunished, and punishes individual sins as much as he ought, will preserve the atonement's fairness according to the extent of the sin, not by holding the penitents back for eternal tortures but by tormenting them with purgatorial[49] pains either in this life or in the future one—if, I say, we have been neglectful in our atonement.

(199) Thus the Apostle says, "If we would judge ourselves, we would surely not be judged." That is to say, if we ourselves punished or corrected our own sins, they would no longer have to be punished by him more seriously. God's mercy is indeed great when he lets us off according to our own judgment, so that he not punish us by a more serious one.

(200) These penalties in the present life whereby we atone for our sins— by fasting, praying, keeping vigil or mortifying the flesh in whatever ways, or by spending on the needy what we take from ourselves—we call "atonement." We know in the Gospel they are called by another name: "penitence's fruits"—where it says, "Make your fruits of penitence worthwhile," as if it were said plainly: "Be so reconciled with God here, by chastising your misdeeds with a worthy atonement, that thereafter he doesn't find anything to punish any more. Forestall graver penalties by gentler ones." For as blessed Augustine says, "The future life's penalties, even though they are purgatorial,[50] are graver than all the present life's ones." Thus great care should be taken with them and great deeds done, so that in accordance with the stipulations of the holy Fathers[51] such atonement might be undergone here that there remains nothing to be expurgated there. So when there are indiscreet priests who are ignorant of these canonical stipulations, so that they exact less atonement than is needed, penitents are thereby put at a considerable disadvantage. For having mistakenly relied on them, they will be punished afterwards with graver penalties for what they could have atoned for here with lighter ones.

(201) There are some priests who deceive their subjects not so much by mistake as through greed, so that for an offering of coins they excuse or relax the penalties of the atonement imposed, not paying attention to what the Lord wants so much as to what a coin is worth. The Lord himself complained*[52]

49. The connection with the doctrine of Purgatory is obvious. But, as the sentence makes clear, the pains described here need not take place in Purgatory after death.

50. And so only temporary.

51. That is, authoritative early Christian writers, not necessarily "Holy Fathers" in the sense of popes.

52. Conjecturing *conquaerens* for the edition's *conquirens*. With the latter, the sentence

about them through the prophet, saying "My priests did not say 'Where is the Lord?' " as if he had gone on to say, "but rather, 'Where is the coin'?"

(202) We know that not only priests but even the very princes of priests (that is, the bishops) are so shamelessly on fire with this greed that while dedicating churches, consecrating altars or blessing cemeteries, or at any solemnities when they have crowds of people from whom they expect an abundant offering, they are lavish in relaxing penances. They grant indulgences to all in general, here a third, there a fourth of the penance, naturally with a certain facade of charity, but in fact with supreme greed.*

(203) They brag about their power, which they say they got from Peter or the apostles, when the Lord said to them, "Those whose sins you will forgive, they will be forgiven them," or "Whatever you will release on earth will be released in heaven too." They glory in what is theirs to do, especially when they distribute this benevolence to their subjects. If only they did it for *them* at least, and not for the cash, so it would appear as a kind of benevolence instead of greed!

(204) But surely, if the fact that they relax a third or a fourth of the penance is supposed to be regarded as grounds for praising their benevolence, then their piety will have to be publicized much more widely if they dismissed half or all of the entire penance, as they claim is allowed to them and was granted by the Lord. The heavens were placed in their hands, so to speak, according to the texts just cited about forgiving or absolving sins. In short, it seems that they are to be charged on the contrary with a great *impiety*. Why don't they absolve all their subjects of all their sins, and so permit none of them to be damned—if, I say, it has been put in their power to dismiss or retain in this way whatever sins they want, or to open or close the heavens to whomever they decide? In any case, they would have to be declared *most* blessed if they could open the heavens to *themselves* when they wanted. But if in fact they can't or don't know how to do this, then certainly, as I judge it, they run up against the poet's remark, "The arts that benefit all do not benefit the Lord." Let anyone (not me!) be eager for the power whereby he can help others rather than himself, as if he has it in his power to save others' souls more than his own—although any prudent person feels otherwise.

---

would start, "Searching, the Lord himself said about them through the prophet." Perhaps an explanation for *conquirens* may be found in the text of Jeremiah, a few verses before the quotation, where the passage is introduced with the question (= the "searching"): "Thus says the Lord, 'What immorality have your fathers found in me, that they have departed from me and have walked after vanity and been made vain?' " (Jer. 2:5).

Do releasing and binding[53] pertain to all prelates in general?

(205) So it seems not a small question when it is asked what that power is—that is, the keys to the kingdom of heaven that the Lord handed over to the apostles and, we read, granted in like manner to their vicars the bishops. For since there are many bishops who have neither religion nor discernment even though they have episcopal power, how will we say that the passage, "Those whose sins you will forgive, they will be forgiven them, and those whose sins you will retain, they are retained," fits them equally as well as it does the apostles? If a bishop wants to increase or relax a sin's penalty indiscriminately or excessively, is this in his power, with the result that God distributes penalties according to the bishop's judgment, so that what should be punished less he punishes more or the other way around—although God should pay more attention to the fairness of the matter than to people's will? What if a bishop, out of rage or the hatred he has for someone, has decreed that he do just as much penance for lighter sins as for more serious ones, or that his penalty extend in perpetuity, or has decided *never* to relax it for him no matter how long he does penance? Will the Lord confirm this sentence of his?

(206) So what the Lord said to the apostles, "Those whose sins you will forgive, they will be forgiven them," etc., has to be referred to their own persons, it seems, and not to all bishops in general. It is like what he said to them elsewhere, "You are the light of the world," and "You will be the salt of the earth," or several other texts that have to be taken with reference to their own persons especially. For this discernment or holiness that the Lord gave to the apostles he did not grant equally to their successors. He did not say equally to all, "Blessed are the eyes that see what you have seen," and again, "Now I called you friends because, whatever things I have heard from my Father, I have made them all known to you." And again, "Now when the spirit of truth will have come, it will teach you every truth."

(207) If perhaps someone raises an objection about Judas, who also was one of the apostles when these things were said, let him know that the Lord didn't fail to know to whom he should aim what he was saying. So too when he said, "Father, forgive them, because they do not know what they are doing," his prayer isn't regarded as having to be applied to *all* those persecuting him. For when 'them' or 'you' is said (these are demonstrative pronouns) the statement is directed, according to the speaker's

---

53. Releasing and binding: that is, forgiving and not forgiving sins.

intention, either to all alike who are present or to some of them whom he determines. So too the passages quoted above are to be referred not to all the apostles in general, but to the elect alone. And it seems that perhaps we should take his statement, "Whatever you will have bound on earth, they will be also bound in heaven," in the same way, where the sense is thought to be similar.

(208) When blessed Jerome, who considered this matter closely, came to explaining the words in Matthew where the Lord says to Peter, "Whatever you will have bound on earth," he said: "Bishops and elders do not understand this text. They take upon themselves some of the Pharisees' haughtiness, so that they either condemn the innocent or else think they release culprits, even though for God the question is not about the priests' judgment but about the criminals' life. We read about the lepers in Leviticus, where they are ordered to show themselves to the priests, and if they have leprosy then they are made unclean by the priest. It is not that the priests *make* them clean or unclean, but rather that they are familiar with lepers and non-lepers and can discriminate who is unclean or clean. Therefore, in the sense in which the priest "makes" the leper unclean, so too the bishop or elder does not here bind or release those who are offenders or are blameless, but rather knows who is to be bound or who is to be released once he has heard their various sins in his official capacity."

(209) Unless I am deceived, it is plain from these words of Jerome that what was said to Peter or likewise to the other apostles about binding or releasing the shackles of sins is to be taken more with respect to their persons than with respect to all bishops generally. This is so unless perhaps, in accordance with what Jerome himself says, we understand this binding or absolving as the judging just mentioned, which was granted generally to all, so that they have the power to judge who is to be bound or absolved by God and to discriminate between the clean and the unclean.

(210) Hence also Origen's remark on the same text in Matthew, where Origen is distinguishing from others the elect bishops who have earned this grace that was granted to Peter. He says the following:

"Whatever you will have bound on earth."[54] People defending the position of the episcopate use this text as Peter did, and teach that the keys of the kingdom of heaven are received from Christ, that those who have been bound by these people are bound in heaven and those who have been released by them (that is, have obtained forgiveness) are released in heaven too. It must be said they speak well—

54. This sentence is the text on which the following commentary is based.

if they have the deeds on the basis of which it was said to Peter, "You are Peter,"[55] *if* they are such that Christ's Church might be built on them, and *if* the gates of hell do not prevail over them. Otherwise it is ridiculous for us to say that one who is bound with the shackles of his sins, who drags his sins behind him like a long cord, and who continually drags his iniquities around like a calf's leash has this kind of power solely because he is called a "bishop," so that those released by him on earth are released in heaven, or those bound on earth are bound in heaven.

So let the bishop who binds or releases someone else be irreproachable—that is, someone who deserves to bind or release in heaven. Let him be one wife's husband, sober, chaste, distinguished, hospitable, easy to teach, not a wine-sot, not a brawler, but modest, not contentious, not a money-craver, one who runs his household well, with his children subject to him in all purity. If he is like that, he will not unjustly bind on earth, and will not release without exercising his judgment. For this reason, whatever someone like this will have released will also be released in heaven, and whatever he will have bound on earth will be bound in heaven too. For if there were some "Peter," if I may so put it, and he did not have the things here attributed so to speak to Peter, and he thought he could bind things so that they are bound in heaven and release things so that they are released in heaven, he is fooling himself. He does not understand the will of Scripture and falls, self-important, into the devil's judgment.

(211) So Origen obviously shows, as also plain reason has it, that in the case of the things we said were granted to Peter, they weren't in any way conferred by the Lord on *all* the bishops, but only on the ones who imitate Peter, not in the exaltedness of his chair but in the worthiness of their merits. For those who follow their own will and turn their backs on God's will have no power against the righteousness of divine justice. When they immorally do something, they cannot incline God to immorality and thus make him so to speak like them.

(212) He himself complains bitterly about people like that, and threatens them severely when he says: "You immorally thought I was like you. I will accuse you and set your deeds before your face. You who forget God, understand these things," etc. For who should be said to forget God and to be given to a "reprobate mind" more than someone who claims such power for himself that he says divine judgment is subject to him in binding and releasing subjects according to his own choice, with the result (he has immorally presumed even this!) that he can subvert God's supreme justice—as though he could make whomever he wanted guilty or innocent?

(213) Lest they ever be that presumptuous, Augustine the great doctor of the Church, famous among the bishops themselves, replied to them in *Sermon*

55. The text of Matthew continues, "and on this rock I will build my Church, and the gates of hell will not prevail over it."

16 on the Lord's words. He said: "You have begun to take your brother as a tax-collector.[56] You bind him on earth. But see that you bind justly; for justice tears unjust shackles apart."

(214) Blessed Gregory as well clearly states and demonstrates by precedents from the Lord that ecclesiastical power is unable to do any binding or releasing if it departs from justice's fairness and doesn't conform to divine judgment. That is why he says in *Sermon 25 on the Gospels:*

> It frequently happens that someone holds the position of judge whose life in no way conforms to that position, and often it turns out that he either condemns those who don't deserve it or else releases others, though he himself remains bound. Often, in releasing or binding his subjects, he follows the impulses of his own will but not the merits of the cases. Thus it comes about that someone who uses it for his own designs, and not for the sake of his subjects' morals, robs himself of the very power of binding and releasing. Often it happens that a pastor is motivated by hatred or kindness toward a neighbor. But those who follow either their hatred or their kindness in dealing with their subjects cannot worthily judge their subjects. Thus, according to the prophet, "They dealt death to souls that are not dying and enlivened souls that are not alive." He who condemns a just person certainly deals death to one who is not dying, and he who tries to release a guilty person from torture is working to enliven what is not about to live.
>
> Therefore, one must consider the cases, and *then* the power of binding and releasing is to be exercised. One must see what the fault is, or what regret followed the fault, so that the pastor's judgment may absolve the people whom the Omnipotent visits through the grace of remorse. For a director's absolution is true when it follows the decision of the inner judge. The resurrection of the man dead for four days indicates this well. It points out, that is, that the Lord called the dead man earlier and revived him, saying, "Lazarus, come out." After that, the man who came forth alive was released by the disciples.

(215) Again,

> Look, the disciples are already releasing the dead man whom the master has raised up. For if the disciples had released[57] Lazarus while he was dead, they would have displayed a stink rather than a power. We should see from this consideration that by our pastoral authority we ought to release those whom we know our author is enlivening by the grace of resurrection. This enlivening is now known without doubt, before anything righteous has been done, in the very confessing of sins. That is also why it is not said to the dead man "Come back to

---

56. That is, as someone to be treated with scorn and abuse. Tax-collectors were not popular people.
57. Here the sense is literal: if they had unbound him from his funeral wrappings.

life!" but "Come out!" It is as if it were being openly said to anyone who has died in a state of fault, "You who by negligence are inwardly hidden from yourself, come out now through confession."

So let him come out—that is, let the sinner confess his fault. But let the disciples release the person who comes out, so that the Church's pastors might relax the penalty of one who was not embarrassed to confess what he did.

(216) Again, "But whether the pastor binds justly or unjustly, nevertheless the flock must fear the pastor's judgment, so that he who is subject to it, even if perhaps he is bound unjustly, should not by another fault *earn* that binding judgment."

(217) Again, "Let whoever is under a pastor's hand be afraid of being bound, whether justly or unjustly, and not heedlessly criticize his pastor's judgment, lest even if he is bound unjustly, the fault that did not exist should come to exist out of the pride of arrogant criticism."

(218) From these statements of Gregory's, and from the examples of divine authority, it is obvious that the bishops' judgment is worthless if it departs from divine fairness, wanting to deal death to or enliven those they cannot, according to the prophet's remark. By a bishops' judgment too, a bishop is deprived of communion with them when he has dared to deprive his subjects unjustly of communion with him.[58] Thus, in Canon 210 of the African Council, "Let a bishop not heedlessly deprive anyone of communion, and as long as an excommunicate's bishop does not communicate with him, let the same bishop not be communicated with by the other bishops, so that a bishop might be more on guard against saying about someone what he cannot demonstrate by other evidence."

(219) Finally, the statements that "Justice tears unjust shackles apart" [(213)], and "Let whoever is under a pastor's hand be afraid of being bound, whether justly or unjustly, and not heedlessly criticize his pastor's judgment, lest even if he is bound unjustly, the fault that did not exist should come to exist out of the pride of arrogant criticism" [(217)], raise a question and in my judgment also open up the way to solve it. For who should fear being bound unjustly if there is no way that this can be unjustly done, since "Justice tears unjust shackles apart"? So, to preserve both quotations intact, someone can be bound unjustly by a human judgment in such a way that divine justice nevertheless tears the unjust shackles apart.

58. Abelard needlessly complicates the sentence by using only the plural throughout: ". . . they [= bishops] are deprived of communion with them when they have dared to deprive their subjects unjustly of communion with them." I have changed some of the plurals to singulars for the sake of clarifying the sense.

(220) When someone who gets into an excommunication he didn't earn is kept out of the Church, so that association with the faithful isn't granted to him, he is indeed bound unjustly. But God tears apart these shackles of anathema, because he voids the pastor's judgment so that it doesn't cut off from grace the person whom the pastor separated from the Church.

(221) Suppose someone wants what was said to the apostles about the power of binding and releasing, the power of forgiving or retaining sins, to be granted to all their vicars alike (that is, to the bishops). It seems to me this must be taken in the sense that their power consists of the choice to impose or relax excommunication, so that, as was already said,[59] they are allowed to keep out of or receive into the present Church whomever they want among their subjects. Thus, when it is said to the apostles, "Whatever you will have bound on earth," etc., in order for us to grant that this was granted to all bishops in general, I think it has to be understood in the sense that whomever the Church's pastors bind or absolve here in any way, the heavenly power confirms their judgment whether it was just or unjust, as was already said,[60] so that this power orders it to be preserved by their subjects through humility. In fact, this is why he said to the corrupt prelates, "Keep and do what they will tell you."[61]

(222) And even though blessed Gregory says above [(214)] that one who binds his subjects unjustly robs himself of the power of binding and releasing—that is, makes himself thus unworthy of it—nevertheless he commands that the pastor's judgment, even though it is unjust, be feared by his subjects and not broken. So let no one banished from the Church by excommunication, for no matter what reason, undertake to intrude into it against the bishop's will or dare obstinately to resist him in this, lest in this way he fall into a fault he didn't have before.

(223) And so we take the keys of the kingdom of heaven, turned over to the apostles or to Peter, to be the power of opening or closing the kingdom of heaven (that is, the present Church) to their subjects, as we said [(221)], as if there is one key for unlocking and another for locking. What we are now saying to have been granted to all alike with reference to the power of binding or releasing can also perhaps be understood with reference to forgiving or retaining sins, so that it is their choice to impose or to relax for their subjects

59. Abelard has not said this outright, but see (216)–(217), (219)–(220).

60. In fact, Abelard has not explicitly said this.

61. In the text of Matthew, this is not said *to* the corrupt prelates, but *to* the multitude and the disciples *about* the "corrupt prelates" (= the Scribes and the Pharisees). This must surely be what Abelard intends as well. But the Latin edition has it as I have translated, and shows no variants.

the penalty of excommunication that is supposed to be exacted for sins. For when the Lord said, "Whatever you will have bound"—not *whomever*—he said *sins* are bound or released, so that these sins' being "released" amounts to their being forgiven, and the same sins' being "bound" amounts to their being retained or imposed.

(224) Nevertheless if we carefully weigh the giving of the former and the latter power, then just as they happened at different times, so too they appear to be different gifts. Indeed, the former power was granted both to Peter and the others before the Resurrection, as Matthew writes. But the latter was granted on the very day of the Resurrection, as John remarks. Finally, it was also before the Resurrection, as Luke relates, that the Lord "called his disciples and chose twelve of them, whom he named 'apostles'." And he said to them, "You are the salt of the earth, you are the light of the world." Sending them out to preach, and entrusting the power of binding and releasing to them, he at that time appointed them bishops, just as he had made them apostles. So when he breathed on them after the Resurrection and said: "Receive the Holy Spirit. Those whose sins you will forgive" etc., it seems that this gift of the Holy Spirit was new, so to speak, and was granted especially to them, or only to those of their vicars who were not unworthy of this grace and who are to be called spiritual rather than animal. And in the things they do, it seems the discrimination through the Spirit that we spoke of earlier [(208)] is observed. So neither Judas the traitor, already dead, nor Thomas, still the unbeliever, was worthy of being in attendance then for the receiving of this grace.

(225) Yet if someone maintains, in accordance with the analysis given above [(221)], that this grace was granted to all the bishops equally with the apostles, we won't begrudge them such a grace distributed to all alike. We don't obstinately resist those who want to be made equal to the apostles in the fullness of power. For me it is enough to set out my opinion in all I write, rather than to promise to define the truth. As for now, the clear reasoning of truth incites even people preeminent in religion's name to enough envy or hatred.

The end of Book One

The Beginning of Book Two

(226) The above book of our *Ethics* was devoted to recognizing and correcting sins. It distinguished those sins from vices that are called the contraries of virtues. But now, after we have discussed turning away from evils, it remains for us to turn the pen of our teaching to doing good. This is the right order, according to the Psalmist: "Turn away from evil, and do good."

(227) Prudence—that is, the discrimination of good and evil—is the *mother* of virtues rather than itself a virtue.[62] To it there pertains the granting of dispensations according to the time, the place or the worthiness of the persons.

(228) Just as we have distinguished vices from sins [(4)–(7)], so too the virtues that are the contraries of those vices appear to differ a little from the goods whereby we win blessedness and that consist of the good of obedience. For just as virtues are contrary to vices, so too sin (which is properly said to be scorn for God) appears antithetical to the good of obedience—that is, to the will that is prepared to obey God. This will, perhaps, can sometimes exist even if after it has been possessed for a while it isn't yet so firm and difficult to dislodge that it can be called a "virtue." For as philosophers hold, something in us shouldn't be called a "virtue" unless it is the best kind of mental habit, or the habit of a well-ordered mind. For what they have called "habit" or "disposition," Aristotle distinguished carefully in the first species of quality. He taught that qualities that aren't in us naturally, but come to us through our own industriousness, are called "habits" or "dispositions." They are called habits if they are hard to dislodge, as he says knowledge and the virtues are. But they are called dispositions if on the contrary they are easy to dislodge.

(229) Therefore, if accordingly every virtue of ours is to be called a "habit," it doesn't seem absurd that sometimes a will that is prepared to obey shouldn't be called a "virtue" or a "habit" before it is firmed up, since it is easy to dislodge then.

(230) Nevertheless, those who finish life with this resolution of will aren't in any way to be regarded as though they are going to be damned. What we read in the book of Wisdom is about such people: "Pleasing God, he was made beloved, and living among sinners, he was transported. He was snatched away, so that maliciousness would not change his understanding, or a fable deceive his soul. Perfected quickly, he lasted a long time. For his soul was pleasing to God. For this reason he was quick to lead him out from the midst of iniquities."

62. Compare Abelard's *Dialogue* (256), (270).

(231) Certainly there are many of the faithful who don't have such perseverance that they can withstand the martyrs' agonies or who would* easily fall short in time of adversities. Foreseeing their feebleness, the Lord doesn't allow them to be tempted above what they can bear. He doesn't try people with calamities whom he regards as timid or weak.

(232) They too, not unmindful of this favor and thus giving no little thanks to God, are humbler insofar as they recognize themselves as weaker. They cannot be strangers to God's love, whose favors they don't remain ungrateful for. They confess that they owe more to him from whom they appear to have received more in these ways.

The end in the exemplar.[63]

63. This is a scribe's note, recognizing that the manuscript he was copying from was incomplete.

Dialogue Between a Philosopher, a Jew and a Christian[1]

[Preface]

(1) I was looking around in a dream one night, and here came three men along another path and stood in front of me. In a dreamlike way, I ask them straight out what their profession is and why they've come to me.

(2) "We are men inclined to different religious faiths," they say. "To be sure, we all alike confess that we are worshippers of the one God, but we serve him by different faiths and different kinds of life. One of us is a pagan, from among those they call philosophers; he is satisfied with the natural law. But the other two have Scriptures. One of them is called a Jew and the other a Christian. After conversing and disputing with one another for a long time about our different religious faiths, we have finally submitted to your judgment."

(3) So I am very astonished at this, and ask who brought or gathered them together for this purpose, and most of all why they picked me as the judge in this affair.

(4) THE PHILOSOPHER replies: "It was begun at my doing," he says. "For it's the philosophers' job to investigate the truth by means of reasons, and in all things to follow not people's opinion but reason's lead. So having devoted myself to our schools for a long time, and having been educated in both their reasons and their authorities, at last I brought myself to moral philosophy, which is the aim of all the disciplines and for the sake of which I judged all the rest should be mere preliminaries.

(5) "After being taught all I could there about ultimate good and ultimate evil, and about things that make a person happy or wretched, I at once went on to explore eagerly for myself the different religious faiths facing me, into which the world is now divided. After looking into all of them and comparing them with one another, I decided to follow the one that is more in agreement with reason.

(6) "I therefore applied myself to the doctrine of the Jews, and of the Christians too, and examined the belief and the laws or reasonings of both

1. I have used the traditional title from the *PL*. The edition has only "The Dialogue of Peter Abelard." The important Balliol MS has "The beginning of the Preface to Peter Abelard's *Conversations*."

groups. I found the Jews were fools and the Christians crazy—so to speak, no offense to you who are called a Christian. I have conversed with both for a long time, and since the debate has not yet brought an end to our discussion, we have decided to submit its parties' reasonings to your judgment. Of course we know you're not unaware of the powers of philosophical reasonings or of each Law's defenses. For the Christian religion relies on its own Law, which they call the 'New Testament,' but in such a way that yet it does not presume to spurn the Old. It devotes a lot of effort to studying both. We had to pick *someone* as our judge, so that our debate would reach an end, and we were unable to find anyone who did not belong to one of these three groups."

(7) Then, as if selling flattery-oil and daubing my head with the salve, he went on at once: "So the more word gets around of your preeminence in mental keenness and in knowledge of all the Scriptures, the more certain it is that you can support or defend your judgment and are able to withstand a revolt by any one of us. That amazing work of theology,[2] which jealousy couldn't bear but was unable to do away with, and instead made it all the more glorious by persecuting it, provided for us a sure test that there is indeed a keenness to your mind, and how much the storehouse of your memory is overflowing with philosophical and sacred teachings beyond the usual studies of your schools. For these reasons, it's obvious you've flourished in both fields beyond all the masters, your own as well as the writers we find in the known sciences."

(8) Then I said: "I'm not soliciting this honor you have saved for me, seeing that in passing over the wise you appoint a fool for a judge. Since I too am used to the empty controversies of this world, therefore, like you, I won't take seriously things I've been accustomed to entertain myself with. Yet don't regard it as a great thing, philosopher, if you appear to win this contest, you who profess no Law but submit only to reasons. For in fact you have two swords for the fight, whereas the others are armed against you with only one. You can go after them with both Scripture and reason, but they cannot use anything in the Law as an objection, because you don't follow the Law. And also, the more extensive the philosophical armor you have, being more accustomed to reasons, the less able they are to argue against you with reasons.

(9) "Nevertheless, because you've settled on this by agreement and common consent, and because I see each of you is confident of his own powers, don't by any means let our modesty get in the way of your ventures, particularly since I think I'll learn something from them. Indeed, as one of our own people

---

2. Presumably either or both of Abelard's *Theologia "Summa boni"* and his *Theologia "Scholarium."*

remarks, 'There is no teaching so false that there is no true teaching mixed in.' And I don't think any argument is so silly that it doesn't have some lesson in it. Thus even the greatest of the wise, getting the attentive reader ready, says at the very beginning of his Proverbs, 'Hearing, the wise person will be wiser; the intelligent will get guidance.' And James the apostle says, 'Let every person be quick to hear but slow to speak.' "

(10) They gladly agree to my agreement.[3]

3. The Balliol MS adds, "The end of the Preface. The beginning of the first conversation, namely between the Philosopher and the Jew."

[Dialogue 1: Between the Philosopher and the Jew]

(11) THE PHILOSOPHER says, "It's my job to question the others first, I who am satisfied with the natural law, which is primary. I gathered you together in order to inquire about the Scriptures that were added on later. I say the natural law is 'primary,' not only in time but in nature as well. For everything simpler is naturally prior to the more multiple. Now the natural law, the science of morals we call 'ethics,' consists of moral lessons alone. But your Laws' teaching adds to them certain commands involving external signs. To us they seem altogether superfluous; we must discuss them too in their place."

(12) They both allow the philosopher to go first in contesting this fight.

(13) "To begin with," he says then, "I ask you together about one thing I see applies to both of you equally, you who rely mainly on Scripture. Did some reason lead you into these religious faiths, or are you here following mere human opinion and the love of your own kind of people? If the first of these alternatives is so, that is certainly to be highly commended, just as the other is to be utterly deplored. Yet I believe no discerning person's conscience will deny that the latter alternative is the true one, especially since we experience it with frequent examples. For it often happens that, among some married couples, when one or the other party converts to a different religious faith, their children hold unshaken the faith of whichever of the parents they are close to. How they were raised has more power with them than does their bloodline or reason, since children would also do this no matter who they were raised by, and would recognize them as 'fathers' in faith as well as in rearing.

(14) "This didn't escape him who said, 'The Son cannot do anything but what he sees the Father doing.' For love of their own kind of people and of those they were raised with is so naturally implanted in all human beings that they shrink from whatever is said contrary to their faith. 'Turning custom into nature,' they stubbornly maintain as adults whatever they learned as children. Before they are able to grasp the things said, they assert they believe them. For as the poet remarks, 'A jug will keep for a long time the odor of what it was once filled with when it was new.' Indeed one of the philosophers argues things like this,* saying, 'If they got something from their childish lessons, they shouldn't regard it as sacred. For surely an advanced treatise of philosophy often gets rid of things fit for tender ears.'

(15) "For it's an amazing fact that, although in all other affairs human understanding increases over the course of life and throughout the ages, there's no progress in faith, where an error* is threatened by extreme peril. Instead young and old alike, yokels as well as the learned, are claimed to have a view about it, and the one who doesn't depart from people's common view is called strongest in the faith.

(16) "This is surely why it happens that among one's own people no one is allowed to inquire about what is to be believed, or to doubt with impunity things said by all. For people are ashamed to be asked about what they are unable to reply to. Certainly no one who distrusts his own powers gladly engages in struggle; it is the one who hopes for victory's glory who voluntarily runs to the battle.

(17) "Often, these people even break into such craziness that they aren't embarrassed to profess they believe what they admit they can't understand— as if faith consists more of uttering words than of the mind's comprehension, and belongs more to the mouth than to the heart. Thus too they pride themselves most when they appear to believe so many things they are unable to discuss orally or conceive mentally. The uniqueness of their own sect even makes them so pretentious and superior that whomever they see divided from them in faith they regard as unfit for God's mercy. Once they have condemned all others, they proclaim that they alone are blessed.

(18) "So after reflecting a long time on this blindness and pride of the human race, I have turned to divine mercy, humbly and continually begging it to see fit to lead me out of so great a whirlpool of errors, so miserable a Charybdis, and to direct me from such great tempests to the harbor of salvation. You see me anxious for this even now and, like a student, fiercely eager for the lessons contained in your answers."

(19) THE JEW: "You have questioned two people at once, but two people cannot properly reply at once. Otherwise the number of speakers interferes with understanding. I'll reply first, if that's all right. For we came first to the worship of God and received the first discipline of the Law. This brother who professes himself a Christian will supply what's missing from my imperfection, wherever he sees me falling short or being less capable. Wearing so to speak two horns in the two Testaments he's armed with, he'll be able to resist and fight the enemy more strongly."

(20) THE PHILOSOPHER: "All right."

(21) THE JEW: "Now I do want to warn you in advance about one thing, before the battle of our proposed debate. If perhaps you seem to overwhelm my simpleness with the power of philosophical arguments, do not pride yourself on having thereby defeated us. Don't turn one little person's weakness into the shame of a whole people, or refute the faith from one person's failing, or accuse it of error because I'm little able to discourse on it."

(22) THE PHILOSOPHER: "That too seems judiciously said. But there wasn't any need to postulate it, since you shouldn't doubt that I'll work toward

searching out the truth, not for showing off superiority, or that I'll not bicker like a sophist but rather explore arguments like a philosopher and, most of all, seek my soul's salvation."

(23) THE JEW: "May the Lord himself—who appears to have inspired you with this zeal so that you inquire about him with such care for the salvation of your soul—bring us this conversation whereby you may profitably be able to find him. For me, to the extent that he grants it, it remains now to reply to your questions."

(24) THE PHILOSOPHER: "That certainly conforms to the agreement before us."

(25) THE JEW: "All human beings, while they are children and haven't yet reached the age of discernment, certainly do follow the faith and custom of the people who take care of them, most of all the ones they love more. But after they've grown up, so that they can now be ruled by their own choice, they should be turned over to their own judgment, not someone else's. It is not as fitting to follow opinion as it is to search out the truth.

(26) "Now I've touched on these matters in advance, because perhaps love for our physical forebears and the custom we first learned did lead us at the outset to this faith. But now reasoning more than opinion keeps us here."

(27) THE PHILOSOPHER: "I beg you, disclose that reasoning to us, and that is enough."

(28) THE JEW: "If, as we believe, the Law we follow is given to us by God, then we're not to be blamed for complying with it. Indeed, we should be rewarded for obedience, and those who scorn the Law are making a big mistake.

(29) "Now if we can't compel you to grant it's been given by God, you aren't able to refute it either. But to take an example from ordinary human life, I beg you to give me some advice. I am a certain master's slave, and am powerfully afraid of offending him. I've many fellow-slaves anxious with the same fear. They tell me that in my absence our master has commanded something* of all his slaves, but I don't know about it.* They're working at it, and urge me to work with them.

(30) "What do you recommend I should do if I have a doubt about that command, at which I wasn't present? I don't believe you or anyone else will advise me to spurn all the slaves' advice and, following my own opinion, set myself apart all alone from what they're doing together and what they all attest the master to have commanded—especially since the command appears to be such that it cannot be refuted by any reasoning.

(31) "What need is there for me to doubt a danger from which I can be free? If the master did command what is confirmed by many people's testimony and has good reason, I who don't obey am altogether inexcusable. But if, deceived by the advice or by the urging and example of my fellow-slaves, I do what wasn't commanded even though it didn't have to be done, that has to be blamed on them, not on me. Respect for the lord prompted me to it."

(32) THE PHILOSOPHER: "Surely you yourself have come up with the advice you asked for, and no discerning person will feel the contrary. But apply the example of the proposed analogy to what we are aiming for."

(33) THE JEW: "Many generations have passed, as you yourself know, during which time our people have obediently maintained the Testament they think was given to them by God. They instructed all their descendants equally in observing it, both by word and by example. Almost the entire world agrees that this Law was given us by God. If perhaps we can't force some unbelievers to agree about this Law, nevertheless there's no one who can refute by any reasoning what we believe.

(34) "Surely it is pious, entirely in agreement with reason, and in accord both with divine goodness and human salvation to hold that God shows so much care for human beings that he also sees fit to instruct them by a written Law and to curb our maliciousness, at least by fear of the penalties. If secular princes' laws have been profitably set up for this purpose, who denies that the highest and kindest prince of all has also taken care of this? For how can one govern a subject people without law if everyone, left to his own choice, pursues whatever he picks? Or how will he restrain their maliciousness by justly punishing evil people, unless a law was set up in advance that prohibits evils from being done?

(35) "For this reason, I believe it is plain that the divine Law first came among human beings so that the world might also take the source and authority of this good from God, since he wanted to bridle maliciousness by setting up *some* laws. Otherwise, it could easily have seemed that God didn't care about human affairs, and that the state of the world is produced by chance rather than ruled by providence. Now if it's believed that *some* law was given to the world by God, which one should we suppose this about more than ours, which has got so much authority from its ancientness and from general human opinion?

(36) "Lastly, suppose it *is* doubtful to me, as it is to you, that God set up this Law, even though it is confirmed by so many testimonies and by reason. Nevertheless, you will be forced by the inference in the assumed analogy [(29)–(30)] to advise me to obey it, especially since my own conscience urges me to do so.

(37) "You and I have a common faith in the truth of the one God. Perhaps I have just as much love for him as you do. In addition, I also show it through

deeds, which you *don't* have. If they do no good, what harm do they do me even if they're not commanded, since they're not prohibited? Who too can fault me, if I labor more for the Lord even when not constrained by any command? Who can fault this faith that most highly acclaims the divine goodness, as was said [(34)], and very greatly kindles our charity for him who is so concerned about our salvation that he saw fit to instruct us by a written Law? So either find some fault in his Law, or else stop asking why we follow it.

(38) "Whoever regards the steadfastness of our zeal, which puts up with so much, as devoid of reward asserts God to be most cruel. Certainly no race is known or even believed ever to have borne so much for God's sake as we endlessly put up with for his sake. There can be no rust of sin that the furnace of this affliction shouldn't be conceded to eat away. Scattered among all the nations, alone without a king or earthly prince, are we not weighed down with such impositions that we pay off the unbearable ransom of our miserable life almost day by day?

(39) "Indeed, we're regarded by everyone as worth so much contempt and hatred that whoever brings some injury upon us believes it's the greatest justice and the supreme sacrifice offered to God. For they assert that the disaster of so great a captivity happened only from God's supreme hatred for us, and whether they are Christians or pagans, whatever violence they practice against us they count as just revenge. The pagans, recalling the ancient oppressions whereby we first took possession of their land and afterwards wore them down and destroyed them in lengthy persecutions, count whatever they inflict on us as due revenge. Christians, on the other hand, seem to have greater cause for persecution against us because, as they say, we slew their Lord.

(40) "Look at the kind of people our wandering banishes us to live among, and in whom we must place our trust for patronage. We turn our life over to our worst enemies, and are forced to believe in the faith of the faithless. Sleep itself, which is the best support and rejuvenation for relieving our nature, makes us restless with so much anxiety that even when asleep we aren't allowed to think of anything but the danger to our throat. No entryway to anywhere but heaven is clearly safe for us; our very dwelling place is dangerous for us. When we're going to go out to any nearby places, we take with us—at no little cost—a hired bodyguard we've little trust in. The princes who preside over us and whose patronage we've bought at high price desire our death to the extent they more freely rob what we possess.

(41) "If we're even allowed to live, constrained and oppressed as much as if the world were plotting against us alone, that itself is amazing. It isn't permitted us to own fields, vineyards or any earthly possessions. For there's

no one who can protect them for us from being openly or secretly destroyed. Thus the main thing left to us is profit, so that we sustain a miserable life on this basis by money-lending to foreigners, which of course makes us especially offensive to them. They regard themselves as very much burdened by this. Our status is itself enough to speak to all, more than language can, about this supreme misery of our life and about the perils under which we labor without ceasing.

(42) "No one who has paid attention to it is unaware how much difficulty the commands of the Law involve. As a result, we're afflicted as much by the Law's yoke as by human oppression. Who doesn't flinch or tremble at receiving the sacrament of our circumcision, both from embarrassment and from the pain? What part of the human body is as tender as that one, on which the Law inflicts that injury even for little infants? What bitterness is as great as that of the wild herbs* we consume in the flavoring of the Passover sacrifice? Who also doesn't see that almost all delicious foods are forbidden to us, and especially those that can be easily gotten? Whatever meats have already been tasted by beasts[4] are unclean for us, and whichever ones are already dead or are from animals that have been strangled are forbidden to us. We aren't allowed to eat beasts except those we ourselves have slaughtered and have cleaned of fat and veins.[5] This too burdens us considerably, most of all because we can't afford to buy the entire animal. As we shun meats slaughtered by Gentiles, so they shun those prepared by us. And we all equally avoid wine prepared by others. It is plainly evident from this how hard our life is, wandering among you for God's sake.

(43) "Finally, who doesn't shrink from the harshness of our legal penalties, not only from undergoing them but even from imposing them on criminals? Who puts up with taking from his brother a tooth for a tooth, an eye for an eye, even a soul for a soul—much less agreeing to tolerate these things applied to his own case too, in order not to run contrary to the Law?

(44) "Surely it's obvious from these and countless other observations that any one of us who complies with the Law rightly confesses to God what the Psalmist says, 'I have kept to the hard ways because of the words of your lips.' "

(45) THE PHILOSOPHER: "This zeal you seem to have for God really does put up with many great things, whatever the intention. But the most important

4. That is, meat from animals killed by predators. See Ex. 22:31.
5. Payer (p. 34 n. 24) observes that while there is a Biblical law about removing blood from meat to be eaten (Lev. 3:17, 7:26, 17:10–14; Deut. 12:16, 23), there is no such law about removing the veins themselves. He plausibly takes the term "veins" here as a metaphorical reference to the blood.

thing is whether this intention is correct or mistaken. Surely there's no religious faith that doesn't believe it serves God and doesn't do for his sake the things it supposes to please him. Yet you don't for that reason approve of all *other* people's sects; you try to defend yours alone, or to put it far ahead of others.

(46) "Nevertheless, I want you to examine the extent to which this disagrees with reason, and to argue from the very written Law you follow."

(47) THE JEW: "I gladly undertake this."

(48) THE PHILOSOPHER: "It is agreed that before the Law or the legal sacraments were handed down, most people were content with the natural law, consisting of love for God and neighbor. They cultivated justice and were most acceptable to God. For example, Abel, Enoch, Noah and his sons, Abraham* too, Lot and Melchizedek. Even your Law recalls and praises them highly. Among them, in fact, Enoch is reported to have so pleased God that the Lord is said to have transported him alive into paradise, even as one of you asserts in the words, 'Enoch pleased God and was transported into paradise, to give an example of penitence to the nations.' And how much the Lord loved Noah—'a just and perfect man among his generations,' as is written—is shown by the plain facts, when the Lord saved him and his household alone as the seed of the human race, while all others drowned in the flood.

(49) "Join to these also your eminent patriarchs, Abraham, Isaac and Jacob, in whom and in whose seed the future blessing of all nations is promised. They too preceded the Law. And look how much superior their standing is to that of others who came after the Law! Thus God is said to be especially 'theirs.' Moses, the lawgiver himself, when God was furious at the people, calmed him down by means of their merits and the promises made to them. For it is written:

> Now Moses prayed to the Lord, saying 'Let your fury be still, and be appeasable concerning your people's viciousness. Recall your servants, Abraham, Isaac and Israel, to whom you swore by your very self, saying "I will multiply your seed like the stars of the heavens. And I will give to your seed the whole of this land I have spoken of, and you will always possess it." ' And the Lord was appeased, so that he did not do the evil he had spoken of.

(50) "From this it is plainly gathered how much the earlier fathers' voluntary compliances were accepted by God, to which no law yet constrained them. We still serve him in this freedom.

(51) "But if you say the Law had in a certain sense begun in Abraham on account of the sacrament of circumcision, you'll certainly find that he gets no

reward from it before God (so that there's no bragging for you from the Law), that he neither got any justification nor was even commended by the Lord for it. Indeed, it is written that like the earlier fathers he was justified through faith while he wasn't yet circumcised, when it is said, 'Abraham believed God, and it was counted as justice for him.'

(52) "Also, his religion had earlier[6] obtained for him and his seed the promise of the land and of future multiplication. Even later, after he was circumcised, when he hears from the Lord that all nations are to be blessed in him and in his seed, he didn't earn this from his circumcision but from the obedience whereby he was willing to sacrifice his son.

(53) "Finally, if you read over the whole story of your Testament, you'll find no reward promised for circumcision, but only that the Lord laid it down that whoever among Abraham's seed wasn't circumcised wouldn't be numbered among his people—that is, among Abraham's sons. Indeed, it is so written when the Lord says to Abraham:

> I will set up my covenant between me and you, and your seed after you, etc. This is the covenant you will observe: Every male among you will be circumcised. The eight-day-old child will be circumcised among you. The male whose foreskin-flesh is not circumcised, that soul will perish from his people, etc.

(54) "Now if you say this 'perishing' is to be understood with respect to the soul's damnation too, then there is less reason for establishing circumcision the more dangerous not having it is; there was no hindrance without it beforehand.[7] This view also closes off the kingdom of heaven to children who die before they are eight days old, although they haven't yet committed any offense for which they deserved to be damned.

(55) "Carefully consider too what reward the Lord promises and arranges in advance for observing the whole Law. You certainly can't expect from him anything but earthly prosperity for this. For you see nothing else promised there. Since it isn't apparent whether you get even this—you who in your own judgment are afflicted more than all mortals—the faith in this obedience to the Law, whereby you put up with so many and such great things, is quite amazing. For you're obviously especially frustrated from gaining the advantage that's to be expected from the very thing owed to you by the promise.

---

6. That is, even before his circumcision. Contrast Gen. 15:7–21 with Gen. 17:10–14.

7. That is, if before the Law was established, being uncircumcised posed no threat of damnation, then why does the Law *make* it a threat, with the result that there is greater risk to the soul than there was before? Why raise the stakes unnecessarily?

(56) "Thus, either you aren't fulfilling the Law, and are thereby incurring the Law's curse of damnation, or else he who promised this to those who fulfill the Law doesn't turn out to be truthful in his promises. Whichever of these you pick, I see nothing for you to be confident of from the Law.

(57) "Also, whatever reward consisted only of earthly things would have so little to do with blessedness that the life expected for you would be no other than it is for draft animals.

(58) "Now if you're confident that observing the Law counts so much in your favor that it earns both prosperity in this life and blessedness in the eternal one, then I ask why it was that when God was urging you to observe the Law on the basis of the reward for doing so, he promised what was least and kept completely quiet about what was greatest? Certainly he wasn't prudently making his case when he entirely omitted what was most obviously able to persuade, if he knew that both were sufficient for obedience to the Law,[8] when he entirely omitted what was obviously most able to persuade. As was said [(55)], nothing at all about that true and eternal blessedness was mentioned there in the reward. Instead, earthly prosperity is announced to such a degree that it alone is set out in making the case for obedience. It is recommended so highly that all inquiry by later people is regarded as being satisfactorily answered by giving this response. Indeed, it is written that the lawgiver Moses himself, when he was instructing the people against all opposition to the Law, said:

> Hear, Israel! Keep the Lord your God's commands, and the testimonials and rites he has commanded you. And do what is pleasing and good in the sight of the Lord, so that it may be well with you and that you may go in and take possession of the excellent land he pledged to your fathers, that he might destroy all your enemies before you, just as he said. When your son questions you tomorrow, saying 'What do these testimonials and rites and statutes mean to us, which the Lord our God has prescribed to us?,' you will say to him: 'We were slaves of Pharaoh in Egypt, and the Lord led us out of Egypt by a strong hand and performed in our sight signs, portents and great and very grievous things in Egypt against Pharaoh and all his house. And he led us out of there to give us the land, once we had been led into it, about which he made a pledge to our fathers. The Lord commanded that we fulfill all these ordinances and fear the Lord our God, and that it go well with us all the days of our life, even as it does today.'

8. The sense seems to have been reversed. The context suggests rather: "if he knew that obedience to the Law sufficed for both." Or perhaps understand: "if he knew that both were sufficient *reward* for obedience to the Law."

(59) "Again:

The Lord your God has picked you among all the peoples on earth to be a special people to him. So keep the commands and rites and statutes I charge you with today so that you fulfill them. If you keep them and fulfill them, the Lord your God will keep the covenant with you and will continue the mercy he pledged to your fathers. He will love and multiply you, and will bless the fruit of your womb and the fruit of your land, the grain and wine, the oil and cattle, and the herds of your sheep on the land he swore to your fathers he would give you. You will be blessed among all peoples. None among you of either sex will be sterile, either among human beings or among your flocks. He will take away from you every weakness, and all the worst ailments you knew in Egypt he will inflict not on you but on all your foes. You will devour all the peoples the Lord your God will give you.

(60) "And again:

He will give our land the timely and the late rain, that you may gather your grain, wine and oil, the hay from the fields to feed your draft animals, and that you yourselves may eat and be filled. And all these blessings will come over you and take hold of you, if only you listen to his commands. You will be blessed in the city and blessed in the field. The fruit of your womb will be blessed, and the fruit of your land and the fruits of your draft animals, the herds of your cattle and the pens for your sheep. Your granaries will be blessed, and your leftovers blessed. You will be blessed coming in and going out. He will bless all your hands' doings. You will lend to many nations, and you yourself will take a loan from no one.

(61) "Look, as reward for fulfilling the Law a blessing is promised to people just as one is to 'the fruits of your draft animals, the herds of your cattle and the pens for sheep'; there is no mention made of a spiritual blessing for the soul. Nothing relevant to the soul's salvation or damnation is promised to the obedient or to the lawbreakers. Instead, only earthly advantages or disadvantages are called to mind; the ones that are greatest are left out altogether.

(62) "I ask too whether even now, after the Law has been given to you, the natural law can suffice for some people's salvation just as it did before, without the outward works characteristic of the Law. There is certainly no reason you can deny this, since it is agreed that this Law was given to you alone, not to other peoples, and that circumcisions weren't imposed on anyone but Abraham and his seed. Now only those born of Isaac belong to Abraham's seed, as the Lord tells him, 'For your seed will be so called in Isaac.' And

afterwards, when he had instituted the covenant of circumcision, he added further down,[9] 'Now I will set up my covenant with Isaac.'

(63) "And the Lord so commended Job the pagan, who you don't doubt was without the Law *after* Abraham, that he said 'that there is none like him on earth, a simple and upright man, fearing God and staying away from evil.' While exhibiting his justice through his very self (may we imitate it!), Job mentions none of the works of the Law, but only the works of the natural law of which natural reason itself persuades absolutely everyone. 'If,' he says, 'I have walked in vainglory or my foot has hastened in guile, if I have denied the poor what they wanted and have made the eyes of the widow to be apprehensive,' etc. In words and examples, he established these things for us, the nations, as a law. Thus Solomon maintains that the pagans' prayers are to be heard too, just like the Jews'. He says:

> Furthermore, when the foreigner too, who is not of your people Israel, comes from a faraway land for your name's sake and prays in this place, you[10] will heed him in heaven, in the firmament of your dwelling place. And you will do all the things for which the foreigner calls upon you, so that all the peoples of the lands may learn to fear your name as your people Israel do.

(64) "See, when it is promised that foreigners' prayers are heeded, even about how all kinds of things might be brought about, and when you make foreigners out to fear God too just as you do, who would despair of their salvation too, since it is written, 'Blessed is the man who fears the Lord'? And again, 'Nothing is lacking to those who fear God.'

(65) "Finally, Scripture relates that your Jeremiah, who was well after the establishment of circumcision and of the legal sacraments and was indeed of Abraham's seed, was sanctified before he was born—where the Lord says to him, 'I knew you before I formed you in the uterus; and before you came forth from the womb I sanctified you.' How, I ask, do you call those things necessary for sanctification or salvation, given that he was sanctified without them when he wasn't even born yet? What was his sanctification then, unless perhaps by God's inspiration he even then already believed and loved him? Indeed, whomever* these two[11] are in, they doubtless make him just, no matter what things are still lacking to him outwardly.

---

9. Apparently this means further down in the text of Genesis. But in fact the passage occurs earlier (Gen. 17:21 rather than 21:12).

10. The passage is addressed to God.

11. That is, belief and love.

(66) "Now if these things are enough for some people's salvation *before* the Law, or even now, why was it necessary to add the Law's yoke and increase the number of crimes by multiplying commands? For where there is no law, neither can there occur a violation of it. Anyone craves something more ardently insofar as he observes that he is more hindered and held back from it, as if by a kind of force. Thus the poem says, 'We strive always for the forbidden, and we desire things denied.'

(67) "In fact even one of your own, carefully considering the matter and attesting that no one is justified by works of the Law, says, 'For the Law produces wrath; for where there is no law, neither is there a violation.' Furthermore, in showing that your Law not only doesn't take away sin but even increases it, he adds a little later: 'Now the Law sneaked in, so that crime would abound.' And again he says:

> I did not know sin except through the Law. For I did not know covetousness, except that the Law had said 'Thou shalt not covet.' Through that decree sin took the occasion to produce every covetousness in me. For without the Law sin was dead. Now at one time I lived without the Law. But when the decree had come, sin was restored to life but I died. The decree that was unto life was found to be unto death for me, etc.

(68) "Surely, even though I know you don't acknowledge these testimonies,[12] nevertheless it's plain that no discerning person's conscience disagrees with them.

(69) "How did he establish you as a people special to himself when the Law was given, and for what reason does he call Israel his firstborn, whom he burdens with so great a weight without cause? Who can excuse you from the Law's curse, you who—as required by your sins, according to your own admission—have forfeited the land of the promise, outside which you can't fulfill the Law at all? You aren't permitted to exercise the vengeances of your judgments, or allowed to celebrate the sacrifices or offerings established to purge away sins, or even to complete the chants of divine praises. Indeed, even you yourselves acknowledge this, saying 'How will we sing a chant to the Lord in a foreign land?'

(70) "It is certain from all this that you've forfeited both the works of the Law and the words, as you have forfeited its reward. Neither you nor your wives can now be cleansed by the forfeited sacrifices or offerings, or be consecrated to the Lord, deprived as you are of priesthood and temple alike. As

---

12. Since they are from the New Testament, and so would not be acknowledged by the Jew.

a result, you don't have the consolation of an earthly dignity, you who never asked for any but earthly things from the Lord and who haven't received any promise except of earthly things, as was stated [(55), (58)–(61)]."

(71) THE JEW: "You've raised many objections in succession. It's not easy to remember them, so that I might respond to them individually in order. Nevertheless I'll try to respond according as they occur to me.

(72) "If we were to grant that people can be saved in the manner of the earlier saints even now, by the natural law alone, without circumcision or the written Law's other observances of the flesh, nevertheless it's not to be granted for this reason that the latter were added on superfluously, but instead that they have a great usefulness for extending or securely fortifying religion and for further suppressing maliciousness. Thus, take some of the reasons you yourself have introduced.

(73) "As long as the faithful lived scattered around, mixed in with unbelievers, and the Lord hadn't yet granted them their own land, they weren't divided by any observance of a law from those they were forced to live with, lest* the very dissimilarity of their life lead to hostilities. But after the Lord led Abraham from his land and from his kinfolk to give him and his seed a land for an inheritance whereby they would be set apart from the nations, he decided to separate them completely by the bodily works of the Law too, so that the more they were distinguished from them both in place and in their bodies, the less the faithful could be corrupted by unbelievers.

(74) "Thus, once the promise of this land was bestowed on Abraham and his seed, the land in which the Lord would gather to himself a people and so to speak establish for himself his own city, he began at once to devise a law according to thich they were going to live there. He began with circumcision.

(75) "Certainly the Lord knew our people were going to have a stiff neck, and also that they were inclined to idolatry and the pagans' depraved practices, as proved to be the case later on. Thus once the legal observances were introduced as a kind of wall, he determined that their rites would so distinguish them that they wouldn't be linked to the pagans in any fellowship of behavior or familiarity. In fact, they would gain endless hostilities thereby against themselves.

(76) "Now the greatest familiarity among people is usually brought about by the bond of marriage and by sharing the table. So in order especially to take these away, the Lord established circumcision and forbade us to eat delicious foods. For the sign of circumcision seems so revolting to other peoples that, if we were to pursue their women, the women wouldn't agree to it with us at all, since they regard the mutilation of such a member as the pinnacle of shamefulness. They detest the divine seal of sanctification like idol-worship. Even if

they did give their consent to it, we would be horrified to mix that member with the shamefulness of women unbelievers, the member sanctified to the Lord especially in virtue of the sign through which we've entered into so great a covenant with him. From respect for this sign, when Abraham was binding his servant with an oath, he made him put his hand under his thigh, so that insofar as he thought about this member's greater sanctification, he would guard himself more carefully against perjury. Thus too, when the Lord several times forbids us to marry the Gentiles, especially those whose land we were going to possess, he says in a certain place, 'Be careful never to join with the inhabitants of the land in friendships that are the ruin of you, or to take a wife for your sons from among their daughters, lest they make your sons fornicate with their gods.'

(77) "Rebekah foresaw this much earlier and made her son Jacob go to Mesopotamia on his father Isaac's authority in order to take a wife from among her clan there. As it is written, 'And Rebekah said to Isaac, "I am tired of my life because of Heth's daughters. If Jacob should take a wife from this land's lineage, I do not want to live." And so Isaac called Jacob,' etc.

(78) "So even if other reasons are lacking, I believe these are enough for the present. All the same, what you're trying to do on the basis of the very authority of Scripture—to eliminate or lessen the merit of circumcision or of the Law—I believe can instead be refuted on that basis if you pay careful attention to things in the course of Scripture that you seem to have slipped past in silence. I believe you saw they will be harmful to your case.

(79) "For when the Lord established through circumcision the covenant that was entered into with him, he said to Abraham, 'I will set up my covenant between me and you and your seed in its generations after you as an everlasting alliance, so that I be your God and your seed's after you.' For when he says 'as an everlasting alliance, so that I be your God and your seed's after you,' he's plainly teaching that we are to be allied perpetually to God by circumcision and that it's through this that we deserve him as God, so that we not be divided from him in this life or in the future.

(80) "He even repeats this to commit it more to our memory and adds, 'And my covenant will be in your flesh as an eternal alliance.' Thus, just as circumcision, once it is performed in the flesh, cannot thereafter be undone, so neither can we be divided any longer from God. Encouraging us specifically, he says, 'You will be to me a people, and I will be God to you.' Thus he calls himself specifically the God of the Hebrews, not just the God of Abraham, Isaac and Jacob. In fact, it is hinted that he *becomes* the God of Abraham and his sons through circumcision to such an extent that before circumcision he wasn't called either their God or any peoples'.

(81) "Now he established circumcision* as an appropriate sign of the alliance between him and us, so that those generated* by the member that is especially consecrated after the obedience of being circumcised are warned to sanctify themselves to the Lord through even the very tool of their generation, so that in their heart they may be inwardly circumcised[13] from vices, just as they are already circumcised outwardly in the flesh. They cut themselves off in their practices from their earlier origin among the Chaldean unbelievers in the same way that they removed from themselves that member's foremost part, going out with Abraham from among those people, not so much in body as in mind. David mentions this too when he summons the faithful soul: 'Forget your people and your father's house,' etc.

(82) "Thus too, comparing the people to a select vineyard, the Lord complains that he had expected it 'to produce grapes, and it produced wild grapes.'[14] Now just as the whole of his people is compared to a vineyard, so the individual faithful are aptly likened to vines, and their sexual organs to the shoots. But unless the vine's offshoot is cut away from it, it brings forth wild grapes rather than grapes, and stays uncultivated. So in accordance with this analogy, the cut off foreskin by which God begins to nurture us signifies the divine cultivation's care for us.

(83) "If you also think over the beginning of human fault in our first parents, and the Lord's judgment of the penalty spoken against the woman when she is told, 'You will bear children in sorrow,' you'll see too that the man who was a participant in the sin was rightly made a partner in the penalty, especially in the genital member, so that driving himself and us alike into this life's tribulations by his own transgression, he may rightly suffer in the member whereby he generates the children who are going to die in the present life's exile. Woman too, who labors in childbirth, rightly suffers in the organ whereby she conceives and generates. She is punished in childbirth for the very pleasure of lust she has in conceiving, and furthermore pays the penalty she acquired by sinning. Because she sinned first, and afterwards drew the man into sin, she not inappropriately went first in this penalty as well.[15]

(84) "Yet God didn't altogether delay in punishing the man. He was put under penalty at once. It was said by the Lord: 'The land is cursed in your

13. Abelard is here appealing to the more general meaning of the verb. It can also mean "cut off," "removed."

14. "Grapes" (*uvas*) and "wild grapes" (*labruscas*) are two entirely different words in Latin.

15. That is, her penalty was assigned first (Gen. 3:16), and then Adam's penalty afterwards (Gen. 3:17–19).

work. You will eat of it in hardships all your life's days. It will put forth thorns and thistles for you,' etc. But when we reached the wealth of the promised land that *doesn't* put forth thorns and thistles, what was removed from the penalty there was not inappropriately compensated by circumcision. Nevertheless, circumcision was begun by the patriarchs right after the *promise* of this land, before it was occupied, in order to transmit a firmer authority to posterity.

(85) "I think these considerations about the reason for circumcision are enough in the present circumstances.

(86) "Now you who are trying to show on the basis of Scripture that circumcision was imposed only on those who are brought out of Abraham's seed [(53)], you aren't noticing that in the same passage those who *aren't* of this lineage are also written about. For when the Lord said, 'The eight-day-old child will be circumcised among you, every male among your generations, both the home-born and the bought slave will be circumcised,'* he at once added, 'and whoever is not of your lineage.'

(87) "So look how much discord there is in your assertion that only Isaac and his seed are relevant to circumcision, and correct yourself on the basis of Abraham's action. He's mentioned as having also circumcised Ishmael, together with himself, 'and all the males of his household, both home-born and bought slaves and foreigners alike,' on the Lord's command. 'At once,' the Scripture says, 'on that very day, as the Lord had commanded him,' even before Isaac had been born, that you might know it began with you[16] and to that extent might appropriate it to yourselves as being more natural.

(88) "So now let's also set out the very words of Scripture, if that's all right. They go like this: 'Now Abraham took Ishmael his son and all the home-born slaves of his house, and circumcised the flesh of their foreskin—at once, on that very day, as the Lord had commanded him.' And again: 'Abraham and his son Ishmael were circumcised on the same day. And all the males of his household, both home-born and bought slaves and foreigners alike were circumcised.'

(89) "There's also nothing to block the point you raised [(62)] when you wanted to understand the words 'Now I will set up my covenant with Isaac' only with respect to the covenant of circumcision, not that of the earthly promise—*if* you agree that it is said, as stated a little earlier,[17] 'I will set up my covenant with him in an everlasting alliance, and with his seed after him.' For even if Ishmael

16. That is, among you Gentiles. The point is that circumcision did not originate with the Jews.

17. That is, a little earlier in the text of Genesis. The passage has not occurred previously in the *Dialogue.*

too was circumcised at the Lord's command, nevertheless the Lord didn't establish circumcision in him, since it didn't persist in his posterity.

(90) "Your bringing in the pagan Job as an example [(63)] is without force, since you can't *prove* he was uncircumcised, or that he lived after circumcision was established. For it is agreed that Ishmael was circumcised by Abraham. So too Esau, Jacob and both the rejected and chosen sons were circumcised by the patriarchs in accordance with the Lord's command so that, from then on, if any of their posterity stuck with God, they would also take on the example of circumcision. So too you yourselves preserve it to this day when, imitating your father Ishmael, you receive circumcision in the twelfth year.[18] We know our people also had many proselytes from among the nations, converts to the Law not out of imitation of their parents so much as from a kindred virtue. This could have happened with Job as well. We see he offered sacrifices accepted by God, in our own fashion, both for his sons and for his friends.

(91) "The objection can easily be refuted that no reward but a temporal and earthly one was promised for observing the whole Law [(55)], and that the Lord wasn't very prudently making his case for believing in or recommending the Law, if fulfilling the legal commandments doesn't earn eternal life too [(58)]. For we're allied with the Lord in perpetuity also through the very circumcision the Law commanded, as I said [(79)]. Also, why did he pick *us* from among all nations of human beings to be a special people to him and give *us* the Law whereby we would be made holy, if it is only the present life's joys, which reprobates possess more than the elect do, that would be owed for the additional observance of the Law? If holiness obtains for you or for any human beings the happy and immortal life of your souls, it's plainly owed especially to us on account of the Law, if observing it makes us holy. Now it certainly does make us holy, as the Lord himself told us through Moses, saying: 'If therefore you hear my voice and keep my covenant, you will be to me a personal treasure among all peoples. For the whole earth is mine. And you will be to me a priestly kingdom and a holy nation.' How then did he pick us as his own special people and make us holy through the Law, if he makes you or others happier?

(92) "Later on, while urging us to obey the Law, he says 'For I am your God, granting mercy for a thousand generations to those who love me and keep my

---

18. There is considerable speculation about the implications of this sentence. Since Ishmael is traditionally regarded as the forebear of the Arabs, perhaps the sentence indicates that Abelard was patterning his "philosopher" after an Arab, a descendant of Ishmael. See Payer (p. 53 n. 70). Note that in the Vulgate, Genesis 17:25 says that Ishmael "had completed thirteen years" when he was circumcised, which would make him thirteen, not eleven (= "in the twelfth year") as the text has it here.

commandments.' Now what is this 'granting mercy for a thousand generations' but granting a complete and total mercy above which no higher mercy
can extend, just as no new names of numbers go beyond a thousand?[19]

(93) "Elsewhere, 'Be holy, because I the Lord your God am holy.' Again,
further down: 'Be sanctified and be holy. For I the Lord your God am holy.
Keep my commandments, and do them. I am the Lord, who make you holy.'
And later on: 'You will be my holy people. For I the Lord am holy. And I have
separated you from other peoples, that you may be mine.' And again, 'I am the
Lord, who sanctify you and led you out of the land of Egypt, that I may be God
to you.' Again, 'If you walk in my commandments, I will pitch my tent in your
midst, and my soul will not cast you aside.' Elsewhere he says, 'Who might
grant that they are of such a mind that they fear me and keep all my decrees all
the time, so that it may go well with them and their children everlastingly?'

(94) "Look, the Lord is clearly offering an everlasting reward for obeying
the Law, not a reward that comes to an end. Moses too, after the earthly
reward you mentioned earlier for those who keep the Law [(58)], added the
mercy that's to be exercised by God toward them. He was plainly holding out
for us another reward than an earthly one. For when he said, 'And that it
go well with you all the days of your life, even as it does today,' he at once
added, 'And he will be merciful toward us, if we keep and do all his commandments, as he has decreed to us.' And after some things in between, when he
had said 'The Lord has picked you, that you may be a special people to him
among all peoples,' he added further down, 'And you will know that the Lord
our God is a strong and faithful God who for a thousand generations keeps the
covenant and continues the mercy toward those who love him and those who
keep his commandments.'

(95) "Now I think it doesn't escape you that the Law itself commands
perfect love of God or neighbor, which is what you say the natural law consists
of [(48)]. Indeed, in summing up the Law at the end of his life, Moses says:

> And now, Israel, what does the Lord your God ask of you but that you fear the
> Lord your God, and walk in his ways and love him, and serve the Lord your God
> with your whole heart and your whole soul, and that you keep the Lord's decrees
> and his rites, which I command today, so that it may go well with you? Come on!
> The heaven, the heaven's heaven, the earth, and all the things in them are the
> Lord your God's. And when the Lord was closely bound to your fathers and loved
> them, he also chose their seed after them—that is, you—from among all peoples,
> as is proved today.

19. In Latin, names for numbers above a thousand are compound expressions of which
the highest component is the word for "thousand."

(96) "The Law so carefully explains that the love of God should be perfect, and so elaborates the point, that it commands that God is to be loved with the whole heart and with the whole soul and with our whole strength. On the other hand, we are ordered to love our neighbor like ourselves, so that the love of God, which extends even *above* ourselves, is contained by no measure. We are also commanded to love the outsiders who abide among us as we do our very selves. The Law expands the bosom of love to such an extent that its benefits are not lacking even to our very enemies or to criminals. Let's now set out some texts on these matters: (a) 'If you run across your enemy's ox or stray ass, return it to him. If you see an ass belonging to someone who hates you collapse under a burden, you will not pass by but will help him lift it up.' (b) 'You will not annoy the wanderer; you were wanderers too in Egypt.' (c) 'Do not look for revenge. You will not be mindful of your fellow-citizen's injuries against you.' (d) 'If an outsider lives in your land and abides among you, do not reproach him. Instead, let him be among you like a native. And you will love him as you do yourselves. For you too were outsiders in the land of Egypt. I am the Lord your God.'

(97) "And elsewhere: 'The poor will not be lacking in the land where you live. For that reason I command you to open your hand to your brother, to the destitute, and to the poor who dwell in the land with you.'

(98) "So I beg you, consider on the basis of these passages how much the Law extends the feeling of love both to human beings and to God, so you may recognize that your law, which you call 'natural,' is included also in ours. Thus if the other commandments were to cease to apply, these belonging to perfect love would be enough for our salvation, even as they are for yours. You don't deny that our early fathers were saved by them, so that a greater certainty of salvation is passed on to us the more the Law's additional commandments establish a more restricted life for us. In fact, this addition seems to me to pertain not so much to religion's holy practices as it does to fortifying it more securely.

(99) "Certainly a true love of God and man is enough for every mental virtue. Even if deeds are lacking, still a good and perfect will is by no means lessened in its merit. But as I said [(73)], just as the Lord wanted to separate us in location from the faithless so that we would not be corrupted by them, so too he decided that this should be done by ritual deeds as well. Therefore, although love's perfection is enough to yield true blessedness, surely the additional commandments of the more restricted life deserved to have gained at least something extra, even in this life, so that we would be made more eager and sure toward God by the solace of an earthly benefit. Since his gifts to us would be increased, our devotion to him would grow, and the outside

population of unbelievers who saw this would be more easily incited by our advantages to venerate God.

(100) "Now as for the fact that the Lord seems to mention earthly benefits as a reward for the Law more often or more plainly than he does eternal ones, understand that this was done mainly on account of a people who were still carnal and rebellious, whom he led out of Egypt's wealth, which they were continually muttering about, into a harsh loneliness. It also seemed pointless, in the promise, to mention the matter of eternal blessedness. It was plain that our ancestors had gotten that earlier, even without the Law's being handed down.

(101) "Finally, infer how great the Law's perfection is from this one concluding remark that Moses writes at the end of his life, in these words: 'And now, Israel, hear the commandments and judgments I teach you, etc. You will not add to or take away from the word I say to you.' And again, 'Do for the Lord only what I command you. Do not add or subtract anything.'

(102) "Surely the perfect is that to which nothing is to be added. Or if any part of perfection *were* lacking, it would be a bad prohibition that forbids what's lacking and blocks the road to blessedness for us.

(103) "Why too does the Law order things in sacrifices or other observances to be done for purifying or cleansing us and for forgiving sins, if this has nothing to do with true blessedness? Surely nothing excludes from true blessedness the people from whom sins have been taken away. Otherwise, it wouldn't be something for *you* to hope for either. Also why does he forbid sins through the Law, unless he's reserving for us what sins bring if they are absent and what they impede if they are present?"

(104) THE PHILOSOPHER: "I'm surprised that you, an expert in the Law, speak so thoughtlessly that you exalt circumcision so much that you're not afraid to lie by saying [(80)] he was called the God of men only *after* circumcision and not before, and only of those who were already circumcised. For example, when he is called the God of Abraham, Isaac and Jacob. Thus the written Law itself plainly rebukes you, since Noah said much earlier, 'Blessed is the Lord, the God of Shem. Let Canaan be his servant.'

(105) "For look here, Noah even calls him 'the God of Shem.' Thus when he is called the God of Abraham, the God of Isaac or of Jacob, it is not inappropriate that the phrase 'and the God of our fathers' is usually added.

(106) "Now if you would also think about the divine benefits you, as his special people, brag of most, notice that Enoch* was transported into paradise more happily than you were led into the land of Canaan. He is mentioned as having earned this, where it's said: 'And Enoch walked with God. And he was

not seen, because God took him.' But Moses denies altogether that you had obtained Canaan by merits. He says:

> When the Lord destroys them, do not say in your heart, 'He has led me in on account of my justice, that I might possess this land.' For these nations were destroyed on account of their irreverences, that he might fulfill his word that was promised to your fathers. Know therefore that the Lord has not given you this best of lands on account of your acts of justice, since you are a most stiff-necked people.

(107) "Now after all human beings except his household were destroyed, Noah was made lord of all things on the earth or in the sea on account of his justness. And all things except blood were allowed him as food. Thus, as for the earthly benefits from God that you want, the earlier faithful's life was happier insofar as it was freer, having dominion over all this earthly dwelling-place's creatures. But to the extent Noah's and his family's life was freer than yours—that is, it was not yet overwhelmed by your Law's yoke—to that extent our life is also freer, that older kind of life that you can't show to be constrained by any of the external works of the dreaded Law.

(108) "Let's carefully consider these works that started with Noah himself, for whom the early law about abstaining from blood was set up. Now I did know that certain commandments of the Law are extended even to foreigners [(95)–(98)]—that is, only to those you have as home-born slaves, or as servants, or who live together with you within your gates or in your land. To be sure, Scripture does carefully delineate them in many passages. And you yourself have shown above, from the very commandment of the Law [(96)–(97)], that they are to be treated mercifully as if they were native-born people. The Law groups them together with you in many observances and plainly distinguishes them from other wandering outsiders. Thus when it says in a certain passage:

> In the seventh year you will have a cancellation of debts, carried out in the following manner. Anyone to whom something is owed by his friend, neighbor, or brother will not be able* to get it back, because it is the Lord's year of cancellation. You will demand it of the wanderer and the outsider.

it plainly teaches that the wanderer and the outsider aren't to be treated as mercifully as a native-born person is. It had also understood this wanderer earlier, where it says: 'Eat everything that is clean. Whatever has died on its own, let no one eat of it. Give it to the wanderer who is within your gates, that he may eat. Or sell it to him. For you are the Lord your God's holy people.' Much earlier in another book of Scripture, it suggests that like what was just said there,[20] even the outsider who wanders in your midst as an inhabitant and is not just passing through should not eat what has died on its own, just as the Law prevents you. It says: 'Whether of native-born people or of outsiders, the soul that has eaten what has died on its own or has been captured by a wild animal will wash his clothes and himself in water. And he will be contaminated until evening. In this manner he will be made clean. But if he will not have washed his clothes and his body, he will carry his iniquity.'

(109) "But sometimes the person it calls in one place a 'wanderer' and an 'outsider' it elsewhere calls a 'stranger.' For example, when it's said 'You will not lend money or crops or anything else on interest to your brother, but to a stranger.'

(110) "In another passage these outsiders who wander around among you (not you among them) are written about, when it says, 'If any person of the house of Israel or among the outsiders who wander among you eats blood, I will set my face against his soul and divide him from his people.'

(111) "Indeed, you will have seen that no other outsider is included in any commandment of the Law, except for him who lives among you and is therefore subject to your control and discipline. Thus with divine grace looking out for us, a grace that has completely taken the possession of any land away from you so that no one wanders among you but rather you among all people, you should know we aren't liable to any of your legal regulations.

(112) "You're trying to push us into circumcision by means of the commandment about circumcision and by Abraham's example, in order also to include people in the Law's sacrament to whom you grant the Law wasn't given, or to whom the promise of land wasn't made, the promise that was established in the covenant of circumcision. Look how invalid your objection is! For when the Lord said, 'Every male among you will be circumcised,' and added, 'every male among your generations, both the home-born and the bought slave, and whoever is not of your lineage,' surely in the phrase 'among you' he included not only Abraham and his posterity but in addition whatever people belong to their family and property so that they could order and force them into circumcision. Thus too, after he said 'among you,' and afterwards appended 'among your generations, both the home-born and the bought slave,' and then added 'and whoever is not of your lineage,' he carefully singled out in the phrase 'among your generations and whoever will not be of your lineage' what he'd included above when he said 'among you': not only their posterity's generations, but also the family of foreigners they owned.

20. That is, earlier in the passage of Leviticus that is about to be cited. See Lev. 17:10, 12–13.

(113) "Also, when he made the statement, 'And my covenant will be in your flesh,' he said 'in your flesh' generally, just as earlier he'd said 'among you.' Otherwise, it would've been highly inconsistent to promise, so to speak, that God's covenant wouldn't appear in *their* flesh unless outsiders were *also* circumcised like the rest. Thus it's plain that in the phrase 'in your flesh' outsiders are included too. How can what was added at the end to complete the statement—'The male whose foreskin-flesh is not circumcised, that soul will perish from his people, because he has made my covenant void'—be related to the remarks that went before in which outsiders were already included too (at least when it says 'among you will be circumcised,' etc.), unless his covenant is with outsiders as well?

(114) "Now it can be shown from the Law itself that what you take pains to affirm [(79), (91)–(94)] is the cheapest kind of conjecture, namely that the souls' eternal blessedness was also promised to you on the basis of your legal regulations. For you understand by the phrase 'with an everlasting alliance' or 'as an everlasting alliance' [(79)–(80)] that those who will be circumcised by God's commandment are allied with him in perpetuity in such a way that they won't be separated from his grace in the future. So there's supposed to be no doubt at all that Ishmael, Esau, and a great many reprobates are going to be saved.

(115) "I'm surprised too that you didn't notice that 'eternal' or 'everlasting' is often taken in the Law in such a way that it doesn't go beyond the present life's duration. Thus when it is said even in the very covenant of circumcision, 'I will give you and your seed the land of your wandering and all the land of Canaan, as an eternal possession,' I don't think you're so deranged that you include in the word 'eternity' a *future* life's blessedness as well. It would be superfluous to stipulate anything about that here. Often too, as you know, with the works of the Law that were observed in this life only, the Law usually adds 'It will be an everlasting legal regulation for you, in all your generations and dwelling-places.' To take one example among several, it added this phrase in the case of observing the festival of Tabernacles. For when it had said,

> You will gather to yourselves on the first day the finest tree's fruits, palm branches, branches of wood dense with leaves, and willows from the stream, and you will rejoice before the Lord your God. And you will celebrate his solemnity for seven days a year

it added right away, 'It will be an everlasting legal regulation for your generations.'

(116) "He also says in a certain passage, when setting up the celebration of the Sabbath on the seventh day, 'It is an everlasting covenant and a perpetual sign between me and the sons of Israel.'

(117) "Then too, when the Lord says of the Hebrew slave who doesn't want to depart as a free man that he will be a slave 'forever,' he includes only his lifetime. For Hebrew slaves, according to the Law, are not passed on to posterity like those taken from foreign nations. Thus it is written:

> Let your slave and handmaid be from among the nations that are in your compass. And from among the outsiders who wander among you or who are born of them in your land, these you will have as servants and will pass on by right of inheritance to posterity and will possess for eternity. But you will not oppress your brothers, the sons of Israel, by your power.

(118) "In rewarding so carnal a people who knew nothing but earthly things, it was surely enough for the Lord to make the reward fit the present lifetime only.

(119) "Now in praising the Law's perfection, you asserted [(**101**)] that only what Moses commanded has to be done. I'm surprised you forgot you'd asserted above[21] that many things were added on to the commandments in a praiseworthy manner, as a mark of favor. It's plain to everyone this is quite true. Thus even *after* the Law, you got some of the basic traditions you regard as most useful. For instance when on the example of Daniel, who spit out kingly foods and wine so he would not be polluted by them, you too abstain from our wine.

(120) "The Rechabites too, abstaining from wine in perpetuity on their father Jonadab's commandment, went beyond both Moses' commandments and all your fathers' traditions. Even Jeremiah, sent to them by the Lord so they might drink wine, wasn't heard out by them. Thus their obedience is praised so much by the Lord's voice that he promised them saying, 'Because of the fact that you obeyed your father Jonadab's commandment and kept all his decrees, there will not fail to be a man standing in my sight from the lineage of Rechab's son Jonadab, throughout all days.'

(121) "And did king Hezekiah, in smashing the brazen serpent, turn out to be a lawbreaker when what was destroyed in praiseworthy fashion *without* a commandment had been usefully made *on the basis of* a commandment?

(122) "When David composed the Psalms for God's honor, or solemnly brought the Lord's ark into Jerusalem, or when Solomon built and dedicated the Lord's temple, they certainly did what Moses hadn't commanded in any way. All the prophets as well were selected without any commandment from Moses or from the Law that was handed down to him. After Moses countless things were done by the holy fathers, either from the Lord's commandment or

---

21. In fact, the Jew has not claimed this earlier in the *Dialogue*.

for the sake of their obvious usefulness, that are in no way contained in Moses' commandments.

(123) "For commandments from the Lord shouldn't be expected in matters that have an obvious usefulness. Sin isn't doing what is not commanded, but rather acting *against* a commandment. Otherwise you couldn't go through a single day of the present life, or carry out your household business for a single day, since we have to do many things—buying, making deals, going from this place to that, or even eating or sleeping—that aren't covered in a commandment.

(124) "Moreover, who doesn't see that if nothing more or less than what Moses commanded is to be done, then all who keep the Law are of equal merit, and among those whose merits cannot be unequal one person is not better than another?

(125) "From the preceding, therefore, it's clear there's no way you can commend the Law's perfection by your understanding that if something is added on that isn't commanded in it, it is against the Law for it to be done. Realize that when the Lord was urging obedience to the Law, you aren't giving him a good enough excuse for leaving out what I said [(58)] is the greatest thing in its reward, if he regarded obedience as enough for him to promise that too.

(126) "But I'm surprised you're sure that spiritual good follows from the purification of sins through sacrifices [(103)], or through *any* of the Law's external works, if—as you yourself acknowledge [(98)] and as plain truth has it—your love of God and neighbor is enough for the justification of holiness. For without the latter, purification will be of no help at all, as far as the soul's salvation is concerned. And there's no doubt that when the love of God and neighbor has made someone just, he's no longer in a state of guilt for sin so as to *need* spiritual purification. Thus you have it written about the repentant sinner, 'An afflicted spirit is a sacrifice to God,' etc. And again, 'I said, "I will confess against myself my injustice, and you took away my sin's impiety." ' Look how the Psalmist commends this sacrifice of the contrite heart. Elsewhere, speaking in the Lord's person, he completely rejects what is external, saying:

Hear, people, and I will speak. I will not take calves from your house, Israel, or goats from your flocks. If I get hungry, I will not tell you. For the earth's globe and its bounty are mine. Shall I eat bull-meat? Or drink goats' blood? Offer God a sacrifice of praise, and carry out your vows to the most high. Call on me in the day of tribulation, and I will rescue you, and you will do me honor.

(127) "The Lord is hungry for the sacrifice of the heart, not of animals, and he's renewed by it. When he finds the former, he doesn't look for the latter;

when he doesn't find the former, the latter is altogether superfluous—I mean as far as the soul's justification is concerned, not for getting around the legal penalties. Nevertheless your sins are said to be pardoned in accordance with these penalties.

(128) "Indeed your Law, which assigns merits for fulfilling or breaking it only in this life, and in either case pays a remuneration only here, fits all things to this bodily life, so that it rates nothing as clean or unclean according to the soul. It doesn't mention any purifications for souls' uncleanlinesses,* which we properly call 'sins.' Thus it calls foods clean or unclean in the same way it does people. Often too it calls beds, chairs, household furniture, or even clothes, and many other inanimate things 'unclean' or 'polluted.' Now if you count the uncleanlinesses of the people for whom purifications were established together with people defiled by sins, do you therefore regard a woman cleansed by a sacrifice after birth as having committed a *sin* by the fact that she gave birth, even though you would better regard her as cursed who *doesn't* leave a seed in Israel?

(129) "What sin does a man who has a seminal flow take on by that fact? Yet the Law regards him as abominable to the extent that the bed he slept in, and wherever he sat, is unclean. Even the clay vase he touched will be smashed; let the wooden one be washed. If any man touched his bed, or sat where he sat, he will wash his clothes. Even when washed with water, he will be unclean until evening. A woman too, when she has a naturally occurring menstrual flow, is regarded as unclean to the extent that where she too slept or sat is so polluted that she pollutes all things by her touch, just as was said above for the man who has a seminal flow.

(130) "Now I ask you, what do these things have to do with defiling the soul, that even someone's touched bed should be polluted? What, pray, are these uncleanlinesses or pollutions? Surely these things are like certain kinds of foods, so that just as you are to shun the latter in eating, so the former in touching. And just as the latter are unclean because they aren't to be eaten, so the former are unclean or polluted because they aren't to be touched. Those who do touch them, even if they do it under compulsion or unknowingly, are likewise declared unclean because they are to be avoided in close dealings until the assigned end of the purification.

(131) "But things that are plain sins, like murder or adultery and the like, are punished by death rather than being atoned for with sacrifices. The medicine of such purifications isn't allowed for them, whereby those who committed them might be saved.

(132) "Understand from this that these purifications are suited more for a kind of honorableness in the present life than for the soul's salvation. When

such people's sins are said to be pardoned, it is plain that it is the bodily punishments established for them that are relaxed for people who are separated from common company. For is a sin's being pardoned to be understood as anything other than the punishment's being relaxed that is due it, whether bodily or perpetual?

(133) "Just as the soul's guilt is brought on by its willing,[22] so it is at once pardoned through its contrite heart and true remorse of penitence, with the result that it isn't condemned for it any longer. As was said [(126)], 'I said, "I will confess against myself." ' For after the repentant sinner has thus decided within himself to accuse himself through confession, by that very fact he permits his perverse will's fault, through which he did wrong, to be now lacking in guilt,[23] and his perpetual penalty is pardoned, although a temporal one may still be kept for the sake of correction, as your same prophet remarks elsewhere, saying, 'Chastising, the Lord chastised me; and he did not turn me over to death.'

(134) "I think in asking these things about my soul's salvation I have conversed with you enough about your faith and my faith. Indeed, in summarizing our conversation, I consider it to have been established that, on your own Law's authority, even if you take it to be given to you by God, you can recognize that I need not submit to its burden, as though something has to be added to the law Job prescribes for us by his example, or to the moral discipline our philosophers left posterity regarding the virtues that suffice for blessedness.

(135) "It remains now to hear the verdict of the present judge on this matter, or else it remains for me to transfer the work of our investigation to the Christian."

(136) THE JUDGE:[24] They both state they will accept our judgment. But, more eager to learn than to judge, I reply that I want to hear all parties' arguments first, in order to be more discriminating in judgment the wiser I become by listening, in accordance with what I mentioned above [(9)] following a proverb of him who is supremely wise: "Hearing, the wise person will be wiser; the intelligent will get* guidance." On fire with the same desire for learning, they all agree to this alike.

22. Contrast *Ethics* (9)–(29), where Abelard insists it is *not* the will but rather *consent* that brings on guilt. Presumably he is only speaking loosely here, and has not changed his doctrine.

23. The Latin from 'by that very fact' to 'lacking in guilt' is awkward, and I am not as confident as I would like to be of the translation. I am grateful to Peter King for help.

24. That is, Abelard himself. See the Prologue, (1)–(10) above.

[Dialogue 2: Between the Philosopher and the Christian]

(137) THE PHILOSOPHER: "Now then, Christian, I urge you also to reply to my investigation according to the agreement in our plan. Your Law should be more perfect, stronger in its reward and more reasonable in its teaching, the later it is. Certainly, the earlier laws would have been written for people to no avail if something hadn't been added to them to complete their teaching. One of our people, thinking this over carefully in the second book of his *Rhetoric,* while preparing a case involving laws contrary to one another, advised that one must pay attention to 'which law was passed later, since whichever is last,' he says, 'carries the greatest weight.' "

(138) THE CHRISTIAN: "I'm surprised you're so shameless in differing from what you claimed at the beginning. For since you first said you had found in your investigations that the Jews were fools and the Christians crazy [(6)], and later said you were not looking for controversy but meeting to investigate the truth [(22)], why in the world do you now expect the truth to be taught by people you've even found crazy? Do you suppose their craziness has stopped now, after your investigations, so that they can suffice now for your education? Certainly, if you suppose the Christian religious faith is craziness, and count the people who follow this sect as crazy, then look, you philosopher! What should be thought of those greatest Greek philosophers who all became the craziest converts to it by means of the rustic and uncouth preaching of simple people—the apostles? This 'craziness' of ours, as you call it, was rooted and fortified among the Greeks to such an extent that both the Gospels' and the apostles' teaching was written down there. Later on, after the great councils were held, it filled the whole world from there and crushed all heresies."

(139) THE PHILOSOPHER: "Sometimes people are more easily provoked by insults and mockeries than they're prevailed upon by beggings and entreaties. Those provoked like this take more trouble over the fight than people are moved by graciousness who are beseeched."

(140) THE CHRISTIAN: "You're to be excused if you did it for that purpose. But now, lest I seem to delay this fight out of timidity, both you and I must pray that the Lord himself, who wishes all people to come to be saved and come to a knowledge of him, might inspire us about what you should ask and what I should reply."

(141) THE PHILOSOPHER: "Amen."

(142) THE CHRISTIAN: "So be it, so be it. Now then please, since you don't take part in the perfection of our Law—that is, of the Gospel's and the

apostles' teaching—let's look at it first and compare it to all other teachings, so that you may prefer it, as you must* do if you see it's more perfect in the commandments and exhortations that justify. Your rhetorician remarked on this above [(137)]. Dealing as you said with contrary laws, he advised, 'If two or more laws cannot be kept because they disagree with one another, let that one be regarded as having most to be kept that seems to deal with the greatest matters.' "

(143) THE PHILOSOPHER: "Nothing is more plausible than this advice, and nothing stupider than to depart from old laws for new ones unless they're stronger in their teaching. Those who put together these new laws were able to write them more carefully and completely insofar as, taught by the earlier laws' discipline and by experience with matters of necessity, they were able by their own talent easily to add what was missing, as happens too in other branches of philosophy.

(144) "Now if modern writers were able to equal the old ones in talents, then the greatest confidence should be placed in the later writers' perfection. But what is to be hoped for if perhaps they even far surpass them? You certainly don't doubt this with the law-giver Christ, whom you call God's very wisdom. You maintain that even our Job celebrated him earlier: 'Behold God in his strength, and there is none like him among law-givers.' And your Apostle, setting out his teaching and plainly showing the first Law's imperfection, says: 'Formerly, God spoke in various and many ways to the fathers by the prophets; in these last days he has spoken to us by his son,' etc. Again further down, while judging the distinction between the Old and the New Law, he says: 'The rejection of the earlier decree came about on account of its weakness and uselessness. For the Law made nothing perfect. But the introduction of a better hope does, whereby we get closer to God.' "

(145) THE CHRISTIAN: "As I see it, ignorance of our faith certainly doesn't condemn you, but more the stubbornness of your disbelief. You've learned our Law's perfection from its writings, and still you're looking for something to follow—as if you don't have there a perfect lesson, more excellent than all others, in the virtues that you don't doubt are enough for blessedness.

(146) "In fact, when the Lord himself handed down the New Testament, filling in things lacking in his old one, he started off right away with this perfection, and said to the disciples, 'Unless your justice is abundant,' etc. Continuing immediately, he carefully portrayed the new Law's abundance through individual examples of where moral perfection was lacking, and summed up a true ethics. Indeed, it can easily be shown in this comparison that whatever things had been handed down by the old fathers or prophets,

about teaching morals and distinguishing virtues, are nothing if we carefully compare them with the earlier ones."[25]

(147) THE PHILOSOPHER: "As you know, only the desire for these comparisons brought me here, and we are all gathered with this purpose."

(148) THE CHRISTIAN: "As far as I see it, we're really proceeding now toward the goal and summation of all disciplines. Surely the discipline you have usually called 'ethics'—that is, morals—we have usually called 'divinity.' That is, whereas we call it such from what it is directed at comprehending, namely God, you do so from the means by which it arrives there, namely the moral goods you call 'virtues.' "[26]

(149) THE PHILOSOPHER: "I agree that's clear. And I very much approve your new terminology. For because you regard the destination arrived at as worthier than the means of getting there, and to have arrived as more felicitous than coming, your terminology is the one for more eminent things, the one that appeals to the reader more from the proper* origin of the word 'divination.' If it is as outstanding on the basis of its teaching as it is on the basis of the word, I think no discipline is to be compared with it. Therefore, we want you now to determine please what the culmination of true ethics consists in, what we are to have in view from this discipline, and how its purpose is achieved when it is arrived at."

(150) THE CHRISTIAN: "The whole culmination of this discipline, I think, is gathered together in this: that it reveal where the ultimate good is and by what road we are to arrive there."

(151) THE PHILOSOPHER: "It's certainly extremely pleasing for the culmination of so great a thing to be expressed in so few words, and for the purpose of all ethics to be so carefully recounted. Indeed, these words describing its purpose so* immediately snatch the hearer to themselves and commend this discipline's study, that in comparison with it all other arts' teachings become vile.

(152) "For insofar as the ultimate good, the enjoyment of which comprises true blessedness, is more excellent than all other things, it's plain without a doubt that its teaching far surpasses other teachings in both usefulness and worthiness. Indeed, the studies of the others stay far below the ultimate good, and don't reach the pinnacle of blessedness. Nothing fruitful is apparent in them, except to the extent that they serve this ultimate philosophy like busy

25. Perhaps "earlier" means the Christian teachings and virtues *mentioned* earlier (although chronologically they were later). But I suspect the word is just corrupt, and should read "later."

26. See Abelard's *Ethics* (1).

maidservants around their mistress. For what is there to the study of grammar, dialectic or the other arts that has to do with seeking out true human blessedness? They all lie far below this pinnacle and aren't strong enough to raise themselves up to such a peak. But they do deal with certain kinds of speech or busy themselves with some of the natures of things, as if providing certain steps up to this loftiness. For we must speak about it and make it known by using some of the natures of things as an example or analogy. Thus through them we reach it, as though reaching the mistress through a kind of escort by the maidservants. In them we have the route for our trip, while in her we achieve peace and an end to our weariness."

(153) THE CHRISTIAN: "I'm glad you've so carefully noted this philosophy's superiority and distinguished it from the others. I gather from this you are mainly occupied in studying it."

(154) THE PHILOSOPHER: "I say 'correctly' occupied. Indeed, this alone is training in the natural law. Directed toward moral commands, it fits philosophers to a greater extent the more they keep using this law and clinging to reasons. As your own teacher mentions, 'For the Jews ask for signs and the Greeks are looking for wisdom.' In fact, only the Jews, because they are animal and sensual and aren't educated in any philosophy whereby they can discuss reasons, are moved to faith by miracles in outward deeds alone. As if God alone can do these things, and no demonic illusion can occur with them! The magicians in Egypt taught them, and Christ especially instructed you, how stupid it is to admit that. Forewarning them about Antichrist's false prophets, he bears witness that such miracles will be done in seducing people 'that even the elect are led into error, if that can be done.'

(155) "So, as if looking for these signs is stupidity, the Apostle cited earlier is thinking of the contrary in the addition, where he adds, 'and the Greeks are looking for wisdom.' That is, they need *reasons*, wisdom's sure instruments, from preachers. Thus your (that is, Christian) preaching is highly praised because it was able to convert those people to the faith who most relied on and abounded in reasons, those who were trained in the studies of the liberal arts and armed with reasons. In fact, they were not only *inquirers* into these studies, but even their *discoverers*. From their fountains, streams have flowed into the whole world. For this reason especially, we even now have confidence that your teaching is more capable in the battle of reasons insofar it has already grown firmer in strength."

(156) THE CHRISTIAN: "On the contrary, after such great philosophers' conversion neither you nor your posterity can legitimately hesitate about our faith, and there seems no need for such a battle. Why do you believe their authority on all matters in the secular disciplines, yet are not moved to faith

by their examples, saying with the prophet, 'Neither are we better than our fathers'?"

(157) THE PHILOSOPHER: "We don't yield to their authority in the sense of not discussing their statements rationally before we approve them. Otherwise we would be ceasing to do philosophy if while disregarding the investigation of reasons we mainly used topics from authority.[27] The latter are declared inartificial[28] and are entirely disconnected from the reality itself, consisting of opinion more than of truth.

(158) "And we might believe that our forebears weren't so much led by reason to confessing your faith as they were dragged by force, as even your histories agree. Indeed, before the emperors' or princes' conversion to your faith—through miracles, you say—your preaching* secured few if any of the wise, even though nations could then easily be pulled away from the most blatant mistakes of idolatry and brought over to any monotheistic cult. Thus your own Paul, shrewdly taking the opportunity of his attack on the Athenians, begins by saying 'Athenian men, I see that you are superstitious about all things,' etc. For knowledge of the natural law and of veneration of the divine had already died out then, and the crowd of mistaken people had wiped out or overcome the few wise ones. To speak from our conscience and acknowledge the not inconsiderable fruit of Christian preaching, we don't doubt that idolatry in the world was wiped out then mainly through this preaching."[29]

(159) THE CHRISTIAN: "Add too that plainly both the natural law was restored and the perfect discipline of morals was handed down by no one but him.[30] You rely on it alone, you say [(11)], and believe it's enough for being saved. Whoever are truly instructed by him as by true *'sophia'*—that is, by God's wisdom—are to be called 'philosophers.' "

(160) THE PHILOSOPHER: "I wish you could establish what you say, to show yourselves truly to be logicians and to be armed as you say with reasons for your words by the supreme wisdom you call *'logos'* in Greek and *'verbum dei'*[31]

27. The reference is to so-called "topical reasoning," as described for example in Cicero's *Topics*. See Abelard's *Dialectica* III. 2. 19, De Rijk ed., pp. 438.23–439.17. For a thorough discussion of topical reasoning in the Middle Ages, including Abelard, see Stump, *Dialectic and Its Place in the Development of Medieval Logic*.

28. A technical term meaning "not in accordance with the rules of the art"—in this case, the art of reasoning.

29. The point of the paragraph is to deny not that large numbers of people were converted (and so idolatry wiped out), but that they were converted by *reasoning*.

30. That is, Christ.

31. *Verbum dei* = God's word.

in Latin. Don't suppose I will offer your Gregory's famous escape for the
wretched: 'Faith for which human reason supplies a test,' he says, 'has no
merit.' Because people among you aren't strong enough to discuss the faith
they affirm, they right away adopt this statement of Gregory's as consolation
for their incompetence. Now what else in fact does this amount to in their
opinion, except that we should be content with *all* kinds of preaching of the
faith, stupid and sound alike?

(161) "For if faith isn't to be discussed rationally at all lest it lose merit, and
the question what has to be believed isn't to be discussed with the mind's
judgment, but instead the things preached have to be agreed with at once no
matter what mistakes the preaching sows, then accepting what is preached is
pointless. For where using reason isn't allowed, refuting anything by reason
isn't allowed.

(162) "Let the idolater say of a stone or piece of wood, or of any creature at
all, 'Here is the true God, the creator of heaven and earth.' Or let him preach
anything blatantly abhorrent. Who will be able to refute him if nothing about
faith is to be discussed rationally? He will right away raise against the person
arguing with him, especially a Christian, the objection just given, 'Faith has no
merit,' etc. The Christian who says his reasonings aren't to be listened to at all
in such matters will be confounded at once by his own defense. He who doesn't
allow himself to be attacked at all can't rightly attack someone with reasons
concerning the faith, where he forbids them to be brought in altogether."

(163) THE CHRISTIAN: "As the greatest of the wise says, 'There are paths
for a person that seem right, yet their last steps lead to his death.' So too, quite
often there *seem* to be reasons—that is, things reasonably and coherently
stated—when that isn't the case at all."

(164) THE PHILOSOPHER: "What about those treated as authorities? Aren't
they often in error? Otherwise, if all people used the same authorities, there
wouldn't be so many different religious faiths. But just as everyone deliberates
with his own reason, individuals pick the authorities they follow. Otherwise all
writings' views would have to be accepted indiscriminately, if reason, which is
naturally prior to them, didn't have the means to judge about them in advance.
For those who wrote only on the basis of reason, whose views are seen to
abound with it, have *earned* their authority, their being worth believing. But
even in their judgment, reason is put *before* authority. Thus as your Anthony
remarks, 'Since human reason's perception was the originator of the writings,
for one whose perception is unimpaired the writings are not needed at all.'

(165) "Authority is regarded as having last place, or none at all, in every
philosophical disputation, so that those who are confident of their own powers
and disdain relying on someone else's ability are completely ashamed to bring

in what are called arguments 'from the judgment of the matter'—that is, from authority.[32] So when the orator is forced to take refuge in them more than the philosopher is, philosophers rightly regarded the topics[33] of such arguments as entirely extrinsic and disconnected from the reality, and as completely devoid of force insofar as they consist of opinion more than of truth, and don't proceed on the basis of any talented skill in finding their arguments. For one who brings them in isn't using his own words, but someone else's.

(166) "Thus, combining in his *Topics* both the Themistian and the Ciceronian division of topics, your Boethius says, 'Arguments that are from the judgment of the matter offer testimony, as it were. They are inartificial[34] topics, and entirely disconnected. They do not follow the reality so much as opinion and judgment.' Again, on the same topic, he says in accordance with Cicero: 'There remains the topic he said is taken from outside. It relies on judgment and authority. It is wholly plausible[35] and contains nothing necessary.' And somewhat later:

> Now this topic is said to be constituted from outside. For the term is not taken from things that belong to the predicate or subject, but comes from a given judgment, from outside. Thus it is also called 'inartificial' and 'lacking,' because the orator does not put the argument together for himself, but uses prepared and given testimonies.

(167) "Your point that errors sometimes occur in distinguishing or recognizing reasons [(163)] is certainly true and obvious. But this only happens to people lacking in experience of rational philosophy and in discerning arguments. The Jews who ask for signs instead of arguments, and those who put their defense in another person's words, admit to being like this—as though it's easier to judge about the authority or text of someone absent than about the reasoning or view of someone present, and as if the former's meaning can be examined better than the latter's can.

(168) "When* we inquire after God as much as we can, anxious about our salvation, his grace surely supplies what our deeds are not enough for. He helps the willing, so they may be able. He even inspires the very fact that they are willing. He who often drags the unwilling along doesn't

---

32. Abelard, *Dialectica* III. 2. 19, De Rijk ed., p. 438.23–24: "Now the topic Themistius calls 'from the judgment of the matter' Cicero calls 'from authority.' " See n. 27 above.

33. See n. 27 above.

34. See n. 28 above.

35. That is, merely persuasive.

reject the willing. He holds out his right hand to one who is trying, whose carelessness he cannot blame. What you call Truth itself, the Christ who makes you safe, tacitly understands this when the apt analogy is given: 'Ask and you will receive. Seek and you will find. Knock and it will be opened to you. For everyone who asks receives, and who seeks finds, and to the knocker it will be opened.'

(169) "Indeed in explaining the above words in a certain work of his *On Mercy*, Augustine says, as I recall, 'Ask by praying, seek by disputing, knock by demanding.' Thus too in the second book of *On Order*, putting the art of argument ahead of the disciplines as if it alone knows or makes people knowers, he says in praise of it: 'The discipline of disciplines they call dialectic. It teaches how to teach; it teaches how to learn. In it reason itself demonstrates what it is; it alone knows what it wants. It not only wants to make people knowers, but is also able to do so.'

(170) "In the second book of *On Christian Teaching*, while showing that dialectic is quite necessary for reading Sacred Scripture, he says:

> There remain matters that do not pertain to the body's senses but to reason, where the discipline of disputation and number rules. Now* the discipline of disputation is of enormous value for going into all the kinds of questions that come up in sacred literature. Yet one has to be careful there of the passion for wrangling and a kind of childish display of deceiving the adversary. For there are many false conclusions of reasonings, called 'sophisms,' and very often they imitate true conclusions so much that they deceive not only slow people, but even clever ones when they are less attentive. As far as I can see, Scripture curses this kind of captious conclusions in the passage where it is said, 'He who speaks sophistically is loathsome.' "

(171) THE CHRISTIAN: "Surely no discerning person forbids investigating and discussing our faith by means of reasons. One does not rationally agree to things that were doubtful without first setting out a reason why one has to agree. When that reason produces faith in something doubtful, it truly becomes what you call an argument. Certainly controversy arises in every discipline, both about the text and about the view. And in any battle of disputation, a declared truth of reason is stronger than pointing to an authority.

(172) "For it isn't what holds in reality that's relevant to affirming the faith, but what can be believed. Many questions come up about the words of the authority itself, so that one must judge *about* them before judging *by means* of them. But after the reason has been declared—even if it's not really a reason but only seems to be—no question remains because there's no doubt left.

(173) "Now the more you rely on reason and the less you recognize Scripture's authority, the less one should deal with you on the basis of authority. Certainly no one can be argued against except on the basis of what he's granted, and he can only be convinced by what he accepts. We must do battle with you differently than we do with one another. We know that what Gregory, our other teachers, or even what Christ himself or Moses affirms doesn't yet affect you so that you are forced into the faith by their statements. Among us who accept them they have a place. Yet sometimes one must affirm or defend the faith mainly by reasons. The second book of the *Christian Theology* discusses these reasons more fully, I recall, against those who deny that faith is to be investigated by reasons, and refutes the rebellious both by the power of reasons and by the authority of the texts.

(174) "Now if it's all right, let's return to our point."

(175) THE PHILOSOPHER: "Indeed. For it *is* all right, and we should resolve to do this above all. Let's try as hard as we can, and attempt to insist on the natural law in the truer ethics' lessons.

(176) "We believe this will be brought to completion rightly and in good order if, in accordance with the summary of ethics recounted by you above [(150)], we discuss what the ultimate good is and by what road one can reach it, so that the treatment of our ethics is divided into these two parts."

(177) THE CHRISTIAN: "I concur with you on your recommendation. But in accordance with our proposal's agreement [(146)–(147)], our views are to be compared with yours so that we can pick the stronger features of each. And you have claimed you get to go first because of the natural law's ancientness [(11)]. Thus you who are content with what you call the 'earlier' (that is, the natural) law and use it alone, it's your task to make your own or your people's views known, and afterwards to hear the reasons for ours if we disagree on anything."

(178) THE PHILOSOPHER: "As a great many of your* own people have remarked, they[36] have defined the ultimate good or final good—that is, its summation or completion—as 'what makes anyone who has arrived at it blessed,' just as conversely the ultimate evil is that the attaining of which makes one wretched. We earn either one of these by our morals. Now it is certain that virtues or the vices contrary to them are called 'morals.'[37] But as Augustine remarks in Book Eight of *On the City of God,* some of our own people have said that virtue itself is the ultimate good, others that pleasure is."

---

36. That is, philosophers. In the passage about to be quoted, Augustine is discussing Socrates and his disciples.

37. See Abelard's *Ethics* (1).

(179) THE CHRISTIAN: "So what, please, did they understand by pleasure?"

(180) THE PHILOSOPHER: "Not the dishonorable and shameful delight of carnal allurements, as many people suppose, but rather a kind of inner tranquillity of the soul whereby it remains calm and content with its own goods in disasters and good fortune alike, while no sense of sin consumes it. Far be it from philosophers, those greatest despisers of earthly happiness, those distinguished flesh-tamers, to set up the ultimate good in *this* life's shamefulnesses! Many people attribute this to Epicurus and his followers (that is, the Epicureans) out of ignorance, not really understanding, as we said, what the latter would call pleasure. Otherwise, as we said,[38] if Epicurus had departed as far as is said from the path of soberness and respectability, then Seneca, that greatest morals-builder, who lived a most self-restrained life as you yourselves acknowledge, would hardly have brought in Epicurus' views so often for moral instruction, as if they were his own master's."

(181) THE CHRISTIAN: "Be it as you suppose. But please answer this: Do those who understand pleasure in this way disagree in meaning too, as they do in words, with those who call the ultimate good 'virtue'?"

(182) THE PHILOSOPHER: "There's little or no distance between them, as far as their overall view is concerned. Indeed, to be strong in virtues is itself to have this tranquillity of the soul, and conversely."

(183) THE CHRISTIAN: "So there is one view for both of them about the ultimate good, but the nomenclature is different. And so the two apparent views about the ultimate good are reduced to one."

(184) THE PHILOSOPHER: "So I think."

(185) THE CHRISTIAN: "And what way have they settled on, I ask, for reaching this ultimate good, namely virtue?"

(186) THE PHILOSOPHER: "Certainly the study of moral literature or exercise in taming the flesh, so that the good will that is firmed up into a habit can be called 'virtue.' "

(187) THE CHRISTIAN: "And whom do they define as blessed?"

(188) THE PHILOSOPHER: "They say the 'blessed' is one who is 'well suited,'[39] so to speak—that is, deals well and easily in all things. Thus being blessed is the same as being strong in good morals, that is, in the virtues."

(189) THE CHRISTIAN: "Do they put any value on the soul's immortality and on a kind of blessedness* in a future life, and expect it in return for their merits?"

---

38. Despite Abelard's claim, he has not said anything like this earlier in the *Dialogue*.

39. Abelard is giving a (spurious) etymology here: *be* + *atus* as short for *bene* + *aptus*. In fact, the word is the passive participle of *beo* = to make happy or blessed.

(190) THE PHILOSOPHER: "Indeed they do, but so what?"

(191) THE CHRISTIAN: "Do they not judge to be greater the blessedness of the life where no suffering's sorrow will afflict them once they've gotten there, so we may look for man's ultimate good and true blessedness there rather than here?"

(192) THE PHILOSOPHER: "Indeed, the utter calm of that life is, as you said, devoid of all suffering. But they say that when affliction stops, blessedness is in no way increased unless *virtue* grows. No one is said by them to become more blessed unless he's made better in virtue. Indeed, they *define* being blessed, as I said [(188)], as being strong in the virtues. Thus while someone is suffering for justice's sake and is said to be of greater *merit* because of the suffering, he's equally as *blessed* in the torments as he's said to be beforehand, because he's equally good. For although his virtue is more apparent now than before, nevertheless it doesn't *grow* at all because of the torment. Rather it appeared from the torment how great the virtue was. For far be it that whatever things pertain to bodily calm or affliction should increase or decrease our blessedness, if the virtue keeps the mind in the same state of resolve. Indeed, did your Christ decrease his blessedness by suffering or increase it by rising again?

(193) "So don't by any means suppose that because these bodily afflictions will cease there, we'll be more *blessed* there if we won't be *better.*"

(194) THE CHRISTIAN: "What if we are?"

(195) THE PHILOSOPHER: "Then certainly we'll be more blessed, because we'll be better."

(196) THE CHRISTIAN: "As I said [(189)], you expect that kind of life as owed because of your merits, as though the battle with the vices were here, but the crown of victory there."[40]

(197) THE PHILOSOPHER: "That's clear to all."

(198) THE CHRISTIAN: "Then how are the rewards for the battles going to be received there, if one isn't going to live more happily there and that life isn't better and more blessed than the present one? But if it *is* more blessed than this one, then surely those who enjoy it are also more blessed than they are seen to be here."

(199) THE PHILOSOPHER: "Certainly they're more blessed if they're better, as I said [(195)]; we don't get it any other way. For one who's obtained the crown isn't thereby endowed with greater virtue than he had in the struggle beforehand; his strength isn't made greater, even though it's more tested and recognized now than* before. Perhaps it's even decreased by the very burden of the battle, and the triumphant person's life is no better than the fighter's, although it's more agreeable."

40. See Abelard's *Ethics* (22).

(200) THE CHRISTIAN: "Your teachers and ours, and everyone else as well, count poverty, illness, death, and other troubles of adversities or sufferings as evils. And because of things contrary to the virtues, there are many vices both of the soul and of the body. They're to be no less regarded as evils. For instance the body's lameness or blindness, the mind's dullness or forgetfulness.[41]

(201) "In fact while discussing contraries in the *Categories* Aristotle says:

> By necessity, the contrary of a good is certainly evil. This is plain through induction from singulars. For instance, faintness is contrary to health, injustice to justice, weakness to strength. Similarly in other cases as well. On the other hand, sometimes a good is the contrary of an evil, sometimes an evil is. For even though poverty is an evil, its contrary is excessiveness—although that is an evil too. But one will observe this kind of thing in few cases. In most cases, however, an evil is always contrary to a good.

(202) "And Cicero in his *Topics*, when he would assign a topic 'from contraries,' says 'If health is good, sickness is evil.'

(203) "The Lord himself too, speaking through the prophet about the peace he bestows on the obedient and the persecution he sends against the rebellious, says 'I am the Lord, making good and creating evil.' And in the Gospel the Lord speaks to the rich person about goods and evils: 'You have received goods in your life, and likewise Lazarus has received evils.'

(204) "And Augustine as well, first yours and later ours,[42] affirms that death is an evil:

> Just as the Law is not evil because it increases sinners' craving, so neither is death good because it increases its sufferers' glory and makes them martyrs. In fact, the Law is good because it is the prohibition of sin, whereas death is evil because it is the payment for sin. But as the unjust use even good things evilly, so too let the just use evil things well. Thus too it comes about that evil people use the Law evilly even though the Law is a good, and good people die well even though death is an evil."

(205) THE PHILOSOPHER: "Please, where are these remarks going?"

(206) THE CHRISTIAN: "They are so that you may understand, I say, that the better life is the one that surely is altogether devoid of these evils and so absolutely removed from sin that not only *does* one not sin but one *cannot* sin there either. Unless it's better or more pleasant than the present life, it's

41. See Abelard's *Ethics* (2)–(3).
42. That is, Augustine was a philosopher to begin with, and was converted to Christianity only later.

pointless to put it forward as a reward. But if it's neither more pleasant nor better, there's no reason it's preferred to this one, and those who desire it more do so uncritically."

(207) THE PHILOSOPHER: "To tell the truth, I'm learning now that you're a first-class philosopher, and it's wrong to resist shamelessly such a plain argument. But according to the argument you've set out, a human being's ultimate good is to be looked for there rather than here. Perhaps this was Epicurus' view when he said the ultimate good is pleasure. For the soul's tranquillity is so great that bodily affliction doesn't disturb it from outside, and neither does any sense of sin disturb the mind nor vice get in its way from inside. Thus its best will is entirely fulfilled.

(208) "On the other hand, as long as something opposes our will or is lacking to it, there's no true blessedness at all. Surely this is always occurring as long as one is alive here, and the soul, weighed down by its earthly body's mass and confined in it as though in a jail, doesn't enjoy true freedom. For who doesn't sometimes want heat when it's too cold, or conversely, good weather when he's tired of rain, or often want more food or clothes than he has? And unless we resist the plain truth, there are countless other things that are pressed upon us against our will or are denied when we want them. Now if as the argument stands the future life's good is to be regarded as ultimate for us, then I think the virtues we are furnished with here are the way to get there. We'll have to discuss them more carefully later on [(253)–(295)]."

(209) THE CHRISTIAN: "See, our disputation has brought us to the point of maintaining that a human being's ultimate good, or 'final good' as it was called [(178)], is the future life's blessedness, and virtues are the way to get there.

(210) "But first I want to compare our (that is, Christian) teaching about this ultimate good with yours, in order that the teaching with the more fertile doctrine or exhortation may be both regarded as more perfect and complied with more fully.

(211) "Now you suppose you've decisively shown [(58)–(61), (114)–(118)], with respect to the Old Law the Jews boast of, that no prize consisting of this blessedness was promised there, and no use is made there of any exhortation based on it. But when he handed down the New Testament, the Lord Jesus put just such a foundation for his doctrine right at the very beginning where he stirred up both contempt for the world and a desire for this blessedness alike, saying: 'Blessed are the poor in spirit. For the kingdom of heaven is theirs.' And later on: 'Blessed are those who suffer persecution on account of justice. For the kingdom of heaven is theirs.' If we pay careful attention to these passages, all his commandments or exhortations are used for the purpose that all good fortune might be despised and adversities put up with in the hope of that higher and eternal life.

(212) "I think your teachers haven't touched on this at all or summoned your souls as much to this final good. But if there were some who did, then run through all the ordinances of your ethics and point them out. Or if* you can't point them out, then confess that Christ's doctrine is the more perfect and better one insofar as it exhorts us to virtues with better reason or hope. For you suppose instead that virtues or their contraries are to be striven after or shunned for their own sakes more than for the sake of something else. Thus you suppose the former should be called 'honorable' and the latter 'dishonorable.' Indeed, you call 'honorable' what is pleasant through itself and is to be striven after for its own sake, not for the sake of something else, just as conversely you call 'dishonorable' what is to be run away from on account of its own shamefulness. For things that are to be either sought after or shunned on account of something else you instead call 'useful' or 'unuseful.' "

(213) THE PHILOSOPHER: "It certainly did seem that way to our forebears, as Cicero describes rather fully in his *Rhetoric*. But surely when it is said that virtue is to be aspired after for its own sake, not for the sake of something else, reward for merits isn't being ruled out entirely; rather the inclination to earthly advantages is taken away. Otherwise we wouldn't have correctly set up blessedness as the virtues' goal—that is, their final cause—as your Boethius remarks in Book Two of his *Topics*, following Themistius. In fact, while giving an example there of the topic 'from the goal,' he says 'If to be blessed is good, justice is good too.' For here, he says, justice's goal is such that if someone lives in accordance with justice, he is led to blessedness. Look, he plainly shows here that blessedness is awarded as payment for a just life, and that our purpose in living justly is that we might reach it. Epicurus I think calls this blessedness 'pleasure'; your Christ calls it 'the kingdom of heaven.'

(214) "But what difference does it make what name it is called by, provided that the thing stays the same, the blessedness is no different, and no other purpose for living justly is proposed for philosophers than for Christians? For we, like you, arrange to live justly here that we may be glorified there. We fight against vices here that we may be crowned there with virtues' merits, receiving the ultimate good as our reward."

(215) THE CHRISTIAN: "On the contrary. As far as I can tell, our purpose and merits are quite different from yours, and we disagree quite a bit too about the ultimate good itself."

(216) THE PHILOSOPHER: "Please explain that, if you can."

(217) THE CHRISTIAN: "No one correctly calls that than which something greater is found the 'ultimate good.' For what is below or less than something

cannot by any means be called 'supreme' or 'ultimate.' But it is agreed that every human blessedness or glory is far and inexpressibly exceeded by the divine one. Therefore, none besides it is to be called 'ultimate.' Nothing besides it is justly said to be the 'ultimate good.' "

(218) THE PHILOSOPHER: "In this context we do not mean the ultimate good absolutely, but the ultimate *human* good."

(219) THE CHRISTIAN: "But neither do we correctly call 'ultimate human good' that than which some greater human good is found."

(220) THE PHILOSOPHER: "That's plain, certainly."

(221) THE CHRISTIAN: "I ask therefore whether in that blessedness [(213)] one person is more blessed than another (as it happens here that one person is more just or holy than another), so that the repayment is different according to the difference in the merits."

(222) THE PHILOSOPHER: "What if that's so?"

(223) THE CHRISTIAN: "Precisely because it is so, you have to grant that one person is made more blessed there than another. And because of this, the person's blessedness that is the less shouldn't be said to be the *ultimate* human good. Thus it's inappropriate for the one who's less blessed than another to be called 'blessed' any longer. For you in fact defined the ultimate good as that whereby someone is blessed when he reaches it [(178)].

(224) "Therefore, either grant that the one who's less blessed there than another has received the ultimate good, or else grant that he is not blessed at all, but rather only the one than whom no one there is *more* blessed. For if what's received makes him blessed, then surely in accordance with the definition given above [(178)], it is properly called the ultimate good."

(225) THE PHILOSOPHER: "Hold on a moment, please! Pay attention to what I now submit in reply to this most recent line of inquiry. It's still legitimate for someone to correct things badly stated, since as was said [(22)], we are having this conversation to investigate what's true, not to show off talent."

(226) THE CHRISTIAN: "I approve, and I grant what you're saying. For it's unseemly for us, who are entirely taken up with the investigation of truth, to squabble with one another like children or with uncouth bawling. Or if things are granted rather incautiously, it's unseemly for one who means to teach or be taught to take the opportunity from that to produce embarrassment where sometimes it's permissible to grant even falsehoods for the sake of arguing. And so we give full license to either completely changing or correcting a view."

(227) THE PHILOSOPHER: "Recall what I said, and remember the condition imposed where it was said, 'What if that is so?' [(221)–(222)]. For it's seemed to many philosophers that all the virtues are present together in all good people, that one who's missing some virtue isn't regarded as good at all, and

that therefore among all good people there's no difference either in their life's merits or in the repayment that is blessedness.

(228) "If perhaps this is so, the same blessedness is given out to all, and all who have equally received the ultimate good become blessed to the same degree. In the second book of his *On Duties*, Cicero plainly professes this view in the following words:

> Although justice without prudence has authority enough, prudence without justice is of no value in producing belief. For the more cunning and sly someone is, the more hateful and suspect he becomes if his reputation for integrity is taken away. For this reason justice conjoined to intelligence will have ever so much force in producing belief; justice without prudence will be able to do a lot; prudence without justice will be capable of nothing.
>
> But lest someone wonder why I am now severing the virtues—as though anyone could be just in such a way that the same person is not prudent—even though* it is settled among all philosophers and I myself have often argued that whoever has one has them all, let me say this: One kind of discourse occurs when truth is being examined in a disputation, but another kind when the discourse is adapted for all people. For this reason we are speaking in this context as the common people do, so that we say some men are strong, others good, others prudent. For when we are speaking in this context, we must use the ordinary, usual words.

(229) "In the *Paradoxes* too, he not only makes good people equal in virtues but also makes evil people equal in sins, so that he asserts all sins are on a par."

(230) THE CHRISTIAN: "I see you're now for the first time not ashamed to get boorish and squabble rather than philosophize. Surely, in order not to appear forced into a confession of plain truth, you turn to the craziness of the most blatant falsehood, so that you regard all good people as equally good, all criminals as equally criminal, and all people as deserving the same glory or penalty to the same degree."

(231) THE PHILOSOPHER: "If only the matter stays at the level of reality, not at the level of people's opinion![43] People judge and repay the effects of deeds more than they do the quality of morals. They judge some people more just, stronger, better, or worse than others according to the things that outwardly *seem* to be performed.

(232) "Actually, I think you're not far from this view, if you consider your own teaching. Indeed as your greatest philosopher Augustine asserts, charity encompasses all the virtues under one name. It alone, as he himself says,

---

43. The sentence is elliptical. The sense is, "What you describe as 'craziness' is in fact the truth, if only . . ."

differentiates between the sons of God and of the Devil. Thus he remarks in a certain passage: 'Where there is charity, what is there that can be lacking? But where there is not, what is there that can help? "In fact, love is the fulfillment of the Law." ' The Apostle himself who says this, in following up on this fulfillment and both removing evils from it and including goods in it, says: 'Charity is patient, it is kind. Charity is not envious, it does not act badly,' etc. Charity is also the topic when among other things it's said that it 'suffers all things' or 'bears all things,' surely even death. Now as Christ remarks, 'No one has more love than this, that someone lays down his soul for his friends.'

(233) "Therefore one person doesn't abound with charity more than another one does, since charity contains in itself all these things and carries them with it. Now if no one surpasses anyone else in charity, surely neither does he in virtues or merits, since charity, as you say, embraces every virtue."

(234) THE CHRISTIAN: "Really, if virtue is understood properly—that is, as what obtains merit with God—then *only* charity is to be called a virtue. But if it's understood as what makes one just or strong or moderate, then it's correct to call it justice, strength or moderation.

(235) "But just as those who have charity are not all equally on fire with it, and not all prudent people understand equally, so not all just people are equally just or all the strong or moderate people equally so. And although we grant that all the virtues, according to the distinction of their species, are present in some people—that is, when any of them is just and strong and moderate—nevertheless we don't agree that they are on a par in virtues or merits, since it happens that one person is more just or stronger or more forbearing than another. For even though we hold that individual people agree in the previously mentioned species of the virtues, there's nevertheless a big difference among the individual instances of those species, since one person's justice or strength or moderation is greater than another's.

(236) "So even though charity brings together all the things you said [(232)], nevertheless it doesn't bestow them all on the individuals it is present in. For just as all things advantageous to the body are imparted by nature, but not all of them to all bodies, so it happens with the soul's goods or virtues too that not all people are enhanced equally by them all.

(237) "So I want you to notice how weak the reasoning is (indeed, the worst sophism!) that the philosopher just mentioned [(228)–(229)] introduces in his *Paradoxes* from the view of other philosophers, in order to convince us that virtues as well as vices are on a par for all people. He said, 'There is no one better than a good man, more moderate than a moderate one, stronger than a strong one, or wiser than a wise one.' For even though there's no one better than a good man, nevertheless there is a better than *some* good man. For what

else is it to say of someone that he's better than a good man, except that he's better than a good man *whoever the latter may be?* For when we call God better than a human being, we understand nothing else but that he transcends *all* human beings. So too, when we* call some good man better than a good man—that is, than a good man is,[44] or than *some* good man is—it seems this shouldn't be taken in any other sense than that he is put ahead of *all* good men in general. But that's entirely false, since he too is one of the good men. For if he's better than a good man (or than some good man is), the consequent seems to be that neither a good man nor *some* good man is as good, but rather if someone is good, that person is *less* good than he. So it seems to make a big difference if one is called 'better than some good man' (or 'better than is some good man').[45]

(238) "Indeed a sophism's trap can occur here in *any* comparison, so that just as they attempt to prove that all good people are equally good, so too all handsome people are equally handsome, since no handsome person is more handsome than the handsome—that is, simply and in general—although he may be more handsome than another handsome person.

(239) "Finally, who is there who doesn't understand how it is the worst craziness to say all sins are on a par? For whether you locate sin in the will or in the doing,[46] it's clear that among evil persons one has a viler will than another, and is more harmful or acts worse. Certainly the will leads to the act, and when the ability is given to do harm, one person does more harm than another, or persecutes some just person more because he hates him and wants to torment him more. Likewise not all good people are beneficial or want to be beneficial equally. It's plain from this that good people aren't on a par with one another and evil people aren't either. Neither should their merits be equated, so that their repayment is understood to be on a par too.

44. The first "than a good man" is expressed by the ablative in the Latin; the second, after the "that is," is expressed by a *quam*–clause. The purpose of the insertion is simply to express the comparison in a syntactically alternative way. The difference cannot be translated into English. The point of the alternative formulation is *not* the addition of the "is."

45. The sentence doesn't mean there is a big difference between the two formulations used there. Instead it means there's a big difference between *either* of those two formulations (in both of which one is compared to some *particular* good man) and the more general formulation discussed earlier (where one is compared to good men at large). Syntactically, the distinction rests on whether the expression describing what one is compared to contains a particular (that is, existential) quantifier.

46. In the *Ethics*, Abelard argues that it's in neither, but in *consent*. See *Ethics* (9)–(29), (35)–(48), and n. 22 above.

(240) "Moreover, disregarding the opinion of fools, if you consider the approved philosophers' lofty doctrines about the virtues, and notice the careful four-part distinction of the virtues given by that most eloquent man Plotinus—he calls some political, some purgatorial, others virtues of the purged soul, and others exemplary—you will be forced by their very names and descriptions to confess at once that people differ greatly in virtues.

(241) "The Apostle too, about whom you raised an objection against us [(232)], doesn't pass over this difference when he's talking about self-restraint and allowing marriage. He says: 'I want all people to be like myself. But everyone has his own gift from God, one person this way, one that way,' etc. He also distinguishes the future life's rewards according to the quality of virtues or merits, saying: 'Star differs from star in brightness. So too will be the resurrection of the dead.' And elsewhere, 'One who sows frugally will also reap frugally.'

(242) "Now the fact that he said the fulfillment of the Law is charity [(232)]—that is, the Law is carried out through charity—doesn't show all people are equal in charity, since charity extends beyond what's decreed. Hence there's also Truth's exhortation, 'When you have done all things, whatever are commanded, say: "We are useless slaves. We have done what we were supposed to do." ' That is, if you carry out only what you're supposed to on the basis of a command, then regard it as little if you don't add something extra, in addition to the command's duty. His expression, 'We have done what we were supposed to do,' is as though he'd said, 'In fulfilling the commands we carry out only our duties, and perform necessary deeds, as it were, not gratuitous ones.' Now when someone perseveres to the pinnacle of virginity, he certainly thereby goes beyond commandment, and isn't compelled to it by commandment. Thus the same Apostle remarks: 'Now I do not have a commandment of the Lord's about virgins; rather I give advice.'

(243) "But even among those who implement the Law but don't go beyond it, charity can be unequal, since in the same deed the disposition of charity is greater in one person than in another. As for what was objected [(232)] on the basis of Augustine's statement 'Where there is charity, what is there that can be lacking,' etc., no one thinks he took this in the sense that he meant to make all people one in virtues and merits. Following both the Lord and the Apostle, he contradicts this interpretation almost everywhere. Surely what he says is like saying 'What is there that can be lacking *to salvation?*' though not to the perfection of the virtues. No one with it perishes, to be sure, but not all are made equal in it."

(244) THE PHILOSOPHER: "Please don't let it be a burden to you that we bring up many views or opinions in order to be able to ascertain from all of

them the truth of their arguments. For those who are searching for a place they don't yet know are forced to explore many roads, in order to be able to pick the more direct one, as I am now compelled to do while I set forth at your own invitation [(177)] our forebears' views, or my own, in inquiring about the ultimate good."

(245) THE CHRISTIAN: "It wouldn't be a burden if some view were brought up that, even if it weren't true, would at least have some plausibility. For what's plainly false doesn't have to be refuted by any reasoning."

(246) THE PHILOSOPHER: "What if we call the future life's state the ultimate human good only by comparison with the present life's goods? For even though you say God set forth two ends for us, namely the ultimate good in heaven or the ultimate evil in hell, you don't take this in any other sense than with respect to the present life's good or evil state.

(247) "Indeed, reason offers us *six* human states: three in this life and likewise three others, corresponding to them, in the future life. The first human state is the one in which a person is born, when he's not yet received free choice by reason's being aroused in him so that he will be called a good or a bad person according to what he picks—although he himself is a good thing or a good substance or creature.

(248) "When he's brought from this earlier human state to the age of discretion, and has knowingly turned himself either to good or to evil, then he's become a good or a bad person and entered into a good or bad human state. Indeed, the first human state is indifferent so to speak—that is, it is to be properly called neither good nor bad. If the second one rises to the virtues, it's good; if it sinks to the vices, bad.

(249) "So too the future life has three states. One is so to speak indifferent, and isn't properly 'blessed,' but isn't miserable either. It belongs to those whose state in this life was indifferent too, as we said—deprived of all virtues and merits, with human reason not yet aroused. Another state, awarded for merits, is the best, and the other the worst.

(250) "Now I think the latter two are called the ultimate good and ultimate evil, in comparison with this life's other two that produce them, insofar as nothing unfavorable or favorable is mixed into them,[47] although the other two[48] are plainly mixed with such things, so that the purity neither of good nor of evil is present in them."

---

47. That is, the ultimate good is the ultimate good insofar as it has nothing unfavorable mixed in with it, and the ultimate evil is the ultimate evil insofar as it has nothing favorable mixed in with it.

48. The ones in this life.

(251) THE CHRISTIAN: "Aha! According to you, ultimate good is to be understood as the repose of the life on high, just as conversely, ultimate evil is bad peoples' future damnation. Both of these we acquire by our merits, as you remarked [(178)], through which we arrive there as if by certain kinds of roads, so to speak."

(252) THE PHILOSOPHER: "So I think, that's plain. Certainly no view is held more strongly by those who embrace the natural law than that virtue is enough for blessedness; and because only the virtues make one 'blessed,' one cannot get the name by any other road. So too it is plain that conversely, no one becomes truly miserable except by vices. Thus it's established that just as the former are the roads to ultimate good, so are the latter to ultimate evil."

(253) THE CHRISTIAN: "Since you seem now to have come somewhat nearer to a person's ultimate good as well as to his ultimate evil, and furthermore to have touched on the roads to them, it's all right to loosen your objections' reins a little on your racecourse, so you might thereby reach your proposed goal more easily and be able to decide more truly and more perfectly when the work is done. So now that you've pointed out what you call a person's ultimate good or his ultimate evil, it also remains [(176)] for you carefully to define and distinguish what you called these 'roads' to them, the virtues and the vices, so that the better known they are, the more they might be desired or avoided."

(254) THE PHILOSOPHER: " 'Virtue,' they say, 'is the mind's best habit.' So too conversely, I think vice is the mind's worst habit. Now we're calling a 'habit' what Aristotle in the *Categories* distinguished when he included habit and disposition in the first species of quality.[49] Therefore a habit is a thing's quality, not implanted in it naturally but sought out by practice and deliberation, and hard to change. Thus we don't count among the virtues the chastity they call 'natural' in some people, arising from the body's frigidness or some physical condition. It never endures any fight against a lust it might triumph over; it obtains no merit. Neither do we count among the virtues any of the soul's qualities that are easy to change.

(255) "Surely where there's no fight against resistance, there's no crown for a virtue that overcomes it, in accordance with your great philosopher: 'No one will be crowned unless he has contended lawfully.' Hence too there is Philosophy's statement to Boethius in the fourth book of his *Consolation*, 'Virtue too is so called from the fact that, relying on its own powers, it is not overcome by adversities.'[50] He also asserts that every virtue is hard to change, when, in the

49. See Abelard's *Ethics* (228).
50. Boethius is giving a false etymology here, deriving *virtus* from *vis/viris*.

treatise on quality just cited, he explains Aristotle's putting sciences and virtues together among the habits: 'For it is not a virtue unless it is hard to change. For someone who judges justly once is not just. Neither is he who commits adultery once an adulterer, but only when this will and thought become permanent.'

(256) "Now the 'mind's best habit' is one that molds us for meriting true blessedness. Individual species of virtue are like this. Some people settled on more of them, some on fewer. Socrates indeed, through whom the study of moral discipline first and mainly got to be strong, distinguishes four species of virtue: prudence, justice, courage, and moderation. Now some people call prudence's discernment the *mother* or *origin* of the virtues rather than itself a virtue.[51] Certainly, prudence is this knowledge of morals that is called, as a certain treatise on ethics transmits to us, the 'science of good and evil things'—discerning goods or evils that in themselves are properly to be called goods or evils.

(257) "For certain things are called goods or evils properly and so to speak substantially. For instance, the virtues and vices themselves. But certain things are so called by accident and through something else, like actions that are our deeds. Although they're indifferent in themselves, nevertheless they're called good or evil from the intention from which they proceed. Frequently, therefore, when the same thing is done by different people, or by the same person at different times, the same deed is nevertheless called both 'good' and 'evil' because of the difference in the intentions. On the other hand, things that are called goods or evils substantially and from their own nature remain so permanently unmixed that what is good once can never become evil, or conversely. And so the discernment of these things, both the goods and the evils, is called prudence.

(258) "In fact, because this discernment can be present equally in perverse people and in good ones, it has no merit, and isn't correctly called a 'virtue' or 'the mind's best habit' [(254)] at all. Thus while distinguishing the sciences from the virtues, Aristotle gives examples of habit in the treatise on quality cited above. He says, 'The sciences or virtues are like this.' Explaining this passage, Boethius says 'For Aristotle does not think virtues are sciences, as Socrates does.'

(259) "So too Augustine, first ours and afterwards yours, as I've already remarked above [(204)], sometimes extends the name 'virtue' even to faith and hope. But sometimes he narrows it down to charity alone, which belongs properly and especially to good people, while the remaining two are common

51. See Abelard, *Ethics* (227).

to reprobates and to the elect. Indeed it is written, 'Faith is idle without deeds,' and 'The hope of the impious will perish.'

(260) "Now just as faith and hope without deeds turn out useless—rather, *harmful* to us—so too does prudence. Surely we're more guilty when we knowingly avoid what's to be done or do what isn't, than if this happened through ignorance, which could* hold out some excuse. Thus there's the passage you know, 'The slave who knows his master's will and doesn't do it will be flogged many times.' And elsewhere, 'It would be better not to have known the road of truth than to turn back after recognizing it.'

(261) "So prudence—like faith and hope, which pertain equally to evil people as to good—aren't to be called virtues[52] so much as offering a kind of guidance to or incentive to the virtues."

(262) THE CHRISTIAN: "I think that's enough for now about prudence. It remains for you now to go on to the other virtues, as Socrates has them [(256)]."

(263) THE PHILOSOPHER: "Justice then is the virtue that bestows on everyone his due while preserving the common benefit—that is, that virtue whereby we want everyone to have what he's worthy of, if this doesn't imply any common injury. For it often happens that when we grant someone what he deserves for his merits, what's done individually for the one person implies a common injury. And so in order that the part not prejudice the whole, and the individual the community, the words 'while preserving the common benefit' are attached. Surely it's appropriate for all the things we do to be rightly referred to this end: that everyone pay attention in all things not so much to his own good as to the common one, that he provide not so much for domestic affairs as for public ones, and that he live not so much for himself as for his country.

(264) "Thus Socrates, the first and greatest teacher of moral philosophy, advised that all things be held in common and be applied to common advantage. As a result, he arranged even for wives to be in common, so that no one would recognize his own children. Everyone would believe they were begotten not so much for himself as for his country. Thus this community of wives is taken not with respect to the flesh's usage but with respect to the enjoyment of descendants.[53]

52. "Aren't to be called virtues": The plural is in the Latin. Although the syntax requires the singular, Abelard seems to be thinking of prudence, faith and hope together.

53. Enjoyment of descendants: Alternatively, "fruit of descendants" (*fructus prolis*). There is a play here on the contrast between using and enjoying (*utor* and *fruor*), distinguished by Augustine, *Christian Instruction*, I. 3. 3, p. 29 (Martin ed., p. 8).

(265) "Aulius Fulvius by both word and deed left an example of this to posterity's memory by killing his own son. He said he'd begotten him not for Catiline against the country, but for the country against Catiline. On fire with zeal for justice, not considering his son as a son but as the country's enemy, he exhibited the above definition of justice not with his mouth so much as by his hand.

(266) "Therefore whoever is steadfast in this will we've been talking about, so that he cannot be easily dislodged from it, is rich in the virtue of justice even if he's not yet accomplished in courage and moderation. But because what's hard to remove is yet sometimes forced to withdraw by some great intervening cause (for example, this good will that's called justice sometimes disappears out of some fear or greed), courage is needed against fear and moderation against desire. Certainly if the fear of a thing we don't want or the greed for what we do want is so great that it overcomes reason, they easily pull the mind away from its good purpose and lead it into contrary ones. Thus courage takes up the shield against fear, and moderation the bridle against greed, so that, strengthened by them too, we're able to attain as far as is in our power the things we already want through the virtue of justice.

(267) "Thus we call both of these a kind of firmness and steadiness of the mind whereby we are enabled to carry out what we want through justice. Their contraries are indeed rightly called a kind of mental weaknesses or inabilities to resist vices. For instance, laziness or faintheartedness, which makes a person neglectful, and immoderation, which turns us loose to obscene pleasures or shameful wants.

(268) "Courage is the considered (that is, reasonable) enduring of hardships and the taking on of dangers. This is the virtue that makes us ready to take on dangers or tolerate hardships, insofar as that's appropriate. It depends especially on the love for justice we call a 'good zeal' in warding off or avenging evils.

(269) "Moderation is the mind's firm and restrained domination of lust and of other mental impulses that aren't right. For we often go beyond restraint while seeming to ourselves to be moderate when we violate the limits of moderation. For example, when we seek self-control we afflict ourselves with unrestrained fasts, and when we want to tame vice we snuff out nature itself. And so going to excess in many ways, we establish the adjacent vices[54] instead of the virtues. Hence after the occurrence of 'firm' in the definition, it's right to add 'restrained.'

54. A vice "adjacent" to a virtue is one that isn't the direct opposite of the virtue (such as *giving in* to the "lust and other mental impulses that aren't right"), but instead borders on or is right next to a virtue. See also (270).

(270) "Certainly, over this reasoning [(263)–(269)] one must set the reasoning of prudence, which we called the mother of virtues [(256)]—that is, their origin and nurse. For unless through it we learn about the virtues in advance, and are able to distinguish them carefully not only from their contrary and plain vices but also from the adjacent vices, we take no pains at all to have and keep virtues we're ignorant of. So whoever is accomplished in these virtues must have prudence present in him. Through it justice, which distributes merits, knows what is due to whom, courage possesses discernment in taking on dangers or tolerating hardships, and moderation, as was just said, possesses restraint in holding back our craving.

(271) "It's therefore clear that a person is accomplished and made perfect in goods in the three virtues we mentioned, among which prudence cannot be lacking. But now it remains to distinguish their species or parts, in order for us to recognize them more attentively and judge their teaching more truly by following them through, one by one."

(272) THE CHRISTIAN: "Certainly we want that to be done. For it seems right, and ought to seem right."

(273) THE PHILOSOPHER: "Thus to speak succinctly, reverence, beneficence, truthfulness, and vengeance pertain to justice, which maintains for everyone what's his own."

What is reverence?

(274) "We call reverence that part of justice whereby on our own we show due veneration to all—that is, to God (this is called religion) as well as to people who deserve it either through power or through some merit (this is called deference). It's clear, therefore, that the virtue of obedience is included here, whereby we give honor to our superiors by complying with their commands because we don't scorn their reasonable ordinances."

What is beneficence?

(275) "Now beneficence is that whereby we're ready to give due support to people's needs—that is, either by giving the poor what they need (this is called liberality, whereas wastefulness involves things that are unnecessary), or by freeing the harshly oppressed (this is called clemency).

(276) "Now our forebears said mercy (so called from 'miseries')[55] is a vice and a kind of mental weakness rather than a virtue. Through it, since we are

55. Abelard is here deriving the etymology of *misericordia* from *miseria*. In fact both are derived from the more basic Latin adjective *miser.*

naturally sympathetic, we want to assist others merely because they're in distress. Clemency, however, is driven to assist people only because of a *reasonable* emotion. It doesn't pay attention so much to the fact that they're in distress as to the fact that they're *unjustly* distressed, with the result that it would comply with justice by preventing injustice. Our deeds don't otherwise belong to justice when we assist others, unless in doing so we render to everyone his own. But since virtue is a mental habit that is obviously had by application or effort rather than by nature, as is plain from the above [(254)], such a natural sympathy isn't to be linked to the virtues—that is, a sympathy whereby through a kind of human or carnal emotion, not a 'reasonable' one, we're busy assisting even criminals who are put in distress. In doing so, we're rather *resisting* justice, in order that the penalties due them not be exacted.

(277) "Finally, no matter what happens, to submit the mind to sorrow belongs to weakness rather than to virtue, to misery more than to blessedness, and to a disturbed mind, not a calm one. For since nothing happens without a cause, because God arranges all things for the best, what is it that occurs that makes a just person have to grieve or be sad,* and insofar as he can to go against God's arrangement for the best, as if he thinks it has to be corrected?"

What is truthfulness?

(278) "Truthfulness is that whereby we strive to abide by what we've made ourselves owe in making a promise. For if we promise what we shouldn't, we aren't made guilty by not fulfilling what a bad promise doesn't in fact make us owe. For one who pursues what ought not to have been promised doubles the bad deed's effect when he adds a twisted act to the twisted promise, and doesn't choose to correct the bad promise by ceasing from doing the deed."

What is vengeance?

(279) "Vengeance is the steady desire for revenge, whereby due penalty is inflicted for evils committed.

(280) "Now in each of these four parts of justice, it's plain that what we stipulated in its definition [(263)]—namely, 'while preserving the common benefit'—is to be implicitly understood. For as we also remarked above [(263)], it's proper for our deeds' goal to be that each person seeks not so much his own advantages as communal ones, and lives not so much for himself as for all, in accordance with what Lucan recites in praise of Cato: 'Surely, to him alone who lacks zeal and hatreds is there time to mourn the human race.' Again, 'These were the morals, this was the unshakable manner of stern Cato:

to keep within measure, to hold to the limit, to follow nature, to dedicate his life to his country, to believe he was born not for himself but for the whole world.' And later on, 'He is a father for the city and a husband for the city, good all around.'

(281) "Surely whoever's concerned about what's for his own advantage is of a weak nature; about what's for the advantage of others, is of outstanding virtue. He who takes care of himself alone, striving for his own advantages, ought to regard his life as of little consequence. He doesn't earn for himself others' thanks and praise. Each one in his own small measure ought to imitate God, who takes no care for himself but for all and doesn't minister to his own needs but to all people's, since he needs nothing and is the overseer of the entire fabric of the world as if it were one great republic.

(282) "There are people who distinguish justice's parts into a greater number, not of things but of names. They distinguish into several the many things included by us under one word. What's comprised in the whole they differentiate into parts: (a) dutifulness toward one's parents; (b) friendship, that is, good will, toward those who love us—friendship for their own sake more than for the sake of hoping for some advantage—together with their own will in like manner toward us; (c) thankfulness in repayment for benefits. But actually it's plain that these three belong under beneficence, whereby the mind is ready to dedicate due beneficence to parents as well as to others."

On natural or positive justice[56]

(283) "Now with matters pertaining to justice, one mustn't depart from the path of either natural or positive justice. For one kind of law is called natural and another kind positive. A natural law is one that reason itself, which is present in all people naturally and is therefore permanently in all people, persuades us must be fulfilled in practice. For example, worshipping God, loving one's parents, punishing the perverse, and whatever things are such that their observance is so necessary for all people that no merits are sufficient without them.

(284) "On the other hand, what belongs to positive justice is what is instituted by human beings to protect either usefulness or honor more surely, or to increase them. It depends either on custom alone or on a written authority. For example, vengeance's penalties or the judgments of the courts in investigating indictments. For some people use duels or a red-hot iron, while among others every controversy is ended by taking an oath and every dispute is consigned to

---

56. Throughout this section, I am translating *jus* as "law" and *justitia* as "justice." Although the words are unrelated in English, they are obviously related in Latin.

witnesses. Thus it comes about that when we have to live with any other people, we keep these ordinances of theirs we spoke of, just as we do natural laws.

(285) "The Laws you call divine, namely the Old and the New Testament, hand down certain natural commandments you call moral, such as loving God and one's neighbor, not committing adultery, not stealing, and not committing murder. But others belong so to speak to positive justice. They are adapted to certain people for a time. For example, circumcision for the Jews, baptism for you, and many others of what you call 'figurative' commandments. Every day, the Roman pontiffs or the gatherings of synods pass new decrees or grant dispensations on the basis of which you affirm that what was legal earlier is now illegal, or conversely—as if God put in their power that by their commands or permission they might make things good or evil that were not so earlier, and as if their authority can prejudge our law.

(286) "After considering justice, it remains now to direct the pen to the two remaining kinds of virtue."

On the parts of courage

(287) "And so courage seems to us to be contained in two parts, namely magnanimity and forbearance."

What is magnanimity?

(288) "Magnanimity, however, is that whereby we're prepared to set about doing difficult things when a reasonable cause is at hand."

What is forbearance?

(289) "But forbearance is that whereby we steadily persist in undertaking this plan."

On the parts of moderation

(290) "Now as far as I can see—and I don't think you reject this—the parts of moderation are these: humility, thriftiness, gentleness, chastity, and sobriety."

What is humility?

(291) "Humility is that whereby we refrain from the desire for empty glory, so that we don't desire to seem more than we are."

What is thriftiness?

(292) "But thriftiness is the brake on superfluous prodigality. Through it we reject the possession of more than is needed. So too gentleness is the brake on wrath, chastity on wantonness, and sobriety on guzzling.

(293) "Note that since justice is the mind's steady will that reserves for everyone what is his own [**(263)**], therefore courage and moderation are certain abilities, a toughness of mind whereby the good will for justice is strengthened, as we remarked above [**(266)**–**(269)**]. For surely it's obvious that things that have inabilities as contraries are abilities. Now the mind's debility, to which courage is contrary, is its kind of weakness and inability that we can call laziness or faint-heartedness. Immoderation too, the opposite of moderation, is a kind of feebleness and inability of a mind that doesn't have the strength to resist its impulses of the unreasonable stirrings whereby, as though by certain accomplices, a weak mind is dragged into vices' miserable captivity, and becomes the handmaid of things it ought to have dominated.

(294) "Now just as justice is the good will we spoke of, so injustice is the contrary will. Justice makes a person good, but courage and moderation make him capable, because what we will through the former we are* able to bring about through the latter.

(295) "I think I've just distinguished virtue's species or parts in such a way that in them there are included all the stages by which blessedness is attained and the ultimate good is grasped, in proportion to one's merits. Now if anything appears to your prudence that you decide to approve or disapprove in all these remarks, or if you think perhaps something has to be added to complete them, we're ready to listen."

(296) THE CHRISTIAN: "That's certainly proper. But before we come to these steps you've postulated toward the ultimate good, let's go back to the dispute about the ultimate good and ultimate evil, which was interrupted but not discontinued [**(253)**]. Let us determine what is called the ultimate good or the ultimate evil absolutely, and whether the ultimate good is other than the ultimate *human* good or the ultimate evil other than the ultimate *human* evil."

Return to the interrupted investigation of the ultimate good

(297) THE PHILOSOPHER: "Surely it's agreed among all those who philosophize rightly that the ultimate good is said and believed to be nothing else but God, whose incomparable and inexpressible blessedness doesn't know beginning or end and can't be either increased or diminished. On the other hand, I think the ultimate evil is the ultimate misery or torture of penalty, no matter whose it is—whether a human being's or another creature's. Now as I've already remarked and settled earlier [(246)–(250)], I understand the ultimate human good or ultimate human evil as the future life's rest or perpetual penalty.

(298) "So I think this is the difference that matters between the ultimate good and the ultimate *human* good: As is plain from the above [(217)], the ultimate good is God himself, or else his blessedness's ultimate tranquillity that nevertheless we do not regard as anything other than him who is blessed from himself, not from something else. The ultimate *human* good, however, is the perpetual repose or joy everyone receives after this life in proportion to his merits, whether in the vision or cognition of God, as you say, or however else it happens. On the other hand, the ultimate evil is the ultimate misery or penalty of any creature whatever, as I just said, undergone in proportion to its merits. We call ultimate *human* evil, however, all the tortures *people* undergo there in proportion to their merits."

On ultimate evil

(299) THE CHRISTIAN: "As far as I can see, you understand both the ultimate evil and the ultimate *human* evil as nothing but the penalties of the future world, exacted in proportion to merits."

(300) THE PHILOSOPHER: "I do indeed."

(301) THE CHRISTIAN: "But penalties imposed in proportion to merits are surely just, because it's just to punish in this way those who've earned it. Now surely whatever is just is good. And so without doubt, the penalties you call 'the ultimate evil' or 'the ultimate human evil' are good. So look! Don't you seem to be granting that what's good rather than evil is the ultimate evil? I don't see why you call what's not evil at all the 'ultimate evil' or the 'ultimate human evil.' "

(302) THE PHILOSOPHER: "You should've remembered that you yourself showed above [(200)–(204)], using both our evidence and yours, that every torment too is an evil rather than a good. Nevertheless, I don't think it has to be granted for that reason that every one of them is evil.[57] Indeed, changing the genders of adjectival names[58] frequently varies the sense, so that it's one thing

57. The distinction is between "*an* evil" (the neuter of the adjective, standing alone) and "evil" (the feminine of the adjective, modifying *afflictio* = torment). Torments are evils, absolutely speaking, even though they are not evil *torments*.

58. That is, of adjectives. In mediaeval grammatical theory, "names" included both what we call nouns and what we call adjectives.

to say a penalty is good and another to say a penalty is *a* good, that is, a good *thing*.

(303) "It's one thing to say this bronze statue is imperishable,[59] which is false, and another to say it's *an* imperishable, some thing that's imperishable, which is true: namely the bronze itself, the nature of which is imperishable and unfailing. Again, although every proposition is a kind of compound,[60] nevertheless we don't call every one of them compound, but only one that has propositions as parts—that is, a hypothetical.[61] Neither do we call every word compound although we know it's a compound thing,[62] or grant that every word we call simple is a simple thing. So too therefore, when we say some penalty is just or good, insofar as it's just or good for him who is tortured to be so tormented, we aren't for that reason forced to grant it's a just or good thing.

(304) "You too, although you maintain every creature is good insofar as there's nothing but good in God's creation, and you also don't deny that this person who is evil is a creature, thereby granting that he who is evil is a good thing, nevertheless you don't for this reason allow that he is a good person. Surely no person should be said to be good but one who is equipped with good morals. Yet even what is irrational and inanimate can be called a good thing or a good creature. Again, while God is said to have created all things as good, and this little person or horse is now created by him, nevertheless, although it is created as a good thing, it is not now created as a good person or a good horse. And God didn't himself create this little person, who will be wicked, as a good person or an evil person; rather, he formed him as a good thing, or as a good nature's substance. Neither did he ever create as a good horse the horse that will never be a good horse—although he does seem to create some vice-ridden horses, those that are said to contract some vice in their very creation and so afterwards turn out to be of little or no use. Plainly too, human beings themselves naturally contract some vices from the mixture of the elements in their very creation, so that they become naturally irascible or wanton, for instance, or tangled up in other vices.

---

59. Throughout this paragraph, I am translating forms of *perpetuus* (= everlasting) by "imperishable," since I needed a word that can be used as both an adjective and a noun. (Later in the paragraph, at "imperishable and unfailing," the word is *perpes*.)

60. Namely, of subject and predicate.

61. In mediaeval (and ancient) terminology, "hypothetical" propositions included not only conditionals (*if . . . then . . .*) but, as Abelard says, *any* proposition containing more than one proposition as component parts.

62. Every word is a compound *thing* insofar as it consists of a sequence of phonemes. But not every word is a compound *word* like, for example, "northeast."

(305) "Perhaps God didn't form as a good angel or good spirit the angel that was put ahead of the others as a 'Light-Bearer,'[63] so to speak, the one you say later apostatized and, you say, God had never established in truth and in the love of God. Most of your own people say* that once charity is had, it is never given up. Surely no angel, rational spirit, or even a human being, who's a stranger to the love of God and to true charity is rightly called good—or evil either, as long as he lacks sin. Therefore, if that angel was created with neither sin nor God's charity, how is he still supposed to be said to have been created as a good or an evil angel? So too individual people, when they are created not yet sharing in reason, shouldn't be called good or evil people by creation, since they didn't get their being good or evil people in their very creation.

(306) "Since some of them too come into being as naturally sick or even stupid, and are born possessed of various vices of the soul as well as of the body, and since all people in general are created mortal, surely human nature's good substance comes to partake in many evils from its very creation. For as Aristotle remarks and as plain truth holds, the contrary of good cannot but be evil. So it's clear that mortality, as well as the other things just listed that we're born with,* should be counted among evils (since no one doubts their contraries are good), and that certain vices or evils are naturally present in certain good substances from their very creation. For example mortality in a human being, irrationality in the horse. For although mortality is not called a vice of a person, since no one is worse than another person with respect to what all participate in equally, nevertheless it's a kind of vice of the nature in a person. For in this respect human nature is worse or weaker than one that's immortal.

(307) "Thus just as we grant that any person is a good thing, no matter how many vices he's disfigured by, and yet don't allow that he's a good person for that reason, so too conversely: we acknowledge that any penalty is an evil thing, even though we maintain that some penalty is good.

(308) "So look, if we set up a good and just penalty as the ultimate human evil, it doesn't follow that we grant for that reason that what's good is his ultimate evil. For even if the penalty is good, as was said, it's not for that reason to be called a good absolutely, a good *thing*."

(309) THE CHRISTIAN: "For now, let it be as you say. That is, from what you've granted you can't be accused of granting that what's good is the ultimate human evil, even though you don't deny that a penalty that's good and just is that ultimate evil. But I ask again, since both the preceding fault and the penalty arising from it are an evil, which of them is to be called the worse and

63. Light-Bearer = *Luciferus*.

greater human evil? Is it his fault that makes the person evil, or the penalty imposed by God that effects a just judgment on him?"

(310) THE PHILOSOPHER: "In my view, his fault is clearly a worse human evil than its penalty is. For since between any evils whatever, there's no doubt that the one more displeasing to God and deserving of penalty is greater than the other, who doubts* that the fault is worse than the fault's penalty? Certainly a person displeases God through the fault whereby he's called evil, not through the penalty imposed for the fault. The former certainly is an injustice; the latter is justice's due effect, arising from a correct intention. So it's clear that what there is in a person that makes him guilty is worse than what inflicts a just judgment on him by punishing him."

(311) THE CHRISTIAN: "Therefore, since a person's fault is a greater human evil than the penalty for it is, how do you call a person's penalty his *ultimate* evil? The fault is a greater evil than that, as was said."

(312) THE PHILOSOPHER: "So if you reject our opinion, please let me hear your view on this. That is, what do *you* think should be called the ultimate human evil?"

(313) THE CHRISTIAN: "What can make him worse, certainly. So too conversely, his ultimate good is plainly that whereby he's made better."

(314) THE PHILOSOPHER: "And what are they, please?"

(315) THE CHRISTIAN: "His ultimate hatred or ultimate love for God. Plainly, through these two we more displease or please him who is simply and properly called the ultimate good. Both of these surely follow after this life. For the more those who are tortured by the greatest everlasting penalties feel themselves burdened thereby, the more they burn from the very despair of pardon with a greater hatred for him by whose judgment they're being punished. They'd want him not to exist at all, so that then at least they could be released from the penalty. So they are much worse there for hating than they were here in scorning.

(316) "So too conversely, those who enjoy the vision of God that the Psalmist speaks of ('When your glory appears, I will be satisfied'—that is, after you've shown me your divinity's majesty through your very self, I will not need to seek anything more) are then made better insofar as they love more fully him whom they see in himself more truly. Thus ultimate love in the enjoyment of the ultimate good which is our true blessedness should rightly be called the ultimate human good.

(317) "Indeed, divine majesty's glory is so great that no one can gaze on it who doesn't at once become blessed in the very vision of it. Hence it's said, 'Let the impious be removed, lest he see God's glory.' Thus when his faithful, who loved him above all things, gaze on such blessedness as they could in no

way have envisioned by faith, this ultimate exultation of theirs will be their everlasting blessedness."

(318) THE PHILOSOPHER: "It's all right to understand ultimate human good or evil as that whereby a person is made better or worse, as you say. But if this comes about in the future life, so that we're made better or worse there than here, then surely we seem to merit something more there than here. For to the extent we're made better or worse than before, we're judged worthy of a greater penalty or reward.

(319) "Now if there's an advance in merits there too, so that the more we know God the more we love him, and if our love for God grows with the repayment as well, so that we're always being made better, then surely the growth in our blessedness is stretched out to infinity, so that it's never complete because it's always being increased."

(320) THE CHRISTIAN: "You don't understand that the time for meriting is in this life only, for reward in that one—that is, here 'for sowing,' there 'for gathering.' Therefore, even though we're made better there by the prize for merits than we were here by the merits themselves, nevertheless it's not necessary that we merit something there all over again. The very fact that we're made better there than here is the reward for merits had here. Although, having been bestowed for merits, it makes us better, it doesn't merit a prize *again*. It's established only as a reward for merits, not as being had for meriting something all over again.

(321) "For among us too, when someone receives from a friend a repayment for friendship and loves him all the more because of it, he's not judged to merit a reward from him again because of the greater love that comes from the prize given—so that the merits are thus stretched out to infinity. For by a kind of* force of necessity, love is increased by the payment of a prize, so that it seems not so much voluntary as necessary. Thus surely there's an emotion naturally implanted in all people, so that the very payment of a prize brings with it a kind of increase in love, and sets us on fire with love for him by a kind of necessity or self-love rather than by virtue or love for the payer.

(322) "Therefore, if among people a friend gets a reward from his friend, and is compelled to love him more by that very reward, yet isn't said to merit all over again from this growth in love, what is there surprising if, in the other life too, we who love God more for the reward received don't in any way turn the reward itself into a merit again?

(323) "Or what in the end prevents it from being granted that the divine majesty's glory is so great that there can always be some advance of ours in seeing it, with the result that the longer we gaze on it and the more it makes itself known to us, the more blessed it makes us? Surely this continual increase

of blessedness is worth more than a lesser blessedness that stays at one level only and doesn't advance by any increment."

(324) THE PHILOSOPHER: "How, I ask you, can there be any advance in seeing God, or any difference among those who see him, since the ultimate good is altogether simple? Nothing but the whole of it can ever be gazed on; neither can something in it be gazed on by one person that isn't gazed on by another."

(325) THE CHRISTIAN: "Surely the diversity isn't in the thing gazed on, but in the *way* of gazing on it, so that our blessedness in seeing him is increased the better God is understood. For in understanding a soul or some spirit we don't all understand equally, even though such incorporeal natures aren't said to have parts in their essence's quantity. And when a body (or some part of one) is looked at by several people at once, it's nevertheless seen better by one person than by another and, in accordance with some nature of the body, is better known by this person than by that one, and is understood more completely. While the same thing is understood, nevertheless it's not understood equally.

(326) "So too, even though it's through understanding that all people see the divine essence, which is altogether indivisible, nevertheless they don't perceive his nature equally. Thus in accordance with their merits, God imparts a better and more complete knowledge of himself to this person than to that one, and shows himself more fully. It surely can happen that even though this person knows all the things that one does, yet this one knows individual details better and more completely than that one does, and even though as *many* things are known by this person as by that one, nevertheless the one doesn't have as much knowledge about the same things as the other one does, or doesn't know the same things as well."

(327) THE PHILOSOPHER: "Did the angels that you call 'fallen' ever have the vision of God that true blessedness consists of, or did the main one, at least, who in comparison with the rest is compared to a 'Light-Bearer'?"[64]

(328) THE CHRISTIAN: "Certainly he shouldn't by any means be believed to have had it! And none of those who failed did either. Even those who didn't fail didn't receive that vision in repayment for their humility until after the others' fall, the vision whereby they were made both blessed and confirmed at once, so they wouldn't be able to fall any more.

(329) "Indeed all the angels, like human beings, were created such that they were able to act both well and badly. Otherwise those who didn't sin would've had no merit from the fact that they didn't accede to the others in sinning.

64. See n. 63 above.

(330) "Now the fact that Lucifer was endowed with the privilege of a kind of excellence came about not so much because of his blessedness as because of the acuteness of his knowledge, insofar as he was made superior to the rest with respect to the light of knowledge, and made more subtle in understanding all the natures of things. Reflecting on this within himself, he swelled up, inflated with the very extent of his knowledge whereby he saw himself set above the others. He ventured greater things than he would've been able to hope for, so that because he knew himself to be set above others, he thought he could become equal to God and* would acquire a kingdom all by himself, just like God. Thus, the higher he raised himself up through pride, the worse he failed through his fault."

(331) THE PHILOSOPHER: "Please settle this too: Should this ultimate human good—I mean that ultimate love of God a person takes on from the vision of God—be called an accident of a human being? Is it appropriate for an accident to be called a substance's ultimate good, as if it should be preferred to the underlying substance?"

(332) THE CHRISTIAN: "When you distinguish accidents and their underlying substances, you're resorting to the vocabulary of philosophical teaching and measuring things belonging only to the earthly life, not the heavenly one. Indeed, this secular and earthly discipline was content only with lessons adapted to the present life's state, not to the future life's quality, where neither this vocabulary nor any human teaching is needed. People applied their arts' rules when they investigated the natures of things, but, as is written, 'He who is of the earth speaks about the earth.' Therefore, if you endeavor to scale the heavenly life's summit that goes far beyond every earthly discipline, don't rely too much on earthly philosophy's rules. Earthly things still haven't been able to be fully comprehended and defined by them, much less heavenly ones.

(333) "Now there's no use in deciding whether the love that's said to be had in the heavenly life is an accident or some kind of quality. It can't be truly known except by experiencing it, since it goes far beyond all sense of earthly knowledge. But what does it matter to blessedness whether we maintain it's an accident or a substance, or neither one? For whatever we say or decide, it isn't changed for that reason, and doesn't diminish our blessedness.

(334) "If you pay careful attention to what your philosophers have said about accidental and substantial forms, you will see it isn't substantial for us human beings, since it isn't present in all of us. It isn't accidental either; for after it is present, it cannot be absent. Thus even your own view describes an accident as what can be present and absent.[65]

---

65. Compare Porphyry's definition of an accident in his *Isagoge*, pp. 12.25–13.8, translated in Spade, *Five Texts on the Mediaeval Problem of Universals*, p. 11, §§ (57)–(58).

(335) "Also, what is there to prevent us if we grant that the future love there, like the present kind we have here, is an accident?[66] For even though our substance is regarded as better or more worthy than any accident of it, nevertheless it doesn't seem incongruous that what renders a person best and most worthy through participation in it, should be called the ultimate human good. To speak more truly and with greater likelihood, let's settle it that God himself, who alone is properly and absolutely called the ultimate good, is also the ultimate human good. That is, we're made truly blessed by the participation we enjoy in the vision of it that we've spoken of [(316)–(317)].

(336) "Indeed, his ultimate love flows to us from him whom we see in himself. So he who isn't from another and makes us so blessed is more rightly to be called the ultimate human good."

(337) THE PHILOSOPHER: "This view about the ultimate good is certainly all right. It's not unknown to our own philosophy. But if this vision of God, as you call it, that makes us blessed is evident only to the mind's eyes, not the body's, what need is there for holy souls, as you call them, to take up their bodies again in the end—as though their blessedness or glory is thereby going to be increased? For since as you say, 'the human measure that is also an angel's,' how is taking up bodies again good for your blessedness? Although they're absent in angels, nevertheless they don't obstruct or diminish their blessedness."[67]

(338) THE CHRISTIAN: "All* the things God does he turns not so much to our blessedness as to his own glory. For example, things that are injurious to some people. Thus Solomon says, 'God created all things for himself, even the impious for an evil day.' Indeed, even the impious person's penalty whereby God punishes his iniquity commends God's justice and thereby glorifies him. So even though we would maintain that the recovery of bodies confers no blessedness on holy souls, nevertheless we don't regard it as superfluous. It's of great value to the praise of divine power. For the more we recognize bodies in advance as weaker and liable to suffering, the more they will show afterwards that God is to be glorified, when we'll see them become so strengthened and indissoluble that no suffering is able to come to us from them, no dissolution to occur in them. Souls also do seem to get some blessedness from this. For the

---

66. The sentence is puzzling since it would seem that what prevents us is the very notion of an accident, as just described in (334). Perhaps the Christian means: "Even if we set that point aside, why should the argument in (331), that this would make an accident preferable to a substance, prevent us?" But although the latter argument seems to be referred to at the beginning of the next sentence, it is never directly answered.

67. Rather, the *absence* of bodies doesn't obstruct or diminish, etc.

more they'll experience the divine power's greatness, the more they'll unde-
niably love him and be blessed."

(339) THE PHILOSOPHER: "Please explain too whether the vision of God that
blessedness consists of can be increased or diminished by some difference of
place, or whether it* can be displayed to all in all places equally, or if some fixed
place is allocated to it, one that all who are to enjoy the vision must reach."

(340) THE CHRISTIAN: "Those who don't doubt God is everywhere
through his power's greatness, but believe all places are present to him in such
a way that in all of them he can do whatever he wants, and in such a way that
the places themselves and all things in them are either brought forth or
arranged by his doing, aren't going to be bothered at all by this question. In
fact he's the one who, remaining without location now just as he did before
time, shouldn't be said so much to be *in* a place (he's in no way 'local') as to
enclose inside himself all places, containing even the very heavens, as is
written, 'in his palm.'

(341) "For he who existed without a place before all things, afterwards
constructed places not for himself but for us. His blessedness cannot be either
diminished or increased, or take on any variation. Surely he has no location
now, just as he didn't before. His eternity persists altogether simple and
incorporeal. Therefore, he is nowhere locally (that is, enclosed by a location)
and yet everywhere (that is, he's said to be both *in* all places and *around* all
places through the power of his operating). For all places are present to him, or
he to them, in such a way that whatever he wants has to come about there. So
he is said to be 'everywhere,' as was said, through his power's greatness.

(342) "Thus he himself speaks through the prophet: 'I will fill heaven and
earth.' And the Psalmist, reflecting that he could nowhere flee his power when
he was enraged, said: 'Where will I go, away from your spirit? Where will I flee
from your face? If I climb up to heaven, you are there. If I go down to hell, you
are present,' etc.

(343) "Now just as he's said to be *in* all places or *inside* them all through his
power's operating—or directing, since all things must be directed through
him there—so too, enclosing those very places, he's nevertheless asserted to
be *around* them, to have them so in his power that nothing can happen in them
without him or without his arranging. And so since God is both inside and
outside all things and penetrates all things by his own power, no matter how
solid they are, as was said [(341)], what place can prevent his being able to
impart a knowledge of himself to all people equally, wherever he wants?
Indeed, in the same way that* he's said to inhere or be present 'in' all places
through his power, not through location, he everywhere has the ability to
impart a knowledge of himself to whomever he wishes.

(344) "That ultimate spiritual power, which has access to all existing places, can't be impeded by any solidity or quality. Surely the sun's brightness penetrates the thickest glass in such a way that it pours its illumination through it onto us. And after the resurrection our bodies will be of such subtlety, we believe, that already somehow made spiritual, no matter can obstruct them. Thus too the Lord's body, which while still mortal was born from a closed womb, went in to the disciples after the resurrection 'with the doors closed,' now completely immortal and impassable. Therefore, it's much more to be believed that the ultimate vision of divine brightness can't be impeded by any obstacle or helped to illuminate[68] by nearness in place. Even fire, which you say is subtler than the other elements, doesn't admit of being cut up, because its parts can't be divided by any interposed body. A spiritual substance, however, which is far subtler than any body, is impeded much less by a bodily obstacle.[69]

(345) "Now since divinity is of such subtlety that any other natures are regarded as corporeal in comparison with it, and it alone is judged incorporeal with respect to the others, how could its ultimate brightness, which considers all things in its knowing, have an obstacle? Those who enjoy it aren't ignorant of whatever it's appropriate for them to know, no matter how far removed it is, since they see the one who sees all things. Otherwise, those who enjoy paradise wouldn't gaze on hell's torments so that they love God more, the more they see they've escaped more grievous things through his grace.

(346) "Indeed, the Lord Jesus plainly implies that this paradise everywhere consists in the very vision of God, when, on the day his soul, having suffered in the flesh, descended into hell to set his own people free from there, he said to the thief who acknowledged him, 'Amen I say to you, today you will be with me in paradise.' In fact, as was said, Christ's soul didn't come out of that paradise even when he descended into hell.

(347) "And so according to our faith and plain reason, whatever place the faithful soul is in, it finds God because he's present everywhere, as was said. Since it's impeded by no obstacle, it persists everywhere equally in its blessedness, which we obtain from the vision of God infused in us by him, not from our own powers. Certainly we don't climb up to apprehend

---

68. Although "ultimate vision" is the grammatical subject, Abelard seems to be treating "divine brightness" as the subject of "illuminate."

69. This puzzling analogy requires that a body can be "cut up" only if it is "impeded" by what cuts it. It cannot pass through the impediment, and so separates to go around it on either side.

the corporeal sun's brightness. Instead, it pours itself out on us, that we may enjoy it. So too we don't so much come close to God as he to us, as if he pours out on us his brightness and his love's warmth from above. If we're said somehow to draw near even to him who isn't anywhere locally, this must be understood as happening with respect not to places but to merits. For instance,* we're made more like him in good or agree more fully with his will. So too we should be understood to withdraw from him the other way around. The venerable teacher Augustine, who was also most expert in your teachings, explained this carefully. He said 'We are near to or far from God, not in places but in morals.'

(348) "Thus although saints' bodies will be of such facility after the resurrection that they're believed to be immediately wherever their souls want, nevertheless no moving away on their part will impede the vision of God so that their souls are less blessed. No quality belonging to any given place will be able to penalize those in whom there is nothing to be punished, just as nothing could be harmful to the first human beings before sin.

(349) "Thus too, when the holy angels sent to us execute his orders, they aren't in any way deprived or emptied of the vision of him whereby they're blessed because of any quality belonging to a place or because of the distance. And even though the demons that linger in the air, and are therefore called 'heaven's flyers,' are seen to be superior to us in their place's position, nevertheless they shouldn't for that reason be said to draw closer than we do to God, who's superior to all natures because of his own nature's worthiness.

(350) "Thus Satan, who came among God's sons and stood in the Lord's view, speaking in conversation with him as is written in the book of Job, isn't released from his misery by his approach so that he becomes more blessed. Higher than the rest, in falling even from heaven he shows plainly that worthiness of place adds nothing to blessedness. For it's not because he comes among God's sons (that is, among the holy angels) and puts himself in God's view that the Lord comes into his view, so that the Lord is viewed by him when he's viewed by the Lord. He is a blind man putting himself among seers, so to speak, set apart from them not by location but by the light's benefit. For what the bodies' quality does in the case of seeing the corporeal sun, the merits' quality does in the case of seeing the spiritual sun. And just as no difference of virtues consists in the quality of bodies or places here, so neither does a difference of repayments there. The divine glory's vision whereby the holy angels become blessed appears all the more marvelous the less it can be impeded or helped in this by any quality or difference of place. Even with those who *aren't* disconnected by place, he acts so that he makes some blessed by

illuminating them, and others he abandons, miserable in their blindness, just as in this life too he doesn't stop acting through imparting his grace.[70]

(351) "In fact God is said to be everywhere through his power, as was said [(341)], in such a way that nevertheless through his grace he's said to be present somewhere and absent somewhere else. Therefore, no matter how divinity's grace is said to be present or absent, or to arrive or withdraw, it doesn't happen locally or corporeally. Instead it comes about spiritually or through some efficacy of its operation. For if it were everywhere locally, where could it arrive locally or where could it withdraw from?

(352) "Yet sometimes he's said to 'descend' to us, either through some benefit bestowed on us from his grace or through some display in a visible sign, or when he does something unusual on earth—as the sun is said to 'descend' to us or to fill up the very world, not locally but effectually, that is, not by its location but by the working of illumination."

(353) THE PHILOSOPHER: "I'm surprised you bring these authorities from your Scriptures to the reasonings whereby you try to argue against me. You don't doubt that I'm not compelled by them in the slightest."

(354) THE CHRISTIAN: "It was proposed to me, as you know, not that I present you with my own views, but that I explain to you our forebears' common faith or teaching.[71] Therefore I produce these witnesses from our own people, not that I mean for you to be compelled thereby, but so you may understand that they come from others rather than my having fabricated them myself."

(355) THE PHILOSOPHER: "Certainly I don't object to it, if your intention ran like that. But let's now hurry along to the remaining items. Therefore, if the divine vision's power is so great, as you assert, that wherever souls are, it can make them equally blessed by participation in it, then why, I ask, is the kingdom of heaven assigned especially to God and holy souls, so that they're said to be mainly in heaven, as though they were more blessed there? Even your own Christ showed this by his own example so much that he ascended bodily into the heavens in the sight of his people. There he remains sitting at the Father's right hand, as is written, and from there, it's promised, he'll come for the judgment of those who run up against him in the air.

(356) "Why then is no region of the world but heaven assigned for the divine dwelling place, if God, existing everywhere as you say [(341)], enjoys his own

70. Despite the "just as," the last clause does not seem to express anything altogether parallel to what precedes it.

71. In fact, this has *not* been proposed to the Christian in so many words. But see (146)–(147), (177), (312).

blessedness equally, and his vision's brightness pours itself out alike, insofar as it wants, on whomever it wants wherever it wants, and makes them everywhere equally blessed? It needs no assistance for this, no quality of place or nearness, but is enough all by itself. Since the Lord, existing everywhere through his power and enclosing his majesty's lodging so to speak in one place, says 'The heaven is my seat,' and since all the writers of both the New and the Old Testament assign no other part of the world but heaven for his dwelling place, it can seem not undeservedly that this higher place's calm confers something of blessedness on them or on us.

(357) "Thus too it's promised through Isaiah that for this blessedness's fullness, the moon's light will be like the sun's light, and the sun's light will be seven times as bright then, and there'll be a new creation both of heaven and of earth, so that our happiness too may be increased by this renewing of things."

(358) THE CHRISTIAN: "If you'd learned how to 'prophetize'[72] rather than 'judaize'[73] over the text of Scripture, and knew that things said of God under a corporeal aspect are understood not literally in the corporeal sense, but mystically through allegory, you wouldn't take things that are said as the vulgar take them. Certainly if you follow the common view of it, your understanding of it won't go beyond the faith of people who conceive with their mind nothing but the corporeal, or after the fashion of a corporeal thing. You'll doubtless be lost in such a great error that you won't be able to understand God at all except as a kind of corporeal thing consisting of certain parts, composed of a head, hands and feet, or of other members, especially since almost all the human body's parts are assigned to him in the Scriptures according to some likeness. For what illiterate or simple person will put up with hearing you if you preach that God doesn't have eyes or ears or the other members that seem necessary to us? In fact, he'll object at once that someone who doesn't have eyes like that can't see at all, and likewise one who lacks ears and hands can't hear or work.

(359) "Therefore, just as you judge that all these things belonging to the body are to be understood in the case of God only in the manner of a parable, don't doubt that whatever things are said about divinity with respect to corporeal location are to be taken that way too. So when you hear Isaiah say:

> The Lord says, 'The heaven is my seat, and the earth the footstool for my feet. What is this house you will build for me? And what is this place of my rest? My hand made all these things,' etc.,

72. That is, to read in a prophetic or allegorical manner.
73. That is, to read in the literal sense, as Abelard thinks the Jews did.

just as you don't understand him to be corporeal in the least, so don't understand heaven as his corporeal seat, the earth as the corporeal footstool for his feet, or any location for him where he's regarded as sitting, any more than you would when his angels are called a 'throne.' For far be it from his majesty to have some weakness, so that he needs to be propped up by some seat or footstool!

(360) "Therefore good and evil souls are distinguished in this passage by the names 'heaven' and 'earth,' as if higher and lower on the basis of their merits. So good souls are said to be like his temple or heaven—according to the Psalmist, 'The Lord in his holy temple; the Lord, in heaven is his seat'—insofar as he sits before those who are loftier in merits, and inhabits them through grace as though in his own house, in a temple sanctified to him.

(361) "He crushes carnal souls—those that gawk at earthly and base desires—like a footstool for his feet. For he doesn't mercifully raise up to himself those he looks down on. He presses down derelicts, as it were, grinds them by crushing, and so to speak reduces them to a loose powder.

(362) "Therefore the Lord, who doesn't inhabit things made by his hand, is saying that since I inhabit such an exalted seat in holy souls and hold carnal and earthly men in such disdain, why do you seek to construct for me an earthly building as a house, as though it were needed, and don't instead build me a spiritual house within yourselves? Otherwise the visible temple's signification is canceled out if the invisible one is absent.

(363) "And so when you hear the future blessedness called 'heaven,' or 'the kingdom of heaven,' understand the future life's sublimeness rather than heaven's corporeal position. Plainly it's sometimes also indicated by the name 'land' on account of its stability, as by the name 'heaven' on account of its worthiness. Thus the Psalmist says, 'I believe I shall see the Lord's goods in the land of the living.' And the Lord himself, promising his elect future blessedness after the resurrection, says through Ezekiel: 'Behold, I will open your burial mounds and lead you out of your graves, my people, and lead you into the land of Israel. And I will bring it about that you rest on your own ground.'

(364) "Now the fact that our Lord Christ ascended bodily and visibly into the corporeal heavens [(355)] didn't benefit the glory of him whom divinity's fullness inhabits bodily, but rather benefits our faith. Therefore, he who by going in to the disciples 'with the doors closed' had earlier shown through his own resurrection the subtleness of the bodies that will be restored, whereby they'll be able to penetrate all things, afterwards displayed in his ascension their future lightness, so great that they'll no longer be impeded from ascending anywhere by any mass of earthliness whereby they were previously

weighted down. As it is written, 'The body that is corrupted adds weight to the soul.' Instead, they will be transported* immediately, without any difficulty, wherever their souls want.

(365) "Now with respect to his being mentioned as having ascended to the Father's right hand, just as the Father's right hand isn't understood as corporeal, so this sitting whereby the Father sits isn't a local position. Instead, his power and equal worthiness of governing together with the Father is expressed thereby, when he's said to have sat together with him by his side on the right. Since indeed this sitting at the right hand can't hold literally in a corporeal sense, what was said above [(355)] about his bodily ascension, even though in reality it happened bodily that way, nevertheless indicates a kind of 'better' ascent on his part in the minds of the faithful. He himself had already spoken of this ascent to Mary earlier: 'Do not touch me. For I have not yet ascended to my Father.' For Christ was taken up from men's eyes to heaven as in a cloud, to remain sitting at the Father's right hand, when in the saints' preaching Christ, having been carried off from the view of the present and wearisome life, is preached as having been raised to glory in such a way that in ruling together with the Father he would command the whole universe and equally govern all things as coequal substance or Son.

(366) "What you suggested [(357)] about multiplying the brilliance of the moon or sun (as if it had anything to do with future blessedness for that to happen corporeally) is easily refuted both on the basis of the very prophet's authority who said it and on the basis of plain reason. In fact afterwards the Lord, speaking to Jerusalem through the same Isaiah and promising it the future life's brightness, says:

> The sun will no longer be for shining on you by day. Neither will the moon's brilliance illuminate you. Instead the Lord will be as an everlasting light, and your God as your glory. Your sun will not set any more and your moon will not wane for you. But the Lord will be as an everlasting light for you, and the days of your distress will be completed. Now your people will all be just; they will inherit the land in perpetuity, etc.

(367) "What except the eternity of future blessedness is this land that's going to be inherited by those who are perpetually just and is going to be illuminated by the divine brightness's presence as by a sun that never sets? Since this brightness is so great that it needs no help in illuminating, surely the sun is rightly said to give up the job of illuminating any more—that is, after our having been made no longer animal but spiritual, we will experience what was said above [(337)]: 'the human measure that is also an angel's.'

(368) "Finally, who doesn't know that lesser lamps set beside greater lamps are at once darkened by the stronger light, or lose the force of their illuminating? Therefore what job of illuminating can a corporeal light have where the divine brightness's presence will so illuminate darkness's secrets that it discloses even the very plans in people's hearts?

(369) " 'We see now through a mirror and in obscurity,' the Apostle says, 'but then face to face. Now I know in part, but then I will know even as I am known.' In fact, all things will be then perfectly, then most truly known by us as by the angels, through the heart's eyes. All sensory and all administrative functions will cease there, when God will be 'all in all.' Indeed the vision of him will so satisfy all our desires in all respects that it will bestow on us by itself all the things needed for true blessedness. The vision of divine majesty itself will be for us unfailing light, ultimate holiness, perpetual repose, peace exceeding every sense, and finally every good, every virtue, every joy.

(370) "Therefore when God will thus be all in all, it's plain that then, as the same Apostle says, every 'principality and power' will be made void, since the only power that will rule through itself then is the one that will furnish all goods to all the elect through the vision of its presence, as was just said. No angelic or human principality will have charge over us any longer in any administration, no power in any government. For nothing will be able to be lacking where God will be all in all, where since what's complete will be present, what's merely partial will be made void. Nothing in fact helps us now except partially, nothing is enough to bestow on us all the things needed. Whatever helps us now toward a teaching, toward some virtue or toward some administering, acts imperfectly. For it's God alone who can do all things. And so whatever things act imperfectly will cease, since he who can do all things will be enough by himself. So the fact that we will there take up again the eyes of the flesh, along with the rest of the body's members, will certainly not come about because of jobs of theirs we need done, but rather for glorifying God, as we've said before [(338)]. That is, we'll experience his power in them all the more, to the extent that we'll sense them to be more capable of doing their jobs if need be, and to the extent that we'll see they have reached a far stronger and better state.

(371) "Even if we take the remark about multiplying the sun's and moon's light [(357)] in a corporeal sense and not just mystically, this is to be referred more to the maker's glory than to a need for their function. So is the fact that the whole state of the world is going to be changed into a better one. With the help* also of the heavenly lamps or the change in the world, God will make plainly known to us that their having less beforehand didn't arise from the maker's inability but because of the necessity of their mortal and weak life, which could in no way bear such great things or even be worthy to use such great favors.

(372) "Yet it's easy to understand mystically the moon's shining then like the sun. That is, the elects' church, like God its sun, has an unfailing light. And yet he, its sun, also then surpasses the moon's light with the result that light's perfection, which is indicated by the sevenfold number, is in him alone."

(373) THE PHILOSOPHER: "As far as I see it, if these things are as you say, then God whose glory you preach above all in everything seems to owe many things to your faith. But now it remains for you also to explain carefully what one's view of hell should be. For just as the ultimate human good will be more striven for the more it's known, so conversely the ultimate evil will be more avoided the less it's unknown."

(374) THE CHRISTIAN: "In fact for a long time now there's been a difference of opinion on this topic, among us as among you. Some people think hell is a kind of corporeal place underground that's called 'hell' because of its location, which is lower than the other parts of the world.[74] Others think hell isn't a corporeal torment so much as a spiritual one. Thus just as we distinguish souls' ultimate blessedness by the name 'heaven,'[75] which is the world's higher part, so too their ultimate misery by the name 'hell,' which is said to lie lower the farther away it's recognized to be from that ultimate blessedness, and the more contrary it's seen to be to it. For just as what's better is called 'high' on account of the excellence of its worth, so conversely what's worse is called 'lowest' on account of its being debased.

(375) "Certainly both the Old and the New Testament narrate many things about hell's pains that it seems can't be taken literally at all. For what's literal in what the Lord says through Isaiah about the just and the impious: 'And they will go out and will see the corpses of those who have transgressed against me. Their worms will not die, and their fire will not go out'? What is this corporeal 'going out' by the saints to see the pains of the impious? What are the corporeal worms in reprobates' bodies that are going to be resurrected whole in all their members just as saints' bodies are? What worms' gnawing will there be, where there will be the immortality of all bodies alike without fail?

(376) "How can what the Lord relates in the Gospel about the rich person and Lazarus, who are dead, be taken literally? For surely the rich man's soul cannot have a corporeal grave in hell. Or what is Abraham's corporeal bosom where Lazarus's soul is said to be carried off by angels? What tongue does the rich man's soul have there, or what finger does Lazarus's soul have? Or what is

---

74. There is some Latin wordplay here. "Hell" (*infernus*) is so called because it is "lower" (*inferior*). The point cannot be easily conveyed in English.

75. The word has both the astronomical and the theological sense in Latin.

the corporeal water there, a drop of which poured on the burning tongue can put out or lessen its fire? Thus, since these things can't happen literally with souls already sweated out of the flesh, neither can what's said elsewhere: 'Bind his hands and feet. Send him into the shadows outside. There will be weeping and gnashing of teeth there.'

(377) "It seems to be implied by both the Old and the New Testament that the things said about hell should be taken mystically rather than corporeally. Thus for example just as Abraham's bosom, where Lazarus's soul is taken, is to be understood as spiritual and not corporeal, so too hell is the spiritual torture where it is recounted that the rich person's soul is buried.

(378) "For as long as souls lack bodies, where can they be carried or moved locally, or forced as if being surrounded by the body? They aren't localized at all, and by their own nature are far subtler than any body. Or what corporeal force of the elements is there, either of fire or the other elements, that can touch or torture souls without bodies? All this can't easily be described or understood.

(379) "Thus even demons after the fall are said to have been spun off into certain airy bodies they took on as a prison, so to speak, so that they can suffer corporeally too. For this reason they were called 'airy powers,'[76] since they can do a great many things in the element they're embodied in, just as people who rule on earth are called 'earthly powers.'

(380) "But if on the other hand the prophet is said to have understood the souls' worms as a kind of inner gnawing in them whereby they're already tortured in their conscience because of despair for forgiveness and the increase in future pain, and as the fire whereby they'll later on be tortured in their restored bodies, then it's easy for both the spiritual and corporeal torment of the damned to be defined as hell by comparing other penalties, whether they're said to be carried out underground or somewhere else, with these that are thus called 'lowest' or 'extreme.'

(381) "For since it's agreed that earth is founded on the waters, how will it be said there's any corporeal fire under the earth, unless perhaps 'under the earth' is understood as whatever depth of the earth is below the earth's surface we live on? But again, since the number of reprobates is infinite, and according to Truth's assertion the number of the elect will be small, perhaps it won't easily be accepted that there's anywhere so large a hollow of the earth that can hold so many bodies.

(382) "Thus if it seems to someone that divine judgment's power is great enough to be able to punish equally in all the places it wants to, and that the

---

76. The phrase has not occurred previously in the *Dialogue*. But compare (349) above.

qualities of places are irrelevant to the penalty or to the glory, then I have no doubt that this view will find assent more easily the more it seems to commend divine power and to come closer to reason. For let's follow the general view of almost all people, who say that some who are put in the same fire are tortured more, some less, in accordance with their merits, not in accordance with the amount of fire. I don't see how so great an adjustment in the *same* fire's pain can come about through divine power, and that power not be more able to afflict people with different torments who're put in *different* places—or even to rack them all, no matter where they are, with any pains he wants and to turn all the elements against them into whatever pains. As it's written, 'The earth's globe will fight for God against the irrational.'

(383) "For by their[77] reckoning the common faith asserts that the bodies of the blessed will stay in the ethereal heaven without any damage, where the fire burns and shines more purely the more acute and intense it is, and this is bestowed on them after the resurrection for their glory. Our weakness couldn't withstand that earlier. So indeed does light restore healthy eyes and aggravate weak ones.

(384) "Also, who doesn't daily experience animals' natures so different that what preserves* the life* of some snuffs out others', and according to the different structure of bodies, what helps one thing hinders another for both animate and inanimate things? Human beings die under water, fish in the air. Salamanders are known to live in fire, which brings a quick destruction to other animals. Venom is the snake's life, a human being's death. The same things provide a needed diet for some animals, but a deadly one for others. There's nothing whatever that can be adapted to all natures. People who come from the same womb, begotten together by the same father, don't live by the same customs at all. They aren't amused or offended alike by the same things, and aren't tormented alike when they're together in the same heat or cold. This difference in their sufferings certainly doesn't come from the quality of the things that do the punishing, but from that of the punished.

(385) "And so why should it be surprising if divine justice's power adjusted the restored bodies for pain according to each person's merits, whether in the same place or different ones, so that all things might be everywhere equally painful to them?[78] He who admitted he could not escape God's vengeance certainly had this in mind when he said, 'Where will I go, away from your

77. The "almost all people" from (382).

78. The idea isn't that all things *are* equally painful everywhere, since Abelard has just been saying that the bodies are punished in accordance with their merits. Rather the point is that how painful something is doesn't depend on *where* it is.

spirit? Where will I flee from your face? If I climb up to heaven, you are there. If I go down to hell, you are present.'

(386) "Finally, who thinks evil people's souls are tortured more in hell than are those spiritual wickednesses that stay in the air and carry their torments around with them everywhere? By all means, they are certainly worthy of a greater torment insofar as they're no doubt more wicked. In the same way, who denies that impious people's souls, taken up again in the bodies, carry their torments with them whatever place they move to, even if no outward torment is inflicted? We certainly see that many sufferings are either inflicted from without on a soul that still remains in the body or else are born within from some disturbance or disequilibrium of the body. Once had, they can't be taken away by any change of place. For to say nothing of other sufferings, how does where you put someone who's now dying, or laboring under the greatest suffering, help cure the pain if that suffering isn't going to be softened because of the place?

(387) "Or since when we're dying, death's suffering is so great in the body that the soul is forced to abandon it for that reason, as blessed Augustine remarks, who doesn't think the suffering by which we're broken apart[79] here in dying is enough for damnation (if it's perpetual there) without any external torture added on, even if there can perhaps *be* some other greater suffering?[80] For what's more fitting to justice than that souls should take up again their own bodies in particular for torment, which they used badly for pleasure?

(388) "Now the suffering in the break-up that is death is certainly so great that no matter how briefly it be imposed, it's nevertheless believed to be enough to purge any sin not worthy of eternal damnation. Thus as blessed Jerome asserts, this is the Prophet's view: 'The Lord will not judge twice on this, and a double distress will not arise.'

(389) "We read too that some damned souls of dead people were unwilling to be returned to the present life in order to be saved by doing good, if they would be forced to end it again when death intervenes. We've also found it written elsewhere that certain souls of dying saints utterly shrank from going out to the blessedness made ready for them, out of fear of pain at the time of their break-up, until the Lord had bid them be taken up by angels without any painfulness.

(390) "It's plain from this how great is this death's suffering, from fear of which one person was unwilling to return for salvation and another was afraid

79. broken apart: The reference, here and in the following paragraphs, is to the soul's being separated from the body at death.

80. That is, even if it is possible that some other suffering be greater, this one is bad enough to count as eternal damnation all by itself, provided only that it be everlasting.

to go out to blessedness, as we said. Nevertheless, it obviously belongs to divine power to take this suffering away altogether from whomever it wants, as the teacher cited above claims, saying that John the apostle was a stranger both to death's painfulness and to the flesh's corruption.

(391) "Therefore he who in death is able to take away completely the ultimate suffering of death, everywhere and for whomever he wants, seems able to apply it much more easily wherever he wants.[81] Certainly a nature capable of suffering is more disposed to incur pain than to lack it.

(392) "From all these things, I now think it's clear that the place's quality is irrelevant to the penalty of the damned and to the glory of the blessed. Rather, being tortured in hell or handed over to perpetual fire is to be racked with the ultimate pains. They are especially compared to fire because torture by this element seems more piercing. Also, it seems to commend the divine power's glory most if he who is no doubt everywhere present* through his power dispenses damnation's penalty and blessedness's glory in all places equally."

(393) THE PHILOSOPHER: "I see you're eager to turn the damned's penalty and the elect's glory equally to the praise of the divine power, in order to proclaim his great goods even in ultimate evils."

(394) THE CHRISTIAN: "And that's certainly fitting. For there're no deeds of his but noble ones, full of amazement. But I think it's superfluous to define the places these things occur in, so long as we can get or avoid them."

(395) THE PHILOSOPHER: "Of course, there's still a discussion to be had after this. Now that in accordance with our plan [(296)] you've described both our ultimate good and our ultimate evil, as they appeared to you, explain no less carefully the roads by which they're reached, so that the more we know them the better we can hold to the former or avoid the latter. But because it seems that what the ultimate good or the ultimate evil is can't be understood well enough yet, I want it first to be determined what should be called good or evil in general; I want you to define that, if you can. Of course, we know many *kinds* of these things, but nevertheless we aren't able to understand or examine well enough *in what respect* things are called good or evil. Indeed, our authors who call some things good, others evil, and others indifferent, didn't distinguish these by any definitions, but were content to illustrate them with certain examples."

(396) THE CHRISTIAN: "I realize how hard they thought it was for things to be defined the names for which seem hardly ever to consist of a single signification. Indeed, when 'good person,' 'good blacksmith,' 'good horse' and

81. This sentence finally expresses the point of the observations in (387)–(390).

the like are said, who doesn't know that the name[82] 'good' borrows different senses from the words joined to it. For we call a person good because of his morals, a blacksmith because of his knowledge, a horse because of its strength and speed or whatever things are relevant to its use. On the other hand, the signification of 'good' is varied so much by what is joined to it that we aren't afraid of attaching it even to the names of vices. We say, for example, 'a good thief' or 'the best thief,' insofar as he's adroit and cunning in performing this maliciousness. Sometimes we apply the expression 'good' not only to the things themselves, but also to things said *about* those things—that is, to the *dicta* of propositions[83]—so that we even say 'It's good for evil to be,' even though we in no way grant evil is good. Indeed, it's one thing to say 'Evil is good,' which is completely false, and another to say 'It's good for evil to be,' which is not to be denied.

(397) "And so what's surprising if, like them, we aren't able to define the signification of these words, which is so unfixed? Nevertheless as it strikes me now, I think that is called 'good' simply—that is, a 'good thing'—which, while it's fit for some use, mustn't impede the advantage or worthiness of anything. Contrariwise, I believe a thing is called 'evil' that necessarily carries one of these features with it. The 'indifferent,' on the other hand—that is, a thing that's neither good nor evil—I think is one such that necessarily no good is delayed or impeded by its existence. For example, the casual movement of a finger or any actions like that. For actions aren't judged good or evil except according to their root, the intention. Rather, by themselves they're all indifferent. If we look into it carefully, things not good or evil by themselves contribute nothing to merit, since they're equally appropriate both to reprobates and to the elect."

(398) THE PHILOSOPHER: "I think we should stop here and linger awhile, to consider if perhaps the things you've said can serve as definitions."

(399) THE CHRISTIAN: "It's extremely difficult to circumscribe* all things with their own definitions, so that they can be separated from all other things—especially now, since we don't have time enough for thinking through the definitions. With most names, we've come to know which things they go together with from their use in speech, although we're unable to determine

---

82. See n. 58 above.

83. The *dictum* of a proposition is the expression formed from that proposition by putting the subject in the accusative case and the main verb in the infinitive mood. Latin routinely uses such constructions in indirect discourse. In English, where only certain pronouns show a distinction between nominative and accusative forms, we can still see this construction in "He maketh *me to lie down* in green pastures" (Ps. 23:2).

what the correct meaning or understanding of them is. We also find many things for which we can't outline the correct nomenclature or meaning in a definition. For even if we aren't ignorant of the things' natures, nevertheless expressions for them are not in use. And often the mind is quicker to understand than the tongue is to utter or discuss what we perceive. Look, from the daily use of the word we all know which things are called stones. Yet I believe we're still unable to determine what the proper differences[84] of 'stone' are, or what the characteristic of this species is, in any expression whereby a definition or description of 'stone' can be achieved. It shouldn't seem surprising to you either if you see me fail in matters on which we know that those great teachers of yours, whom you boast of as philosophers, weren't adequate. Yet I'll try to say what I can in reply to any objection raised by your investigations of these definitions I've offered."

(400) THE PHILOSOPHER: "What you're now saying too seems reasonable and likely enough. But really, unless things that are said are understood, they're uttered in vain. They can't teach others unless they can be discussed. Now, if you please—rather, because you've agreed to do so—I want you to clear up a little the things you've said. Why then didn't it seem enough, I say, for you to say 'what's fit for some use'—that is, suited for some usefulness— when you were defining a 'good thing'?"

(401) THE CHRISTIAN: "It's a common and likely proverb that there's scarcely any good that does no harm, or an evil that does no good. For instance here's someone who, a long time ago now, trained himself in good deeds so much that, being praised quite often for it, either he's lifted up to pride, confident of his virtues, or else someone else is thereby set on fire with envy. And so it's plain that evil thus comes out of good, and often good is even the *cause* of evil. Indeed, our vices or sins, which are what are properly to be called evils, are unable to exist except in souls—that is, in good creatures. Neither can corruption arise except from a good. Conversely, who doesn't see that often after great catastrophes of sins people arise stronger or better through humility or penitence than they were before?

(402) "Finally, it's plain that penitence for sins is an evil rather than a good because it's a mental affliction and, since it induces sorrow, cannot go together with perfect blessedness. Yet no one doubts it's necessary for forgiveness. Who also doesn't know that God's ultimate goodness, which permits nothing to happen without a cause, preordains even evils well, and even uses them for the

---

84. That is, "differences" in the sense in which a species is said to be defined by *genus + difference*. See Porphyry's *Isagoge*, translated in Spade, *Five Texts on the Mediaeval Problem of Universals*, pp. 7–10, §§ (39)–(55).

best, to such an extent that it's even good for evils to exist, although nevertheless evil isn't good at all? For just as the Devil's ultimate wickedness often uses
even goods for the worst in such a way that he turns them into causes of the
worst effects, and so he does the worst kinds of things through things that are
good, so God acts the other way around,* namely making many goods come
out of evils and often using for the best what the Devil strives to use for
the worst.

(403) "Both the tyrant and the prince, in fact, can use the same sword evilly
and well, the former for violence, the latter* for redress [(279)]. There aren't
any instruments or any things adapted for our uses, I believe, that we can't use
both evilly and well according to our intentions' quality. For this it isn't relevant
what is done, but rather *with what mind* it's done.[85]

(404) "Thus all men, both good ones and perverse, are the causes of both
good and evil things, and through them it comes about that both goods and
evils exist. For the good man doesn't seem to be at variance with the evil one
insofar as he does what's good, but rather in that he does it *well*. For even if
nowadays conversational usage holds that 'doing well' and 'doing good' are the
same, nevertheless perhaps the peculiar force of the phrase doesn't work like
that. For just as 'good' is often said where 'well' isn't—that is, 'with a good
intention'—so too it seems that good can be done although it isn't done well.
Indeed it often happens that the same thing is done by different people in such
a way that the one does it well and the other evilly, according to their intention.
For instance, if two people hang some criminal, the one solely because he hates
him but the other because he has to carry out this justice, this hanging is
accordingly done justly by the latter, because it was done with the right
intention, but unjustly by the former, because it was done not out of love of
justice but out of fervor for hatred or wrath.[86]

(405) "Sometimes too, evil men, or even the Devil himself, are said to work
together with God in doing the same deed, in such a way that the same thing is
asserted to be done both by God and by them. For look, we see the things Job
possessed taken away from him by Satan, and nevertheless Job himself
professes they are taken away from him by God. He says, 'The Lord has given,
the Lord has taken away.'

(406) "But let's move from that to what Christians' minds embrace more
dearly, even if it seems laughable to you and to those like you. The Lord Jesus
Christ's being handed over into the Jews' hands is mentioned as being done by
Jesus himself, by God the Father, and by the traitor Judas. For the Father is

85. Compare Abelard's *Ethics* (57).
86. Compare Abelard's *Ethics* (58).

said to have handed over the Son, and the Son to have handed over himself, and Judas the same man. Yet although in such doings either the Devil or Judas did the very same thing God did, nevertheless they shouldn't be said to have done *well*, even if perhaps they seem to have done something *good*.[87] Even if they did or wanted to be done what God wants to be done, or have the same will as God has in doing something, should they for that reason be said to do *well* because they do what God wants to be done? Or do they have a good will because they want what God wants? Of course not! For even if they do or want to be done what God wants to be done, nevertheless they don't do or want to do it because they believe God wants it to be done. Their intention isn't the same as God's in the same deed. And although they want what God wants, and God's will and theirs can be called the same because they want the same thing, nevertheless their will is evil and God's is good since they want it to be done for different causes. So too, although different people's action may be the same because they do the same thing, nevertheless according to the difference in intention this one's action is good and that one's evil. For although they accomplish the same result, nevertheless this one does the selfsame thing well, that one evilly.

(407) "And, it's surprising to say, sometimes there's even a good will when someone wants evil to be done by someone else, because he wants it with a good intention. For the Lord often decided to torment, through the Devil or through some tyrant, people who are either innocent or else didn't deserve that torment for purging some sin of theirs. They're tormented either to increase their merit or to give others an example of patience, or for whatever reasonable cause, even though it's hidden from us. Thus Job remarks on the fact that with the Lord permitting well, the Devil acted evilly. He says 'As it pleased the Lord, so it was done.' In giving him thanks, he shows he doesn't doubt how well this was permitted by the Lord, when he adds, 'Blessed be the name of the Lord.'

(408) "Also, the Third Book of Kings[88] teaches that the lying spirit had been sent by the Lord to deceive impious Ahab. For when the Lord said, 'Who will deceive Ahab?' the lying spirit came out and stood before the Lord and said, 'I will deceive him.' The Lord said to him, 'With what?' And he said, 'I will go out and be a lying spirit in the mouth of all his prophets.' And the Lord said, 'You will deceive and prevail over him. Go out and do so.' Indeed the

---

87. Compare Abelard's *Ethics* (57).

88. In the Latin Vulgate, the first and second books of Samuel are called 1 Kings and 2 Kings, with the result that what are otherwise counted as 1 Kings and 2 Kings become 3 Kings and 4 Kings.

prophet Micaiah, when he had explained before Ahab himself that this had been revealed to him, added 'Then look now, the Lord has allowed a lying spirit in the mouth of all your prophets who are here, and the Lord has spoken evil against you.'

(409) "Now whether the Lord permits the Devil to rage against the saints or against the impious, it's surely plain he only permits well what's good to be permitted, and the Devil only does the evil that nevertheless is good to be done and that has a reasonable cause why it's done, although one unknown to us. For as that great philosopher of yours remarks in his *Timaeus*, when he proves God does all things for the best: 'Everything begotten is begotten from some necessary cause. For nothing happens for which a lawful cause and reason does not precede its arising.'

(410) "It's plainly shown in this that no matter what things are done, no matter by whom, because they occur from divine providence's best governance, they take place reasonably and well in the way they turn out. For they have a reasonable cause why they're done, even though he who does them may not do them reasonably or well, or in doing them pay attention to the same cause God does.

(411) "So since plainly nothing is done except with God's permitting it—indeed nothing *can* be done if he's unwilling or resists—and since in addition it's certain that God never permits anything without a cause and does nothing whatever except reasonably, so that both his permission and his action are reasonable, surely therefore, since he sees why he permits the individual things that are done to be done, he isn't ignorant *why* they should be done, even if they're evil or are evilly done. For it wouldn't be good for them to be permitted unless it were good for them to be done. And he wouldn't be perfectly good who would not interfere, even though he could, with what wouldn't be good to be done. Rather, by agreeing that something be done that isn't good to be done, he would obviously be to blame.

(412) "So obviously whatever happens to be done or happens not to be done has a reasonable cause why it's done or not done. And for that reason it's good for it to be done, or good for it not to be done, even if it's done by someone by whom it's not done well, or evilly not done by the one by whom it's not done—that is, its being done is renounced because of an evil intention. Thus it's good even for evils themselves to be or to be done, although the evils themselves aren't good at all. Truth itself plainly acknowledges this when it says: 'For it is necessary that scandals come about. But woe to the man through whom a scandal comes about'—as if saying openly: 'It's useful and in keeping with human salvation that some people, offended or enraged because of me, thereby fall into scandal of the soul (that is, damnation), so that through some people's

maliciousness that deed should be done whereby all are saved who are predestined to be cured. But nevertheless woe to (that is, there will be damnation for) the one by whose advice or persuasion the scandal is instigated. So the scandal is evil, but it's good for the scandal to exist. So too it's good for any evil to exist, although nevertheless no evil is good.'

(413) "Noticing this and reflecting how much God orders even these evils for the best, Augustine, the great disciple of truth, says the following about God's goodness and the Devil's wickedness, 'Just as God is the best creator of good natures, so he is the most just orderer of evil wills,* so that while they use* good natures evilly, he uses even evil wills well.'

(414) "Again, the same man says about the Devil, 'When God created him, he was not ignorant of the latter's future wickedness, and foresaw what good he himself was going to make out of the latter's evils.'

(415) "Again, later on, 'For God would not have created any human beings or angels he foreknew to be evil, I say,* unless he likewise knew which uses of good things he would adapt them to.'

(416) "Again, elsewhere, 'They are good as individuals, but together universally they are *very* good, because the universe's admirable beauty consists of all of them.'

(417) "Again,

What is called evil commends goods more highly when it is well ordered and put in its place, so that the latter are the more pleasing and praiseworthy when it works together with goods. For almighty God, since he is good to the ultimate degree, would in no way permit there to be anything evil among his works unless he were so almighty and good that he would do well even with evil.

(418) "Again,

It is not to be doubted that God does well even in permitting to come about whatever evils do come about. For he does not permit this except by a just judgment, and what is just is certainly good. Therefore, although things that are evil, at least to the extent they are evil, are not goods, yet it is good that there be not only goods but also evils. For unless it were good that there be evils too, they would not be permitted by almighty God at all, for whom not permitting to exist what he does not want is no doubt as easy as it is easy to do what he does want. For he is not truly called almighty for any other reason except because he can do whatever he wants. Neither is the almighty will's effect blocked by any creature's will.

(419) "Look, you've heard it shown by plain reason that it's good for there to be evil too, although it isn't true that evil is good. Surely it's one thing to

say it's good for there to be evil, and another thing to say evil is good. For in the latter 'good' is applied to an evil thing, in the former to there being the evil thing—that is, in the latter to the thing, in the former to the thing's occurrence.

(420) "As was said [(397)], we call a thing good that, while it's fit for some use, mustn't impede the advantage or worthiness of anything. Now a thing's being impeded or lessened would indeed be necessary if through its contrary or lack the worthiness or advantage would necessarily not remain. For example, life, immortality, joy, health, knowledge, and chastity are such that although they have some worthiness or advantage, it plainly doesn't remain when their contraries overtake them. So too any substances whatever are plainly to be called good things because, while they're able to impart some usefulness, no worthiness or advantage is necessarily hampered through them. For even a perverse man whose life is corrupt, or even *causes* corruption, could be such that he were not perverse, and so nothing's* being made worse would be necessary through him.

(421) "Now I think this is enough at present for describing a 'good thing.' But when we apply the expression 'good' to the *occurrences* of things—that is, to what are said by propositions and what they 'propose' as occurring, so that we call it good for this to be or not to be—it's as though the occurrence were said to be necessary for filling out some optimal arrangement of God's, even if that arrangement is completely hidden from us. For it's not good for someone even to do well, if his doing it doesn't agree with but rather opposes some divine ordering. For what doesn't have a reasonable cause why it should be done cannot be done well. But if something arranged by God were necessarily hampered if a thing came about, then it doesn't have a reasonable cause why it should be done.

(422) "So often we're deceived when we say it's good for us to do this or that which is regarded by all as having to be done. But since it disagrees with the divine ordering, we 'lie' out of error. But, as we say, we're not *guilty* of a lie in having this opinion.

(423) "In prayer too, we often through error ask for many things that won't be beneficial to us at all. They're most appropriately denied to us by God in the divine arrangement of things. He knows what's necessary for us better than we do. Thus the main thing is Truth's lesson, whereby in prayer one must always say to God, 'Your will be done.'

(424) "Unless I'm mistaken, in the present circumstances it's enough for me to have said these things to show how the name 'good' is to be understood when it's taken simply for a good thing, or when also it's applied to the *occurrences* of things, which* are said by propositions.

(425) "If there's anything left over that depends on investigating the ultimate good,* and that you think ought to be asked further about it, it's all right to add it, or else hurry on to the remaining points."[89]

89. The text ends apparently incomplete. One manuscript adds "The end of the conversation of the philosopher with the Christian."

References

Paragraph references to the translations above are given in parentheses in boldface. References for multiple passages within a single paragraph are separated by a bullet (•) and are given in the order in which they occur. Semicolons separate alternative references for a given passage. If necessary, I have given a short identifying phrase in boldface to indicate where in the paragraph the reference goes.

Whenever possible, I have included standard references to internal divisions of a work. References to chapters and verses of Scripture are given according to the New Revised Standard Version, although in every case I have translated directly from Abelard's Latin. When a translation of a work is listed in the Bibliography below, I have referred to it here by its translated title, and have given a page or other reference to the translation, followed in parentheses by a page or other reference to the Latin edition listed. Otherwise, when there is no readily available English translation, I have given only the Latin title and a reference to the edition cited in the Bibliography.

Ethics

(5) Prov. 16:32 **(6)** 2 Tim. 2:5 **(16)** Matt. 26:52 **(18)** Phil. 1:23 • 2 Cor. 5:4 **(19)** Augustine, *Homilies on the Gospel of John* CXXIII. 5, pp. 446–47 (pp. 679–80) • John 21:18 • Matt. 26:39 • Isa. 53:7 • Ps. 115:3 **(26)** John 6:38 Luke 14:26 **(27)** Ecclus. 18:30 **(30)** Augustine, *On Free Choice of the Will* I. 3. 8, p. 6 (p. 215) **(41)** 1 Cor. 7:3 **(43)** Ps. 51:5 • 1 Cor. 7:5 • 1 Cor. 7:6 **(44)** Job 14:4–5 (Septuagint), quoted in Jerome, *Commentariorum in Hiezechielem* VI. 18, p. 228 • Ibid. IV. 16, p. 168 **(50)** Deut. 5:21 • Matt. 5:28 **(52)** Deut. 5:17 Deut. 5:20 **(53) the Law forbids** Deut. 27:22; Lev. 20:17 **(55)** Augustine, *Christian Instruction* III. 10. 15, p. 130 (p. 87) • Gal. 5:14 • Rom. 13:10 **(57) Doctor** Augustine, *In epistolam Joannis ad Parthos* VII. 4. 7, cols. 2032–33. See Augustine, *Expositions on the Book of Psalms* LXVI. 7, pp. 281–82 (LXV. 7, p. 846), and XCIV. 28, pp. 379–80 (XCIII. 28, pp. 1328–29). • **Apostle** Rom. 8:32; Gal. 2:20 **(60)** Mark 7:36 **(63)** Gen. 22:12 **(68) we say** Augustine, *Commentary on the Lord's Sermon on the Mount* I. 12. 34, pp. 53–54 (pp. 36–38); Gregory the Great, *Forty Gospel Homilies* 14, p. 102 (I. 16, col. 1135c); compare Gregory the Great, *Morals on the Book of Job* IV. 27. 49, p. 215 (p. 193). **(70)** 1 Cor. 10:13 **(71) who said** Ps. 25:17 **(72)** 1 Cor. 10:13 **(75)** Vergil, *Georgics* IV. 281–85 **(80)** Augustine, *In epistolam Joannis ad Parthos* VII. 4. 8, col. 2033 **(83) heart and reins** Jer. 20:12 • **see in darkness** Ezek. 8:12 **(84)**

Gal. 5:17 (85) Jer. 20:12 • Matt. 18:15 (90) Augustine, *Faith, Hope and Charity*
3. 11, p. 376 (p. 53), and 8. 27, p. 393 (p. 64); Augustine, *The City of God* XXI.
1, p. 416 (p. 806); Augustine, *Opus imperfectum contra Julianum* V. 60, col. 1495
(106) Aristotle, *Categories* 5 4a23–b1 (107) John 16:2 • Rom. 10:2 (108) Matt.
6:22; Luke 11:34 (111) 1 John 3:21 (112) Luke 23:24 • Acts 7:60 (114) 2 Cor.
5:21 (115) See Rom. 5:12, 19; 1 Cor. 15:22 (116) (Pseudo-) Athanasius,
Symbolum "Quicumque" § 76. 40–41, p. 42 (118) **Stephen calls** Acts 7:60 • **of**
whom he said John 9:3 (119) Acts 7:60 (120) Luke 23:24 (121) 1 Kings
13:11–12 (122) Gregory the Great, *Morals on the Book of Job* XVI. 10. 14, p. 233
(p. 806) • **Abraham** Gen. 22:11–12 • **Ninevites** Jon. 3:4 • **elsewhere** Wisd.
of Sol. 12:15 (123) Luke 23:24 (124) John 3:18 • 1 Cor. 14:38 (125) Aristotle,
Categories 7 6b36–39 (126) Rom. 10:14 • **Cornelius** Acts 10:1–46 (127) Ps.
36:6 • **offered himself** Matt. 8:19; see Luke 9:57 • **other man** Matt.
8:21–22 • Matt. 11:21 (132) **promised** Matt. 11:30 • Acts 15:10 (133) James
3:2 • Ibid. • 1 John 1:8 (136) Ps. 14:1 (139) (Pseudo-) Cicero, *Rhetorica ad*
Herennium IV. 4. 6 (140) **encourages** Matt. 11:28–30 • **suffers** 1 Cor. 13:7
(142) 1 Cor. 13:5 • 1 Cor. 10:24 (143) Horace, *Epistles* I. 16. 52 (146) Rom.
13:10 (150) The reference to Jerome has not been located. (151) Wisd. of Sol.
5:2–3 • **Judas'** Matt. 27:3 (152) **reprobate mind** Rom. 1:28 (153) Augustine, *Letter 153*, p. 296 (153. 6. 20, p. 419) (154) Luke 12:20 • Matt. 25:40
(156) The reference to Jerome has not been located. • Luke 16:19–31 (157)
Ascribed to Apollonius of Rhodes in Cicero, *De inventione* I. 56. 109, p. 163.
(159) Ps. 140:4 • 1 Cor. 14:38 • Ps. 21:8 • Ps. 139:7–8 (160) Hos. 4:9 • Ecclus.
34:24 • Matt. 9:13 (161) Rom. 2:4 • Rom. 2:5 (163) Mal. 1:6 (164) Rom. 2:4
(165) Ezek. 33:12 (166) 1 Cor. 15:22 (167) Gregory the Great, *Forty Gospel*
Homilies 34, p. 294 (II. 34. 15, col. 1256b) (168) John 14:23 (173) Matt. 10:22;
Matt. 24:13 (176) Matt. 12:31–32 • Mark 3:30 (178) Matt. 12:31 • Matt.
12:32 (180) Luke 11:15 (181) Ps. 51:17 • Isa. 35:10 • Rom. 8:28 • Abelard,
Theologia "Scholarium" III, pp. 148–49 (182) James 5:16 (183) Ps. 32:5 (184) 2
Sam. 12:13 (185) 2 Cor. 2:11 (186) Luke 22:62 • Ambrose, *Expositio Evangelii*
secundum Lucam X. 88, p. 371 (188) Luke 22:32 • Luke 19:14 (190) James 5:16
• Ibid. (191) Matt. 15:14 • Ibid. (195) Matt. 23:2–3 (199) 1 Cor. 11:31 (200)
Matt. 3:8 • Compare (Pseudo-) Augustine, *Liber de vera et falsa poenitentia* 18,
col. 1128. (201) Jer. 2:8 (203) John 20:23 • Matt 18:18; compare Matt. 16:19[1]
(204) Ovid, *Metamorphoses* I. 524 (205) John 20:23 (206) Ibid. • Matt. 5:14 •
Matt. 5:13 • Luke 10:23 • John 15:15 • John 16:13 (207) Luke 23:34 • Matt.

---

1. In the Latin Vulgate, the two passages differ in that Matt. 16:19 is in the singular,
while Matt. 18:18 is in the plural. I have not preserved this nuance in the translation.
Abelard sometimes cites it the one way, sometimes the other.

18:18 **(208)** Matt. 16:19 • Jerome, *Commentariorum in Matheum* III. 16. 19, p. 142 • Lev. 13:1–59 **(210)** Origen, *Commentary on the Gospel of Matthew*, p. 459 (XII. 14, vol. 40, pp. 98. 28–100. 26). • Matt. 16:18 **(212)** Ps. 50:21–22 • **reprobate mind** Rom. 1:28 **(213)** Augustine, *Sermon* 82. 7, p. 373 (82. 4. 7, col. 509) **(214)** Gregory the Great, *Forty Gospel Homilies* 26, pp. 204–5 (II. 26. 5, col. 1200a–c) • Ezek. 13:19 • John 11:43 **(215)** Gregory the Great, *Forty Gospel Homilies* 26, pp. 205–6 (II. 26. 6, cols. 1200c–1a) **(216)** Ibid., p. 206 (col. 1201b) **(217)** Ibid. **(218) prophet's remark** Ezek. 13:19 • Probably the Council of Carthage in 419. See Dionysius Exiguus, *Codex canonum ecclesiasticorum* 133, col. 223B.[2] **(219)** Augustine, *Sermon* 82. 7, p. 373 (82. 4. 7, col. 509) • Gregory the Great, *Forty Gospel Homilies* 26, p. 206 (II. 26. 6, col. 1201b) **(221)** Matt. 18:18 • Matt. 23:3 **(223)** Matt. 18:18 **(224)** Matt. 16:19; Matt. 18:18 • John 20:23 • Luke 6:13 • Matt. 5:13–14 • John 20:22–23 **(226)** Ps. 32:27 **(228)** Aristotle, *Categories* 8 8b26–9a13 **(230)** Wisd. of Sol. 4:10–11, 13–14

Dialogue between a Philosopher, a Jew and a Christian

(9) one of our own Augustine, *Quaestiones evangeliorum* II. 40, p. 98 • Prov. 1:5 • James 1:19 **(14)** John 5:19 • **nature** Sallust, *The War with Jugurtha* 85. 9 • Horace, *Epist.* I. 2. 69 • **philosophers** The philosopher referred to here has not been identified. **(44)** Ps. 17:4 **(48)** Ecclus. 44:16 • Gen. 6:19 **(49)** Exod. 32:11–14 **(51)** Gen. 15:6 **(53)** Gen. 17:7, 10, 12, 14 **(58)** Deut. 6:4, 17–24 **(59)** Deut. 7:6, 11–16 **(60)** Deut. 11:14–15, 28:2–6, 12 **(62)** Gen. 21:12 • Gen. 17:21 **(63)** Job 1:8 • Job 31:5, 16 • 1 Kings 8:41, 43 **(64)** Ps. 112:1 • Apparently a paraphrase of Ps. 34:10 **(65)** Jer. 1:5 **(66)** Ovid, *Amores* III. 4. 17 **(67)** Rom. 4:15 • Rom. 5:20 • Rom. 7:7–10 **(69)** Ps. 137:4 **(76) oath** Gen. 24:2–4 • Exod. 34:12, 16 **(77)** Gen. 27:46–28:1 **(79)** Gen. 17:7 **(80)** Gen. 17:13 • Exod. 6:7 **(81)** Ps. 45:10 **(82)** Isa. 5:2 **(83)** Gen. 3:16 **(84)** Gen. 3:17–18 **(86)** Gen. 17:12 **(87)** Gen. 17:27 • Gen. 17:26–27 **(88)** Gen. 17:23 • Gen. 17:26–27 **(89)** Gen. 17:21 • Gen. 17:19 **(91)** Exod. 19:5–6 **(92)** Exod. 20:5–6 **(93)** Lev. 19:2 • Lev. 20:7–8 • Lev. 30:26 • Lev. 22:32–33 • Lev. 26:3, 11 • Deut. 5:29 **(94)** Compare Deut. 6:24 • Deut. 6:25 • Deut. 7:6 • Deut. 7:9 **(95)** Deut. 10:12–15 **(96)** Exod. 23:4–5 • Exod. 23:9 • Lev. 19:18 • Lev. 19:33–34 **(97)** Deut. 15:11 **(101)** Deut. 4:1–2 • Deut. 12:32 **(104)** Gen. 9:26 **(106)** Gen. 5:24 • Deut. 9:4–6 **(108)** Deut. 15:1–3 • Deut. 14:20–21 • Lev. 17:15–16 **(109)** Deut. 23:20 **(110)** Lev. 17:10 **(112)** Gen. 17:10 • Gen. 17:12 **(113)** Gen. 17:13 • **complete the statement** Gen. 17:14 **(115)** Gen. 17:8 • Lev. 23:40–41 • Lev. 23:41 **(116)** Exod. 31:16–17 **(117)** Exod. 21:5–6 • Lev. 25:44–46 **(119)** Dan. 1:8 **(120)** Jer.

2. For a discussion of the identity of this canon, see Luscombe, p. 122 n. 2.

35:18–19 (121) See 2 Kings 18:4, Num. 21:9 (126) Ps. 51:17 • Ps. 32:5 • Ps. 50:7, 9, 12–15 (128) polluted See Lev. 15 (133) Ps. 32:5 • Ps. 118:18 (137) Cicero, *De inventione* II. 49. 145 (142) Ibid. (144) Job 36:22 • Heb. 1:1–2 • Heb. 7:18–19 (146) Matt. 5:20 • Continuing Matt. 5:21–48 (154) 1 Cor. 1:22 • Matt. 24:24 (155) 1 Cor. 1:22 (156) 1 Kings 19:4 (160) Gregory the Great, *Forty Gospel Homilies* 26, p. 201 (II. 26. 1, col. 1197c) (162) Ibid. (163) Prov. 14:12 (164) Athanasius, *The Life of Antony* 73, p. 84 (45, col. 158c) (166) Boethius, *De topicis differentiis* II, p. 61 (col. 1195a) • Ibid. III, p. 70 (col. 1199C) • Ibid. (168) Matt. 7:7–8 (169) (Pseudo-) Augustine, *Tractatus de oratione et eleemosyna*, col. 1227 • Augustine, *Divine Providence and the Problem of Evil* II. 13. 38, p. 315 (p. 174) (170) Augustine, *Christian Instruction* II. 31. 48, pp. 102–3 (pp. 65–66) • Ecclus. 37:20 (173) Abelard, *Theologia christiana* II, pp. 132–93 (178) Augustine, *The City of God* VIII. 3, p. 26 (p. 219) (201) Aristotle, *Categories* 11 13b36–14a6. (202) The example is not in Cicero, but is used to illustrate a point in Cicero by Boethius, *De topicis differentiis* III, p. 67 (col. 1198a) (203) Isa. 45:6–7 • Luke 16:25 (204) Augustine, *The City of God* XIII. 5, p. 306 (p. 389) (211) Matt. 5:3 • Matt. 5:10 (213) Cicero, *De inventione* II. 52. 157–58 • Boethius, *De topicis differentiis* II, p. 53 (col. 1189d) (228) Cicero, *De officiis* II. 9. 34–II. 10. 35 (229) Cicero, *Paradoxa stoicorum* 3. 21 (232) Augustine, *Tractates on the Gospel of John* LXXXIII. 3, p. 131 (p. 536) • Rom. 13:10 • 1 Cor. 13:4 • 1 Cor. 13:7 • John 15:13 (237) Cicero, *Paradoxa stoicorum* 3. 21 (240) Macrobius, *Commentary on the Dream of Scipio* I. 8. 5, p. 121 (Willis ed., p.37); see Plotinus, *Enneads* I. 2. 3–7 (241) 1 Cor. 7:7 • 1 Cor. 15:41–42 • 2 Cor. 9:6 (242) fulfillment of the Law Rom. 13:10 • Luke 17:10 • 1 Cor. 7:25 (254) Boethius, *On Division*, p. 27 (col. 885b) • Aristotle, *Categories* 8 8b26–9a13 (255) 2 Tim. 2:5 • Boethius, *The Consolation of Philosophy* IV. pr. 7 • Boethius, *In Categorias* III, col. 242b (256) Cicero, *De inventione* II. 53. 160 (258) Aristotle, *Categories* 8 8b29 • Boethius, *In Categorias* III, col. 242c (259) James 2:17 • Prov. 10:28 (260) Luke 12:47 • 2 Pet. 2:21 (265) Valerius Maximus, *Factorum et dictorum memorabilium libri novem* V. 8. 5, p. 578 (280) Lucan, *The Civil War* II. 377–78 • Ibid. II. 380–83 • Ibid. II. 388–90 (306) Aristotle, *Categories* 11 13b36 (316) Ps. 17:15 (317) Isa. 26:10 (320) Eccles. 3:2, 5 (332) John 3:31 (337) Rev. 21:17 (338) Prov. 16:4 (340) Isa. 40:12 (342) Jer. 23:24 • Ps. 139:7–8 (344) John 20:26 (346) Luke 23:43 (347) Augustine, *Christian Instruction* I. 10. 10, p. 34 (p. 12) (350) Job 1:6 (355) as is written Mark 16:19; Col. 3:1 • it's promised 1 Thess. 4:17 (356) Isa. 66:1 (357) Isa. 30:26 (359) Isa. 66:1–2 • throne Col. 1:16 (360) Ps. 11:4 (363) Ps. 27:13 • Ezek. 37:12, 14 (364) John 20:26 • Wisd. of Sol. 9:15 (365) John 20:17 (366) Isa. 60:19–21 (367) Rev. 21:17 (369) 1 Cor. 13:12 • 1 Cor. 15:28 (370) Col. 2:15 (375) Isa. 66:24 (376) rich person and Lazarus Luke

16:19–26 • Matt. 22:13 **(381) small** See Matt. 22:14 **(382)** Wisd. of Sol. 5:20
(385) Ps. 139:7–8 **(387)** No such passage has been found in Augustine **(388)**
Jerome, *Commentariorum in Naum* 1. 9, pp. 534–35. See Nah. 1:9 **(405)** Job
1:21 **(407)** Job 1:21 (Vulgate) • Ibid. **(408)** • 1 Kings 22:20–22 • 1 Kings
22:23. **(409)** Plato, *Timaeus* 28a. See Plato, *Timaeus a Calcidio translatus,* p. 20.
(412) Matt. 18:7 **(413)** Augustine, *The City of God* XI. 17, p. 213 (pp. 336–37)
(414) Ibid. (p. 337) **(415)** Ibid. XI. 8, p. 213 (p. 337) **(416)** Augustine, *Faith,
Hope and Charity* 3. 10. p. 376 (p. 53) **(417)** Ibid. 3. 11, p. 376 (p. 53) **(418)**
Ibid., 24. 96, pp. 448–49 (pp. 99–100) **(423)** Matt. 6:10

Bibliography

Note: When one of the items listed below is said to be "translated in" another, or to be a "translation of" another, I mean only that the two contain versions of the same work. I do *not* necessarily mean that the translation was based on the particular edition cited of the Latin text.

Abbreviations:

CCCM = *Corpus christianorum continuatio mediaevalis.* Turnholt: Brepols.
CCSL = *Corpus christianorum series latina.* Turnholt: Brepols.
CSEL = *Corpus scriptorum ecclesiasticorum latinorum.* Vienna: F. Tempsky.
FOC = *The Fathers of the Church.* Washington, D.C.: Catholic University of America Press.
LOF = *Library of the Fathers of the Holy Catholic Church Anterior to the Division of the East and West.* 41 vols., Oxford: John Henry Parker (etc.), 1839–69.
PL = Migne, Jacques-Paul. *Patrologiae latinae cursus completus . . . series latina,* 221 vols., Paris: J.-P. Migne, 1844–64.

(1) Abelard. *See* Peter Abelard.

(2) Ambrose. *Expositio Evangelii secundum Lucam, Fragmenta in Esaiam.* M. Adriaen, ed. CCSL 14 (1957).

(3) Athanasius. *The Life of Antony and The Letter to Marcellinus.* Robert C. Gregg, tr. ("The Classics of Western Spirituality"). New York: Paulist Press, 1980. Translation of (5).[1] The section numbers differ from those in (5). Both will be cited.

(4) Athanasius, (Pseudo-). *Symbolum "Quicumque."* In Heinrich Joseph Denzinger and Adolf Schönmetzer. *Enchiridion symbolorum definitionum et declarationum de rebus fidei et morum.* 34th ed. Freiburg: Herder, 1967, §§ 75–76, pp. 40–42.

(5) Athanasius. *Vita beati Antonii . . . interprete Evagrio.* PL 73, cols. 125–70. Translated in (3). The section numbers differ from those in (3). Both will be cited.

---

1. The English translation was made from the original Greek text, not from Evagrius' Latin translation in (5).

(6) Augustine. *Christian Instruction.* John J. Gavigan, tr. In (7), pp. 19–235. Translation of (12).

(7) Augustine. *Christian Instruction; Admonition and Grace; The Christian Combat; Faith, Home and Charity.* FOC 8 (1950). See also (6), (18).

(8) Augustine. *The City of God, Books I–VII.* Demetrius B. Zema and Gerald G. Walsh, trs. FOC 8 (1950). *Books VIII–XVI.* Gerald G. Walsh and Grace Monahan, trs. FOC 14 (1952). *Books XVII–XXII.* Gerald G. Walsh and Daniel J. Honan, trs. FOC 24 (1954). Translation of (9).

(9) Augustine. *De civitate dei.* B. Dombart and A. Kalb, eds. CCSL 47–48 (1955). Translated in (8).

(10) Augustine. *Commentary on the Lord's Sermon on the Mount with Seventeen Related Sermons.* Denis J. Kavanagh, tr., FOC 11 (1951). Translation of (28).

(11) Augustine. *Divine Providence and the Problem of Evil.* Robert P. Russell, tr. FOC 2 (1948), pp. 227–332. Translation of (26).

(12) Augustine. *De doctrina christiana.* Joseph Martin, ed. CCSL 32 (1962). Translated in (6).

(13) Augustine. *Enarrationes in Psalmos.* D. E. Dekkers and J. Fraipont, eds. CCSL 38–40 (1956). Vol. 38 = Ps. 1–50, vol. 39 = Ps. 51–100, vol. 40 = Ps. 101–50. Translated in (17). The numbering of the Psalms is not the same as in the translation. Both forms will be cited.

(14) Augustine. *Enchiridion ad Laurentium de fide et spe et caritate.* E. Evans, ed. CCSL 46 (1969), pp. 21–114. Translated in (18).

(15) Augustine. *In epistolam Joannis ad Parthos tractatus decem.* PL 35, cols. 1977–2062.

(16) Augustine. *Epistulae.* Al. Goldbacher, ed. CSEL 34.1 (*Ep.* 1–30, 1895), 34.2 (*Ep.* 31–123, 1898), 44 (*Ep.* 124–84a, 1904), 57 (*Ep.* 185–270, 1911), 58 (*Praefatio editoris et indices,* 1923).

(17) Augustine. *Expositions on the Book of Psalms.* 6 vols., LOF, vols. 24 (Ps. 1–36, 1847), 25 (Ps. 37–52, 1848), 30 (Ps. 53–75, 1849), 32 (Ps. 76–101,1850), 37 (Ps. 102–25, 1853), 39 (Ps. 126–50, 1857). Translation of (13). The numbering of the Psalms is not the same as in the Latin edition. Both forms will be cited.

(18) Augustine. *Faith, Hope and Charity.* Bernard M. Peebles, tr. In (7), pp. 355–472. Translation of (14).

(19) Augustine. *On Free Choice of the Will.* Thomas Williams, tr. Indianapolis: Hackett, 1993. Translation of (24).

(20) Augustine. *Homilies on the Gospel of John.* In Philip Schaff, ed. *A Select Library of the Nicene and Post-Nicene Fathers of the Christian Church,* 14 vols. Grand Rapids, MI: W. B. Eerdmans, 1956 (reprint of the original edition. New York: The Christian Literature Co., 1887–94), vol. 7, pp. 7–452. Translation of (21).

(21) Augustine. *In Iohannis evangelium tractatus CXXIV.* D. R. Willems, ed. CCSL 36 (1954). Complete translation in (20). Translation in progress in (31).

(22) Augustine. *Letters.* Sister Wilfrid Parsons, tr. *Letters 1–82,* FOC 12 (1951). *Letters 83–130,* FOC 18 (1953). *Letters 131–64,* FOC 20 (1953). *Letters 165–203,* FOC 30 (1955). *Letters 204–70,* FOC 32 (1956).

(23) Augustine, (Pseudo-). *Liber de vera et falsa poenitentia.* PL 40, cols. 1113–30.

(24) Augustine. *De libero arbitrio.* W. M. Green, ed. CCSL 29 (1970), pp. 209–321. Translated in (19).

(25) Augustine. *Opus imperfectum contra Julianum.* PL 45, cols. 1049–608.

(26) Augustine. *De ordine.* Pius Knöll, ed. CSEL 63 (1922), pp. 121–85. Translated in (11).

(27) Augustine. *Quaestiones evangeliorum.* Almut Mutzenbecher, ed. CCSL 44b (1980).

(28) Augustine. *De sermone domini in monte libri duo.* Almut Mutzenbecher, ed. CCSL 35 (1967). Translation included in (10).

(29) Augustine. *Sermones 1–340.* PL 38. Partially translated in (30).

(30) Augustine. *Sermons 51–94.* Edmund Hill, tr. ("The Works of St. Augustine: A Translation for the 21st Century," 3. 3). Brooklyn: New City Press, 1990.

(31) Augustine. *Tractates on the Gospel of John.* John W. Rettig, tr. *Tr. 1–10* FOC 78 (1988), *Tr. 11–27* FOC 79 (1988), *Tr. 28–54* FOC 88 (1993), *Tr. 55–111* FOC 90 (1994). Ongoing translation of (21).

(32) Augustine, (Pseudo-). *Tractatus de oratione et eleemosyna.* PL 40, cols. 1225–28.

(33) Boethius. *Boethius's De topicis differentiis.* Eleonore Stump, tr. Ithaca: Cornell University Press, 1978. Translation of (35). With notes and essays on the text.

(34) Boethius. *In Categorias Aristotelis libri quattuor.* PL 64, cols. 159–294.

(35) Boethius. *De differentiis topicis.* PL 64, cols. 1173–216. Translated in (33).

(36) Boethius. *On Division.* In Norman Kretzmann and Eleonore Stump, eds. & trs. *The Cambridge Translations of Medieval Philosophical Texts.* Volume One: *Logic and the philosophy of Language.* Cambridge: Cambridge University Press, 1988, pp. 12–38. Translation of (37).

(37) Boethius. *Liber de divisione.* PL 64, cols. 875–92. Translated in (36).

(38) Boethius. *The Theological Tractates. The Consolation of Philosophy.* H. F. Stewart and E. K. Rand, trs. (of the *Tractates*), "I. T.," tr. (of the *Consolation*) ("The Loeb Classical Library"). Cambridge, Mass.: Harvard University Press, 1968. Latin text and English translation.

(39) Cicero. *De inventione, De optimo genere orationum, Topica.* H. M. Hubbell, tr. ("The Loeb Classical Library"). Cambridge, Mass.: Harvard University Press, 1949. Latin text and English translation.

(40) Cicero. *De officiis.* Walter Miller, tr. ("The Loeb Classical Library"). Cambridge, Mass.: Harvard University Press, 1947. Latin text and English translation.

(41) Cicero. *Paradoxa stoicorum.* In Cicero. *De oratore, Book III; De fato; Paradoxa stoicorum; De partitione oratoria,* H. Rackham, tr. ("The Loeb Classical Library"). Cambridge, Mass.: Harvard University Press, 1968, pp. 251–303. Latin text and English translation.

(42) Cicero, (Pseudo-). *Rhetorica ad Herennium = Ad C. Herennium de ratione dicendi.* Harry Caplan, tr. ("The Loeb Classical Library"). Cambridge, Mass.: Harvard University Press, 1989. Latin text and English translation.

(43) Dionysius Exiguus. *Codex canonum ecclesiasticorum.* PL 67, cols. 135–230.

(44) Douglas, Mary. *Purity and Danger: An Analysis of Concepts of Pollution and Taboo.* London: Routledge & Kegan Paul, 1966.

(45) Gregory the Great. *Forty Gospel Homilies.* David Hurst, tr. ("Cistercian Studies Series," vol. 123). Kalamazoo: Cistercian Publications, 1990. Translation of (48). The numbering of the sermons differs from that in the edition. Both forms will be cited.

(46) Gregory the Great. *Moralia in Job.* M. Adriaen, ed. CCSL 143 (*Lib.* 1–10, 1979), 143a (*Lib.* 11–22, 1979), 143b (*Lib.* 23–35, 1985). Translated in (47).

(47) Gregory the Great. *Morals on the Book of Job.* 4 vols., LOF, vols. 18 (Bks. 1–10, 1844), 21 (Bks. 11–22, 1845), 23 (Bks. 23–29, 1847), 31 (Bks. 30–35, 1850). Translation of (46).

(48) Gregory the Great. *XL homiliarum in evangelia libri duo.* PL 76, cols. 1075–312. Translated in (45). The numbering of the sermons differs from that in the translation. Both forms will be cited.

(49) Horace. *Satires, Epistles, Ars poetica.* H. Rushton Fairclough, tr. ("The Loeb Classical Library"). Cambridge, Mass.: Harvard University Press, 1966. Latin text and English translation.

(50) Isidore of Seville. *Isidori Hispalensis episcopi etymologiarum sive originum libri XX.* W. M. Lindsay, ed., 2 vols. Oxford: Clarendon Press, 1911.

(51) Jerome. *Commentariorum in Hiezechielem libri XIV.* F. Glorie, ed. CCSL 75 (1964).

(52) Jerome. *Commentariorum in Matheum libri IV.* D Hurst and M. Adriaen, eds. CCSL 77 (1969).

(53) Jerome. *Commentariorum in Naum prophetam.* M. Adriaen, tr. CCSL 76a (1970), pp. 525–78.

(54) Lucan. *The Civil War.* J. D. Duff, tr. ("The Loeb Classical Library"). New York: G. P. Putnam's Sons, 1928. Latin text and English translation.

(55) Macrobius.*Commentarii in somnium Scipionis libri duo.* Jacob Willis, ed. Leipzig: B. G. Teubner, 1970. Translated in (56).

(56) Macrobius. *Commentary on the Dream of Scipio.* William Harris Stahl, tr. ("Records of Western Civilization"). New York: Columbia University Press, 1990. (Originally published 1952.) Translation of (55).

(57) Origen. *Commentary on the Gospel of Matthew.* John Patrick, tr. In Alexander Roberts, James Donaldson, and A. Cleveland Coxe, eds. *The Ante-Nicene Fathers.* Vol. 10: *Original Supplement to the American Edition.* Allan Menzies, ed. Grand Rapids: W. B. Eerdmans, 1980, pp. 409–512. (Fragments of Dks. 1, 2, 10–14.) Partial translation of (58).

(58) Origen. *Origenes Matthäuserklärung.* Erich Klostermann, ed. *Die griechischen christlichen Schriftsteller der ersten drei Jahuhunderte.* Vols. 40 (Leipzig: J. C. Hinrich, 1935), 41 part 1 (Leipzig: J. C. Hinrich, 1941), 40 part 2 (Berlin:

Akademie-Verlag, 1955), 38 (2nd ed., Berlin: Akademie-Verlag, 1976).[2] Partially translated in (57).

(59) Ovid. *Heroides and Amores.* Grant Showerman, tr. ("The Loeb Classical Library"). New York: The Macmillan Co., 1914. Latin text and English translation.

(60) Ovid. *Metamorphoses.* Frank Justus Miller, tr., 2 vols. ("The Loeb Classical Library"). Cambridge, Mass.: Harvard University Press, 1984. Latin text and English translation.

(61) Peter Abelard. *Commentaria in Epistolam Pauli ad Romanos. Apologia contra Bernardum.* Eligius M. Buytaert, ed. CCCM 11 (1969).

(62) Peter Abelard. *Dialectica.* L. M. De Rijk, ed. 2nd, rev. ed. Assen: Van Gorcum, 1970.

(63) Peter Abelard. *A Dialogue of a Philosopher with a Jew and a Christian.* Pierre J. Payer, tr. ("Mediaeval Sources in Translation," vol. 20). Toronto: Pontifical Institute of Mediaeval Studies, 1979. Translation of (64).

(64) Peter Abelard. *Dialogus inter Philosophum, Iudaeum et Christianum.* Rudolf Thomas, ed. Stuttgart–Bad Cannstatt: Friedrich Frommann Verlag (Günter Holzboog), 1970. Translated in (63).

(65) Peter Abelard. *Peter Abelard's Ethics.* D. E. Luscombe, ed. & tr. ("Oxford Medieval Texts"). Oxford: Clarendon Press, 1971.

(66) Peter Abelard. *Petri Abaelardi opera.* Victor Cousin, ed. 2 vols. Paris: Aug. Durand, 1849–59. Reprinted Hildesheim: Georg Olms, 1970. See also (69).

(67) Peter Abelard. *The Story of Abelard's Adversities.* J. T. Muckle, tr. Toronto: Pontifical Institute of Mediaeval Studies, 1964.

(68) Peter Abelard. *Theologia christiana.* Eligius M. Buytaert, ed. In CCCM 12 (1969), pp. 5–372.

(69) Peter Abelard. *Theologia "Scholarium."* Printed under the title *Introductio ad theologiam* in (66), vol. 2, pp. 1–149.

2. Abelard (*Ethics* (210)) quotes from Origen's so-called *Series Commentary on Matthew.* Trigg, *Origen,* p. 211, says, "At Caesarea Origen continued his exegetical work with a five-volume *Commentary on Luke* and a twenty-five-volume *Commentary on Matthew.* . . . [E]ight books of the *Commentary on Matthew* have survived in Greek and a good deal more in a reliable anonymous Latin translation known as the *Series Commentary on Matthew.* We thus have a continuous commentary from Matthew 13:36 to 27:66."

(70) Plato. *Timaeus a Calcidio translatus.* J. H. Waszink, ed. ("Plato Latinus," 4). London: The Warburg Institute, 1962.

(71) Plotinus. *Plotinus.* A. H. Armstrong, tr. ("The Loeb Classical Library"), vol. 1. Cambridge, Mass.: Harvard University Press, 1978.

(72) Porphyry. *Isagoge.* In *Porphyrii Isagoge et in Aristotelis Categorias commentarium.* Adolfus Busse, ed. ("Commentaria in Aristotelem Graeca," Vol. 4.1). Berlin: George Reimer, 1887. Translated in (74), pp. 1–19.

(73) Sallust. *The War with Jugurtha.* In *Sallust.* J. C. Rolfe, tr. ("The Loeb Classical Library"). Cambridge, Mass.: Harvard University Press, 1971. Latin text and English translation.

(74) Spade, Paul Vincent, tr. *Five Texts on the Mediaeval Problem of Universals: Porphyry, Boethius, Abelard, Duns Scotus, Ockham.* Indianapolis: Hackett, 1994. Contains a translation of (72) on pp. 1–19.

(75) Stump, Eleonore. *Dialectic and Its Place in the Development of Medieval Logic.* Ithaca: Cornell University Press, 1989.

(76) Trigg, Joseph Wilson. *Origen: The Bible and Philosophy in the Third-Century Church.* Atlanta: John Knox Press, 1983.

(77) Valerius Maximus. *Factorum dictorumque memorabilium libri novem.* Joannes Kappius, ed. ("The Delphin Classics," vols. 112–13). London: A. J. Valpy, 1823.

(78) Vergil (= Virgil). *Virgil.* Vol. 1: *Eclogues, Georgics, Aeneid I–VI.* H. Rushton Fairclough, tr. ("The Loeb Classical Library"), rev. ed. Cambridge, Mass.: Harvard University Press, 1986. Latin text and English translation.

Index

The index below includes an index of persons and places, of quotations and allusions, and of main topics. (Marilyn Adams's Introduction is not included.) References to books of Scripture are arranged alphabetically rather than by their order of occurrence in the Bible. For the conventions regarding citations of works by their English or Latin titles, see the list of References, above. Entries are separated from page numbers by a bullet (●). Subentries are separated from one another by semicolons.

A

Abel ● 69

Abraham ● 69–70, 72, 73, 75, 76, 77, 78, 79, 82, 84, 136, 137; sacrifice of Isaac ● 13–14, 26

Accident: definition of ● 126, 127; *vs.* substance ● 126–27

Action: bad, not same as sin ● 1, 17; commands and prohibitions addressed to consent rather than to ● 12; does not add to merit ● 6; does not increase sin ● 7, 8–10, 17; sin sometimes called ● 25; sometimes called sin ● 25–26, 27–28

Adam ● 15, 25, 35, 77

Adjacent vices ● 114, 115

Adjectival names ● 120

Adultery ● 7, 11, 30, 31, 32, 88, 112, 118

African Council (= Council of Carthage) ● 54

Ahab ● 144, 145

Alms, giving ● 12, 28, 34, 35

Ambrose, *Expositio Evangelii secundum Lucam* ● 44

Angels ● xxix, 42, 122, 125, 127, 130, 133, 134, 135, 136, 146

Anthony, St. ● 96

Antichrist ● 94

Apollonius the rhetorician (= of Rhodes) ● 35

Arab, is philosopher in Abelard's *Dialogue* patterned after an? ● 79

Aristotle ● 112; *Categories* ● 23, 27, 57, 102, 111, 112, 122

Ark (= of the Covenant) ● 86

Ascension of Christ ● 131, 133, 134

"Assume," use of term in theology of Incarnation ● 5, 22, 41

Athanasius, (Pseudo-), *Symbolum "Quicumque"* ● 25

Athanasius, *Life of Antony* ● 96, 155

Athenians, St. Paul's attack on ● 95

Atonement ● 17, 33, 38, 41, 43, 44, 45, 46, 47, 48, 88

Augustine ● 12, 99, 112, 139; *Christian Instruction* ● 12, 98, 113, 130; *The City of God* ● 20, 99, 102, 146; *Commentary on the Lord's Sermon on the Mount* ● 15; *Divine Providence and the Problem of Evil* ● 98; *In epistolam Joannis ad Parthos* ● 12, 17; *Expositions on the Book of Psalms* ● 12; *Faith, Hope and Charity* ● 20, 146; *On Free Choice of the Will* ● 7; *Homilies on the Gospel of John* ● 5; *Letters* ● 34; *Opus imperfectum contra Julianum* ● 20; *Quaestiones evangeliorum* ● 61, 151; *Sermons* ● 53, 54; *Tractates on the Gospel of John* ● 107, 109

Augustine, (Pseudo-): *Liber de vera et falsa poenitentia* • 48; *Tractatus de oratione et eleemosyna* • 98

Aulius Fulvius' execution of his own son • 114

B

Balliol MS of Abelard's *Dialogue* • 59, 61

Beelzebub • 42

Beneficence • 115–16, 117; definition of • 115

Bethsaida • 28

Bible: 1 Corinthians 1:22 • 94; 7:5 • 9; 7:7 • 109; 7:25 • 109; 10:13 • 15, 16; 10:24 • 31; 11:31 • 48; 13:4 • 107; 13:5 • 31; 13:7 • 31, 107; 13:12 • 135; 14:38 • 27, 36; 15:22 • 25, 39; 15:28 • 135; 15:41–42 • 109; 1 John 1:18 • 30; 3:21 • 24; 1 Kings 13:11–12 • 26; 19:4 • 95; 22:20–22 • 144; 22:23 • 145; 1 Thessalonians 4:17 • 131; 2 Corinthians 2:11 • 43; 5:4 • 5; 5:21 • 25; 9:6 • 109; 2 Kings 18:24 • 86; 2 Peter 2:21 • 113; 2 Samuel 12:13 • 43; 2 Timothy 2:5 • 2, 111; Acts 7:60 • 24, 26; 10:1–46 • 28; 15:10 • 29; Colossians 1:16 • 133; 2:15 • 135; 3:1 • 131; Daniel 1:8 • 86; Deuteronomy 4:1–2 • 82; 5:17 • 11; 5:20 • 11; 5:29 • 80; 6:4, 17–24 • 71; 6:24 • 80; 6:25 • 80; 7:6 • 80; 7:6, 11–16 • 72; 7:9 • 80; 9:4–6 • 83; 10:12–15 • 80; 11:14–15 • 72; 12:16, 23 • 68; 12:32 • 82; 14:20–21 • 83; 15:1–3 • 83; 15:11 • 81; 23:20 • 84; 27:22 • 11; 28:2–6, 12 • 72; Ecclesiastes 3:2, 5 • 124; Ecclesiasticus 18:30 • 6; 34:24 • 36; 37:20 • 98; 44:16 • 69; Exodus 6:7 • 76; 19:5–6 • 79; 20:5–6 • 79; 21:5–6 • 86; 22:31 • 68; 23:4–5 • 81; 23:9 • 81; 31:16–17 • 85; 32:11–14 • 69; 34:12, 16 • 76; Ezekiel 8:12 • 18;

13:19 • 53, 54; 33:12 • 38; 37:12 • 133; Galatians 2:20 • 12; 5:14 • 12; 5:17 • 18; Genesis 3:16 • 77; 3:17–18 • 77; 3:17–19 • 77; 5:24 • 82; 6:19 • 69; 9:26 • 82; 15:6 • 70; 15:7–21 • 70; 17:7 • 76; 17:7, 10, 12, 14 • 70; 17:8 • 85; 17:10 • 84; 17:10–14 • 70; 17:12 • 78, 84; 17:13 • 76, 85; 17:14 • 85; 17:19 • 78; 17:21 • 73, 78; 17:23 • 78; 17:25 • 79; 17:26–27 • 78; 17:27 • 78; 21:12 • 72, 73; 22:11–12 • 26; 22:12 • 14; 24:2–4 • 76; 27:46–28:1 • 76; Hebrews 1:1–2 • 92; 7:18–19 • 92; Hosea 4:9 • 36; Isaiah 5:2 • 77; 26:10 • 123; 30:26 • 132; 35:10 • 42; 40:12 • 128; 45:6–7 • 102; 53:7 • 5; 60:19–21 • 134; 66:1 • 132; 66:1–2 • 132; 66:24 • 136; James 1:19 • 61; 2:17 • 113; 3:2 • 29, 30; 5:16 • 43, 45; Jeremiah 1:5 • 73; 2:5 • 48; 2:8 • 49; 20:12 • 18; 23:24 • 128; 35:18–19 • 86; Job 1:8 • 73; 1:16 • 130; 1:21 • 143; 1:21 (Vulgate) • 144; 14:4–5 (Septuagint) • 9; 31:5, 16 • 73; 36:22 • 92; John 3:18 • 27; 3:31 • 126; 5:19 • 63; 6:38 • 6; 9:3 • 26; 11:43 • 53; 14:23 • 39; 15:13 • 107; 15:15 • 50; 16:2 • 23; 16:13 • 50; 20:17 • 134; 20:22–23 • 56; 20:23 • 49, 50, 56; 20:26 • 129, 133; 21:28 • 5; Jonah 3:4 • 26; Leviticus 3:17 • 68; 7:26 • 68; 13:1–59 • 51; 15 • 88; 17:10 • 84; 17:10, 12–13 • 84; 17:10–14 • 68; 17:15–16 • 84; 19:2 • 80; 19:18 • 81; 19:33–34 • 81; 20:7–8 • 80; 20:17 • 11; 22:32–33 • 80; 23:40–41 • 85; 23:41 • 85; 25:44–46 • 86; 26:3, 11 • 80; 30:26 • 80; Luke 6:13 • 56; 9:57 • 28; 10:23 • 50; 11:15 • 42; 11:34 •

Bible *(cont.)*
24; 12:20 • 34; 12:47 • 113; 14:26 • 6;
16:19–31 • 35; 16:25 • 102; 17:10 •
109; 19:44 • 45; 22:32 • 45; 22:62 •
44; 23:24 • 24, 26, 27; 23:34 • 50;
23:43 • 129; Malachi 1:6 • 37; Mark
3:30 • 41; 7:36 • 13; 16:19 • 131;
Matthew 3:8 • 48; 5:3 • 103; 5:10 •
103; 5:13–14 • 50, 56; 5:20 • 92; 6:10
• 147; 6:22 • 24; 7:7–8 • 98; 8:19 •
28; 8:21 22 • 28; 10:22 • 40; 11:21 •
28; 11:28–30 • 31; 11:30 • 29; 12:31 •
41; 12:31–32 • 41; 12:32 • 41;
13:36–27:66 • 160; 15:14 • 46; 16:18
• 51; 16:19 • 49, 51, 56, 150; 18:7 •
145; 18:15 • 19; 18:18 • 49, 51, 55, 56,
150; 22:13 • 137; 22:14 • 137; 23:2–3
• 47; 23:3 • 55; 24:13 • 40; 24:24 •
94; 26:39 • 5; 26:52 • 4; 27:3 • 33;
Nahum 1:9 • 139; Numbers 21:9 •
86; Philippians 1:23 • 5; Proverbs 1:5
• 61; 10:28 • 113; 14:12 • 96; 16:4 •
127; 16:32 • 2; Psalms 11:4 • 133; 14:1
• 30, 89; 17:4 • 68; 17:15 • 123; 21:8
• 36; 23:2 • 141; 27:13 • 133; 32:5 •
43, 87, 89; 32:27 • 57; 34:10 • 73;
36:6 • 28; 45:10 • 77; 50:7, 9, 12–15
• 87; 50:21–22 • 52; 51:5 • 9; 51:17 •
42, 87; 112:1 • 73; 115:3 • 5; 118:18 •
89; 137:4 • 74; 139:7–8 • 128, 138;
140:4 • 35; Revelations 21:17 • 127,
134; Romans 1:28 • 34, 52; 2:4 • 36,
37; 2:5 • 37; 4:15 • 74; 5:12 • 25;
5:20 • 74; 7:7–10 • 74; 8:28 • 42;
8:32 • 12; 9:13 • 36; 10:2 • 23; 10:14
• 28; 13:10 • 12, 32, 107, 109; 19:1 •
25; Wisdom of Solomon 4:10–11,
13–14 • 57; 5:1 • 33, 5.2–3 • 33, 5.20
• 138; 9:15 • 134; 12:15 • 27
Blasphemy against Holy Spirit • 41–42
Blessed, who is defined as? • 100
Blessedness • 106; in future life •
100–101, 103; is goal of virtues • 104;
none in this life • 103; not affected by
difference of place • 128–31; not
increased unless virtue grows • 101
Boethius: *In Categorias* • 112; *Consolation
of Philosophy* • 111; *On Division* • 111;
De topicis differentiis • 97, 102, 104
Bolyard, Charles • xxx

C

Caesarea • 160
Canaan • 82, 83, 85
Carthage, Council of • *See* African
Council
Catiline • 114
Cato • 116
Chaldean unbelievers • 77
Charity • 12, 14, 17, 31, 38, 49, 67, 107,
109, 112; alone is properly a virtue •
107; encompasses all virtues • 106,
107; once had is never given up • 122
Chastity • 118, 147; definition of • 119;
natural • 111; part of moderation •
119
Chorazin • 28
Christians • 59, 60, 64, 67, 91–148
Cicero • 97, 102; *De inventione* • 35, 91,
92, 104, 112; *De officiis* • 106;
Paradoxa stoicorum • 106, 107; *Topics* •
95
Cicero, (Pseudo-), *Rhetorica ad
Herennium* • 31
Circumcision • 68, 69–70, 72, 73,
75–79, 82, 84–85, 118
Clemency, definition of • 115
Commands, addressed to consent, not to
action • 12
Comparisons, logical analysis of • 107–8
Confession • 33, 38, 42–47, 54
Consent: commands and prohibitions
addressed not to action but to • 12;
improper • 2, 4, 7, 10, 24, 25;
improper, is properly called sin • 2,
10, 14, 89, 108

Contraries, Aristotle's discussion of • 102
Cornelius • 28
Council of Carthage • *See* African Council
Courage • 114, 115, 119; definition of • 114; parts of: magnanimity and forbearance • 118
Crime, definition of • 30
Currency, units of • 4, 36

D

"Daimonas," meaning of Greek term • 16
David • 9, 10, 43, 77, 86
Day of Judgment • 38
Death: fear of • 4, 5, 139; suffering of • 139–40
Deference, definition of • 115
Demons • 16, 17, 42, 94, 130, 137. *See also* Devil
Despair of forgiveness • 41, 137
Devil • 13, 15, 25, 42, 52, 107, 143, 144, 145, 146. *See also* Demons
Dictum of proposition • 141
Dionysius Exiguus, *Codex canonum ecclesiasticorum* • 54
Disbelief: not a fault • 29; not properly called sin • 24–25, 27
Dishonorable, definition of • 104
Disposition, definition of • 57
Divinity, also called ethics • 93
"Doctor," meaning of term • 12
Duress: killing under • 3–4, 8; sin under • 5

E

Eating delicious food • 6–7, 8, 9, 10, 68, 75
Egypt • 16, 71, 72, 80, 81, 82, 94
Enjoyment *vs.* use • 113
Enoch • 69, 82
Epicureans • 100

Epicurus • 100, 103, 104
Esau • 79, 85
Essence, divine, is indivisible • 125
Ethics: also called divinity • 93; same as natual law • 63; science of morals • 63; treatment of divided into two parts • 99; whole culmination of • 93, 99
Etymology: of "divination" • 93; of "mercy" • 115; of *"misericordia"* • 115; of *"virtus"* • 111
Evagrius' translation of Athanasius' *Life of Antony* • 155
Eve • 15
Evil: action, so called from intention • 112; by accident • 112; definition of • 140, 141; difference between being evil and being *an* evil • 120–23; speaking substantially • 112; ultimate • 59, 110–11; ultimate, definition of • 99; ultimate, is ultimate misery or torture of penalty • 120; ultimate, method of reaching • 140; ultimate, vices the road to • 111; ultimate, *vs.* ultimate *human* evil • 119, 120; ultimate human • 123, 136, 140; ultimate human, found in next life • 120, 123, 124
Excommunication • 54–56
"Excused," usual meaning of word • 24

F

Faith, not a matter of pronouncing words • 64
Fault is worse than penalty for fault • 123
Forbearance: defined • 118; part of courage • 118
Foreign • 74, 86. *See also* Foreigners
Foreigners • 68, 73, 78, 83, 84. *See also* Foreign

Foreknowledge • 16, 26, 146. *See also* Foresight
Foresight • 19, 29, 41, 45, 58, 76, 146. *See also* Foreknowledge
Forgiveness • 9, 10, 15, 24, 25, 26, 27, 30, 38, 44, 49, 50, 82, 137, 142; despair of • 41
Fornication • 7, 9, 10, 19, 37, 39, 76
Fruits of penitence • 48
Fruor vs. utor • *See* Enjoyment *vs.* use

G

Gates of hell • 52
Gehenna • 35, 38
Gentleness: definition of • 119; part of moderation • 119
Gift of Holy Spirit • 56
Gluttony • 6–7
Good: action, so called from intention • 112; added to good, value and merit of • 20–21, 22; by accident • 112; definition of • 140–47; difference between being good and being *a* good • 120–23; every creature is • 121; occurrence of things • 147; speaking substantially • 112; ultimate • 59, 93, 99, 104, 106, 110–11; ultimate, definition of • 99, 105; ultimate, found in next life • 103; ultimate, is God • 119, 120, 127; ultimate, is simple • 125; ultimate, method of reaching • 100, 140; ultimate, not that than which something greater is found • 104–5; ultimate, view that pleasure is • 99–100, 103, 104; ultimate, view that virtue itself is • 99–100; ultimate, virtues are the road to • 111; ultimate, *vs.* ultimate *human* good • 105, 119–20; ultimate human • 123, 126, 136, 140; ultimate human, found in next life • 120, 123, 124; ultimate human, is God • 127

Goodness: God's, is what is meant by Holy Spirit • 41, 42; of intention and of deed • 20, 22–24; of intention, believing one is acting well not sufficient for • 24
Goods: bodily • 1; mental, unconnected to morals • 1
Greed • 12, 13, 35, 36, 48, 49
Greek language • 16, 35, 95
Greeks • 16, 43, 91, 94
Gregory the Great • 54, 55, 99; *Forty Gospel Homilies* • 15, 39, 53, 54, 96; *Morals on the Book of Job* • 15, 26

H

Habit: definition of • 57, 111; includes sciences and virtues • 112
Hanging of one criminal by two people • 12, 143
Heaven, how to understand • 131–36
Hebrews • 76, 86. *See also* Jews
Hell, how to understand • 136–39
Heresies • 91
Heth • 76
Hezekiah • 86
Holy Spirit: blasphemy against • 41–42; gift of • 56; God's goodness what is meant by • 41, 42
Homicide • 30, 31, 39, 88, 118. *See also* Killing
Honorable, definition of • 104
Horace, *Epistles* • 32, 63
Humility: definition of • 118; part of moderation • 118
Hypocrites • 13

I

"I want you to have my cap" • 4
Idolatry • 75, 76, 95, 96
Ignorance, not a sin • 24–25
Immortality of soul • 100
Inartificial • 95, 97
Incarnation • xxix, 5, 22, 41
Incorporeal, only God is • 129

Indifferent, definition of • 141
Induction • 102
Indulgences • 49
Indulging • 10
Intention • 12, 13, 14, 18, 20, 22, 23, 24, 25; goodness of, believing one is acting well is not sufficient for • 23–24; speaker's • 51
Isaac • 69, 72, 73, 76, 78, 82; Abraham's sacrifice of • 13–14, 26
Ishmael • 78, 79, 85
Isidore of Seville, *Etymologiae* • 16
Israel • 9, 69, 71, 74, 80, 82, 84, 85, 86, 87, 88, 133

J

Jacob • 69, 76, 79, 82
Jerome • 33, 35, 51; *Commentariorum in Hiezechielem* • 9; *Commentariorum in Matheum* • 51; *Commentariorum in Naum* • 139
Jerusalem • 86, 134
Jesus • xxix, 5, 12, 25, 41, 44, 103, 129, 143
Jews • 25, 26, 59, 63–89, 91, 94, 97, 103, 118, 132, 143. *See also* Hebrews; actions prohibited to • 8; ordeals suffered by • 67–68, 70
Job • 73, 79, 89, 92
John the apostle • 140
Jonadab • 86
Judas • 12, 33, 50, 56, 143, 144
Judgment Day • 38
Justice • 113–14, 115–18, 119; beneficence part of • 115; definition of • 113, 114, 116; natural • 117, 118; positive • 117–118; reverence part of • 115; truthfulness part of • 116; vengeance part of • 116

K

Keys of kingdom of heaven • 50, 51, 55
Killing • 6, 11, 34, 36, 114; by mistake in role as judge • 11; one's master in order not to be killed • 3–4; under duress • 3–4, 8, 10
King, Peter • xxx, 89

L

Law • 2, 8, 9, 11, 12, 13, 17, 18, 29, 31, 32, 47, 59, 60, 63, 91, 92; Christians' is the Gospel's and apostles' teaching • 91; Jewish • 64, 65–89, 92, 103; natural • 28, 59, 72, 73, 75, 89, 94, 95, 99, 111; natural, consists of love for God and neighbor • 69, 80; natural, consists of moral lessons • 63; natural, included in Jewish Law • 81; natural, is science of morals • 63; natural, prior to Scriptures • 63; natural, same as ethics • 63; no infractions without • 74
Lazarus • 35, 53, 102, 136, 137
Lending • *See* Money-lending
Lepers • 51
Liberality, definition of • 115
Light-Bearer (= *Luciferus*) • 122, 125
Logicians • 95
"*Logos*," Greek term • 95
Lot • 69
Lucan, *The Civil War* • 116–17
Lucifer • 126. *See also* Light-Bearer
Luscombe, D. E. • xxvii, 38, 44, 151
Lust • 5, 6, 8, 10, 11, 15, 17, 18, 114

M

Macrobius, *Commentary on the Dream of Scipio* • 109
Magicians • 16, 94
Magnanimity • 118; definition of • 118; part of courage • 118
Martyrs • 4, 23, 24, 58, 102
Mary (Magdalene) • 134
Masses, sale of • 36
Master, killing in order not to be killed by him • 3–4
Melchizedek • 69

Mercy, definition of • 115
Merit not increased by action • 6
Mesopotamia • 76
Micaiah • 145
Miracles • 28, 45, 94, 95; forbidden to be revealed • 13
Moderation • 114, 115, 119; definition of • 114; parts: humility, thriftiness, gentleness, chastity, sobriety • 118–19
Money-lending • 68, 72, 84
Monotheism • 95
Morals, definition of • 1
Mortality, not a vice of the person but of the nature • 122
Moses • 16, 47, 69, 71, 79, 80, 82, 83, 86, 87, 99
Murder • *See* Homicide, Killing

N

Names in mediaeval grammatical theory • 120, 141
Nathan • 43
Natural Law • *See* Law
Ninevites • 26
Noah • 69, 82, 83
Numbers above a thousand, Latin words for • 80

O

Obedience: definition of • 115; included in reverence • 115
Origen, *Commentary on the Gospel of Matthew* • 51–52, 160
Original sin • 9, 25, 35, 77
Ovid: *Amores* • 74; *Metamorphoses* • 49

P

Paradise • 9, 69, 82, 129; consists of vision of God • 129
Pardon for sin, definition of • 38, 39
Parts, none in incorporeal nature • 125
Passover • 68
Payer, Pierre • xxvii, 68, 79

Penalty: for sin sometimes called sin • 25–26; imposed where there is no fault • 18, 26, 27
Penitence • 33–42, 142; definition of • 33, 39; fruits of • 48
Perfect is that to which nothing is to be added • 82
Performance • *See* Action
Perjury • 30, 31, 32, 76
Peter Abelard: *Dialectica* • 95, 97; *Dialogue*, cross-reference to • 12, 57; *Ethics*, cross-reference to • 89, 93, 99, 101, 102, 108, 111, 112, 143, 144, 160; *Theologia "Scholarium"* • 42, 60; *Theologia "Summi boni"* • 60; *Theologia christiana* • 99
Peter, St. • 5, 19, 28, 29, 44, 45, 49, 51, 52, 55, 56
Pharaoh • 71
Pharisees • 47, 51. *See also* Scribes and Pharisees
Philosophers, instructed by God's wisdom • 95
Philosophy: moral • 59; task of • 59
Place: difference of does not affect blessedness • 128–31; difference of does not affect penalty • 138; enclosed in God • 128; God is in by his power • 128, 131, 132
Plato, *Timaeus* • 145
Pleasure: as ultimate good • 99, 103, 104; definition of • 100; increases sin? • 10
Plotinus, *Enneads* • 109
Porphyry, *Isagoge* • 126
"Praelatus," sense of Latin word • 43
Predestination • 40
"Princeps," sense of Latin word • 44
Prohibitions, addressed to consent, not to action • 12
Proposition: conditional • 121; *dictum* of • 141; hypothetical • 121; is kind of compound • 121

Providence • 40, 66
Prudence • 112–13, 114–15; definition of
• 57; mother of virtues rather than a
virtue • 57, 112, 115; not a virtue, but
a guide or incentive to virtue • 113;
science of good and evil things • 112
Purgatory • 38, 48

Q

Qualification, attributions with and
without • 4
Quality, species of • 111

R

Ransom • 4, 67
Rebekah • 76
Rechab • 86
Rechabites • 86
Reconciliation, three steps of: penitence,
confession, atonement • 33
Relapsing after repenting • 40
Relation, Aristotle's discussion of • 27
Religion, definition of • 115
Resurrection • 39, 53, 56; at end of
world • 109, 127–28, 129, 130, 133,
136, 137, 138, 139; Jesus' • 129, 133
Reverence • 115; definition of • 115

S

Sabbath • 85
Sacraments • 25, 27, 68, 69, 84
Sacrifice for sin • 25
Sallust, *The War with Jugurtha* • 63
Samaria • 26
Satan • 9, 43, 130, 143
Scandal, punishment for • 20
Scorn for God • 2, 3, 7, 8, 10, 14, 18, 19,
20, 24, 25, 26, 27, 28, 30, 32, 37, 38,
39, 42, 57
Scribes and Pharisees • 47, 55
Scriptures, added to natural law later •
63
Seneca • 100
Sex • 5, 8, 9, 10, 11, 19

Shadows defined negatively • 3
Shem • 82
Sidon • 28
Signification, variation in • 23
Simple, prior to multiple • 63
Sin: action sometimes called •
25–26, 27–28; against our will •
7; against Son of Man • 41; comes
about by suggestion, pleasure and
consent • 15; consists of non-being
rather than of being • 3; criminal
• 30, 31, 32; damnable or serious
• 30; defined negatively • 3;
definition of • 2–3; disbelief not
properly called • 24–25, 27; guilt
of without performance • 7, 11;
has no substance • 3; how
voluntary? • 7, 8; ignorance not •
24–25; in thought, speech or
action • 29; increased by pleasure
• 10; inexcusable • 41–42; located
in will or in doing • 108; not
increased by action • 7, 8–10, 17;
not same as bad action • 1, 17; not
same as bad will • 3–7; not same
as vice inclining one to evil • 1–2;
original • 9, 25, 35, 77; pardon
for, definition of • 38; penalty for
sometimes called sin • 25–26;
sacrifice for • 25; senses of word •
25; sometimes action called • 25;
sometimes called action • 25;
spiritual *vs.* carnal • 18; theory
that all sins are on a par • 106–8;
under duress • 5; venial • 29, 30,
31, 32; without bad will • 3–5
Sobriety: definition of • 119; part of
moderation • 119
Socrates • 23, 99, 112, 113
"Socrates is sitting" • 23
Sodom • 26
Solomon • 2, 73, 86
Son of Man, sin against • 41

Sophia, that is, God's wisdom • 95
Spade, Paul Vincent • 126, 142
States, six human: three in this life, three in next • 110
Stephen, St. • 24, 25, 26
Stump, Eleonore • 95
Substance, spiritual, not impeded by any bodily obstacle • 129
Suffering only occurs against one's will • 5
Suggestion • 14–15, 16–17. *See also* Suggestion, pleasure, consent
Suggestion, pleasure, consent: three phases of performing a sin • 14–15

T

Tabernacles, Festival of • 85
Temple, Jewish • 74, 86
Temptation • 14–16; comes about by suggestion, pleasure and consent • 15; definition of • 15
Testament: New • 60, 74, 92, 103, 118, 132, 136, 137; Old • 60, 66, 70, 92, 118, 132, 136, 137
Themistius • 97, 104
Thomas the apostle • 56
Thomas, Rudolf • xxvii, xxviii
Thriftiness: definition of • 119; part of moderation • 119
Topical reasoning • 95, 97; extrinsic • 97; from authority • 95, 97; from contraries • 102; from the goal • 104; from the judgment of the matter • 97
Trigg, Joseph Wilson • 160
Trinity • xxix, 5
Truthfulness • 115; definition of • 116
Tyre • 28

U

Unuseful, definition of • 104
Use *vs.* enjoyment • 104
Useful, definition of • 113
Utor vs. fruor • *See* Use *vs.* enjoyment

V

Valerius Maximus, *Factorum et dictorum memorabilium libri novem* • 114
Vengeance • 115, 117; definition of • 116
Venial sin • 29, 30, 31, 32
"Verbum dei," Latin phrase • 95
Vergil, *Georgics* • 17
Vices: adjacent to virtues • 114, 115; bodily • 1; definition of • 111; dispose us to sin • 2, 14; mental • 1–2; mental, contrary to virtues • 1, 57; mental, unconnected to morals • 1; the road to ultimate evil • 111
Virtue: as ultimate good • 99–100; definition of • 111, 112; philosophical sense of term • 57; properly understood, only charity is a • 107; prudence the mother of • 57, 112, 115; species of: prudence, justice, courage, moderation • 112
Virtues: all contained in charity • 106, 107; as means to ultimate good • 103; contrary to mental vices • 1, 57; Plotinus' division of • 109; road to ultimate good • 111; theory that all good people have equally • 105–9; vices adjacent to • 114, 115
Voluntary: not same as sin • 7; senses of term • 8; sin as • 7, 8
Vulgate version of Bible • 27, 79, 144

W

Want one thing because of another • 4
Wantonness • 2, 6, 7, 119
Wastefulness, definition of • 115
Will: bad • 3, 4, 5, 6, 8; bad, sin not same as • 3–7; bad, sin without • 3–5; divine • 5, 6; not same as the voluntary • 7; to escape death • 4, 8, to kill one's master • 4
Wine • 52, 68, 72, 86
Witness, bearing false • 11, 17
Wives held in common • 113